Productivity, Technology, and Industrial Development

A World Bank Research Publication

Productivity, Technology and Industrial Development

A Case Study in Textiles

Howard Pack

Published for the World Bank

OXFORD UNIVERSITY PRESS

Oxford University Press

NEW YORK OXFORD LONDON GLASGOW
TORONTO MELBOURNE WELLINGTON HONG KONG
TOKYO KUALA LUMPUR SINGAPORE JAKARTA
DELHI BOMBAY CALCUTTA MADRAS KARACHI
NAIROBI DAR ES SALAAM CAPE TOWN

Manufactured in the United States of America
First printing June 1987

Library of Congress Cataloging-in-Publication Data

Pack, Howard.
Productivity, technology, and industrial development.
(A World Bank research publication)
"Published for the World Bank."
Bibliography: p.
Includes index.
1. Cotton textile industry—Labor productivity—
Case studies. I. Title. II. Series.
HD9870.5.P25 1987   331.11′8   86-33271
ISBN 0-19-520543-X

Contents

Preface

TO EVALUATE project proposals that would establish new factories, the World Bank follows well-defined steps to determine the proposed plant's economic viability and rate of return. These evaluations typically assume that there is little scope for altering the productivity of existing plants in the same sector or for modifying the choice of technology to accommodate the circumstances of the host country. This book arose from efforts to examine those assumptions and to encourage a dialogue on the design of industrial projects. The particular issues of contention arose in regard to loans for the construction of cotton textile plants, hence the focus of this book on that specific industry.

As I worked on these issues, I realized that economists and industrial engineers had devoted relatively little effort to either measuring or understanding the sources of low productivity in manufacturing in developing countries. I have attempted in this book to fill that gap and to shed light on other issues in industrial development, as well as to suggest ways in which national governments and international lenders can improve the design of projects. The suggestions involve orthodox macroeconomic policies such as import liberalization, as well as microeconomic policies that are less conventional.

The research was funded by the Research Committee of the World Bank and jointly sponsored by the Industry and Development Research departments. The manuscript was completed while I was a Eugene M. Lang Faculty Fellow at Swarthmore College.

My greatest debt is to Janet Rothenberg Pack, who took time from her own research schedule to accompany me on all the field visits to factories and who helped extensively in the interview process. R. H. Grills, a textile engineer and analyst at the Shirley Institute in Manchester, England, also visited the factories and ensured that the answers received during interviews were consistent on technical issues. He was also an invaluable guide to the uncodified knowledge on textile manufacturing. In Kenya I had considerable help in arranging interviews from Hayley Goris, the head of the World Bank resident mission. In the Philippines the way was smoothed by the Ministry of Industry and the Board of Investment. Bobby Bernardo and Gloria Santos of these organizations were instructive and pleasant guides.

I am especially grateful to the large number of people from each of the textile mills who cooperated with this study. Not only did they willingly provide information, but they also offered insightful observations on technical issues and government policies.

I received useful comments on an early draft from Janet Pack, Gustav Ranis, Yung Rhee, Bernard Saffran, Gene Tidrick, and five anonymous referees. Peter Bocock was a careful and congenial editor. Larry Westphal, who helped to initiate the project, provided helpful conversations and incisive comments on the final draft.

CHAPTER ONE

Introduction

THIS BOOK has its origins in the need to make informed choices about the desirability of proposed industrial projects in developing countries. The past fifteen years have seen an enormous growth in the literature suggesting precise analytic methods for evaluating an individual project whose operating characteristics are known. Nevertheless, one of the most important elements of the decision process—the establishment of a plausible range for these characteristics—has been largely ignored in most formal discussions. It is generally believed that manufacturing plants in developing countries operate at lower levels of productivity than those in developed countries, but relatively little is known of the current magnitude of the difference, its evolution over time, or its sources. Although a few authors, notably Leibenstein, have called attention to this phenomenon, it is still most often treated as a curiosity, outside the mainstream of development thought. Yet the large difference between productivity in industrial and developing countries is inextricably related to such major concerns as the choice of technology and the validity of special support for infant industries. Productivity differences between technically similar plants in different countries are of interest in themselves for the insight they provide into the industrialization process; they also suggest that there may be high social rates of return from industrial projects that improve performance.

A comprehensive approach to the design of industrial projects requires consideration of the optimal choice of technology or capital-labor ratio in a new plant if the correct benefit-cost ratio from additional capacity is to be obtained. Because optimal capital intensity depends partly on the productivity with which specific equipment is employed under actual operating conditions, the choice of technology and the level of productivity are closely related.

Most analyses of technology choice rely on labor and capital productivities that apply only in advanced countries or solely in developing countries. The productivity assumptions embedded in feasibility studies, for example, particularly when equipment of advanced design is one of the alternative technologies, often reflect idealized working conditions in industrialized countries that have had long experience in the manufacture of a particular product. Although the standard input coefficients presented by consulting engineers or machinery producers may offer a useful guide to prospective equipment purchasers in Lyons, Antwerp, or Raleigh, the typical producer in a developing country will fall short of the envisaged productivity. Sophisticated equipment that exhibits a lower unit cost of production (at developing country factor prices) than more conventional machinery in feasibility studies that assume high productivity for both may result in greater cost when the production parameters used are more realistic for developing countries. The unit input requirements in a developed country do not necessarily translate into similar ones when the technology is transferred to a different setting. The calculation of the least-cost technology is sensitive to the specific set of productivities used; the choice of technology and differences in productivity between operating developing country plants and best-practice ones are inextricably linked.[1] Input coefficients specific to the developing country must be used if realistic rather than fanciful project evaluations are to be obtained.

Productivity Comparisons in the Literature

There have been two types of comparative international productivity studies of specific manufacturing branches, and they have drawn mainly on evidence from developed countries.[2] The first uses sectorwide measures of output and input to derive comparisons of labor productivity, whereas the second compares one or two plants in an industry in each of two or three countries. Both sets of analyses typically investigate sectors or firms in developed countries and consider labor productivity differences; they provide little guidance on the probable range of results in developing countries or on differences in total-factor productivity (TFP).[3] There have also been a few comparisons of developed and developing countries with respect to differences in TFP at a point in time.[4] In contrast, the present study analyzes data from a large group of individual plants in Kenya and the Philippines and compares their total-factor productivity with that of best-practice plants in a developed country using identical equipment. Knowledge about the performance of a large number of factories in each developing country permits the measurement and analysis of intracountry as well as international productivity variations. In this and other respects the present study is closer to the emerging literature on frontier production functions than to the studies cited in the preceding footnote or those surveyed by Kravis.[5]

Analyses of Technology Choice

The main empirical question considered in past analyses of the choice of technology has been whether a choice in fact exists or whether the newest technology dominates older ones in the sense of requiring less of both capital and labor per unit of output.[6] A substantial body of work has shown that in many industrial processes the technology permits considerable substitution of labor for machinery and that, in general, newer technologies do not dominate older ones.[7] The analysis of the cotton textile sector presented in the following chapters confirms these earlier findings. Comparison of the most modern technologies and currently available conventional technologies for both spinning and weaving shows that the former have higher production costs at market prices for the factors of production; the discrepancy would be greater at shadow prices. The magnitude of the cost difference between the technologies varies considerably with the productivity with which each technology is used in particular developing country settings.

Productivity Differences and the Transfer of Technology

Evidence about productivity differences and their evolution is critical for evaluating industrialization strategies and methods for effecting the successful transfer of industrial technologies to developing countries.

Productivity in Developing Country Plants

It has often been asserted that the establishment of manufacturing capacity behind tariff or quota barriers enables individual firms to improve their productive abilities gradually and to move toward best practice.[8] Although firms do not need to attain best practice to compete internationally—lower prices for some factors can offset some productivity disadvantage—it is nevertheless of considerable interest to determine how close to best practice textile firms are in the highly protected economies of Kenya and the Philippines. Although it was not possible to obtain adequate time-series data of technical coefficients from the firms, the data collected do permit an analysis of the nature of the gap still to be closed fifteen to thirty years after production started in each country.

The approach followed in this book, particularly the disaggregation of the sources of productivity differences between operating developing country plants and best-practice plants in developed countries, permits the analysis of issues that standard criteria of competitiveness do not consider. In particular, estimates of effective protection rates or domestic resource cost cannot discriminate between a number of microeconomic factors that generate the summary measures. A firm may have successfully mastered its own technologies according to its expectations and may come close to best engineering practice, for example, but may still not be able to match the total-factor productivity of better developed country firms because of excessive product variety—which in turn stems from the particular market structure that has evolved, perhaps in response to protection. A high rate of measured effective protection cannot discriminate between this possibility and substantial technical inefficiency within the firm, yet the two phenomena may have different implications for the success of infant industries.

Disaggregated analysis of the sources of productivity differentials also permits detailed analysis of policy questions with respect to improving industrial sector performance. Much effort has been expended on measuring the level of effective protection but little on finding out why firms (and industries) need such protection. Although there is clearly some validity in the view that protection itself is a source of inefficiency,[9] it is possible that the removal of protection alone will not provide a magic corrective to existing deficiencies; some specific technological intervention or effort at rationalizing the organization of an industry may also be required. These questions are discussed in chapters 8 and 9, using the results of the preceding chapters.

Transfer of Technology

Within the strictly neoclassical framework of a freely available international technology, observed differences in total-factor productivity between actual- and best-practice firms—particularly those attributable to variations in activities controlled by firms—are anomalous. To account for international differences in productivity, it is necessary to postulate differential costs of acquiring technical information, variations in the marginal productivity of utilizing such information, or some combination of the two. Moreover, to the extent that total-factor productivity of firms with identical equipment differs within a country, similar questions arise about the intracountry diffusion of technology.

Although some of the literature on the transfer of technology has documented the substantial expenses that may be incurred in implanting an existing technology in another environment (see Teece 1976), the intracountry dispersion of productivity has received little attention. The data collected in Kenya and the Philippines for this book, plus an unusual body of technical engineering information collected from a sample of major textile-producing nations, permit a number of issues that arise under the catchall phrase "transfer of technology" to be addressed more fully than is usually the case.

One related question—whether local or foreign managers are likely to achieve greater productivity when new firms are established—will also be considered. A priori arguments can be made in favor of both: domestic managers are more familiar with local customs and probable reactions of workers to specific requests, whereas expatriates bring superior technical knowledge. The data available and the analysis performed with them suggest at least preliminary answers to questions about relative productivity performance—answers that also have policy implications in the debate about the desirability of permitting direct foreign investment.

Issues in Industrial Strategy

The typical industrial project, financed by international lending institutions and by industrial development banks in developing countries, allows the borrower to establish or expand a factory. In a country that already possesses a significant amount of manufacturing capacity, existing plants may be inefficient, and much greater output could be obtained if firms could eliminate part of the gap between their current productivity and that realized by the better plants in other countries. The additional output obtained from such an improvement project may eliminate the need for additional physical investment in a particular industry. Any proposal to expand capacity in a sector with existing plants should be viewed as implying an alternative project against which it should be compared, namely an improvement project for the sector in question and, more generally, for other sectors as well. The choice of the optimal project must then be based on a comparison of the social benefit-cost ratio of capacity expansion with that of productivity enhancement.

To design an improvement project requires a substantial amount of detail about the economic and technical engineering characteristics of existing plants. Such information is also a useful check on the plausibility of performance projections for new factories. If insights are to be obtained about the probable magnitudes involved, the relevant analysis must proceed within a specific national and industrial context. The present analysis considers the cotton textile sector in Kenya and the Philippines; the reason for focusing on textiles is discussed in the next section. Detailed data at each processing stage have been collected from textile plants in the two countries. Comparable data from plants in developed countries make it possible to calculate the total-factor productivity of mills in the developing countries and of their counterparts in developed countries using ostensibly identical equipment. The rich data base also makes it possible to identify and measure sources of productivity differences between the two sets of plants. This decomposition in turn makes it possible to address such questions as whether the lower productivity in developing country manufacturing is attributable to the poor labor force skills that may characterize the early stage of industrialization or whether other features of developing economies—such as insufficient product specialization by firms or managers' inadequate technical knowledge—are responsible.

Any effort to improve productivity within a framework of general trade liberalization raises a number of difficult issues, such as the sequencing of tariff reductions, the timing and nature of technical assistance, and the utility of improving or adding to the equipment of existing firms. The information obtained from detailed analysis of the level of productivity and its determinants provides useful insights into these more general policy questions.

The Cotton Textile Industry

The cotton textile industry was chosen for investigation for a number of reasons. The industry is currently among the larger industrial subsectors in many developing countries in terms of employment and share of industrial value added; it is thus high on the list of sectors in which higher productivity could sharply raise output. It is also a sector in which many new plants are being planned. A considerable body of literature indicates both that a substantial range of technology exists and that careful evaluation of alternative technologies is imperative, as the capital required per worker may exceed US$30,000 if machinery is chosen from the higher end of the technology spectrum (see Amsalem 1983; Pack 1975; Pickett and Robson 1981).

The relevant technical characteristics of the industry include the following: it has a largely mechanical—as opposed to biological, chemical, or electronic—technological base; production is machine paced, but the abilities of operatives and technical managers affect the quantity and quality of output per unit of time; and the size of the production run is an important determinant of unit cost. More generally, the textile manufacturing process bears many similarities to such industries as food processing and the manufacture of paints, pharmaceuticals, and ball bearings; some of the methods of analysis followed here should therefore, with suitable modification, be useful in studying these sectors as well.

The choice of countries was largely dictated by the need for the cooperation of individual firms. The selection does not seem to have led to any particular bias; major variables have been roughly checked against less comprehensive plant-level data obtained by consulting engineering firms in other countries. At the time of data collection for the study, both Kenya and the Philippines had long been engaged in encouraging industrialization through comprehensive protection of local firms from import competition. Exports are not, in the aggregate, important for either country's textile sector, though some firms do export part of their output. The two countries differ significantly in that multinational firms dominate the Kenyan textile sector, whereas the Philippine industry is owned domestically. As I shall show, this difference manifests itself in a number of ways.

The Analytic Model

A simple model can be used to analyze the implication of many of the issues that I have raised so far. In the following discussion, "technology" is used to describe a relatively homogeneous set of production methods that differ distinctly from each other; for example, a variety of looms used for weaving differ mainly in the principle by which the weft is inserted into the warp. Semiautomatic, automatic, and water jet looms are three of the many technologies available, though there are several relatively minor variations of the basic loom within each category, depending on the particular loom manufacturer. For any technology, a specific technique indicates the labor-to-capital ratio—each type of loom can be used with varying amounts of labor, depending upon the wage-rental ratio facing the firm. The ex ante unit isoquant facing a firm about to purchase new equipment consists of the envelope of best-practice coefficients of each of the technologies, or EABCE' in figure 1-1, in which the axes measure unit input requirements, k the capital-output ratio, and z the labor-output ratio. Once a particular technology has been chosen by a firm, for example, technology A, ex post variation in technique is possible. If the firm can achieve best practice, this variation occurs along aa. In developing countries, where plants typically exhibit total-factor productivity below that of best practice, ex post substitution occurs along $a'a'$. As drawn in figure 1-1, the ex post elasticity of substitution is less than that holding ex ante, the latter including as it does the possibility of choosing among different technologies designed to be optimal for any given factor price ratio.

Given the preceding definitions and assumptions, we may identify three separate features that are compressed into one in most analyses of the

Figure 1-1. *The Effect of Productivity on the Choice of Technology*

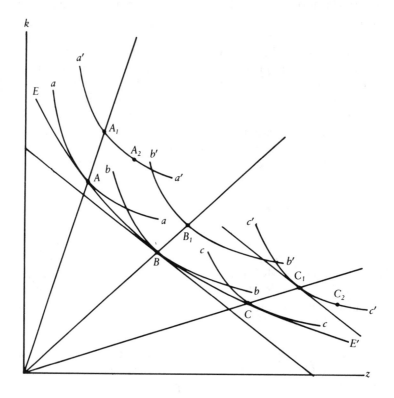

choice of the optimal capital-labor ratio: (1) the choice between ex ante technologies, *A, B, C*; (2) the level of efficiency with which the chosen technology is operated (if each of the isoquants, *aa, a'a'*, and so forth depicts requirements for a unit of output, then efficiency relative to best practice is measured by OA/OA_1, and so forth; the lower the ratio, the lower is relative total-factor productivity [RTFP] in the developing country); and (3) the choice of technique within any technology (for example, operation along *a'a'* at *A* or A_2).[10] For any given factor price ratio, the three characteristics of production jointly determine the least-cost production method; the framework employed here is expanded in chapter 3.

This book systematically explores the above-mentioned aspects of factor choice and productivity and takes the cotton textile sector in Kenya and the Philippines as the concrete setting. The questions addressed include the appropriate ex ante choice of factor proportions at current relative factor prices, both when current productivity generates the relevant set of choices and when developing country firms are postulated to realize productivity close to that on the best-practice frontier. The ex ante choice of technologies includes: (1) the most technologically advanced equipment currently available; (2) machinery currently being manufactured that is of modern but conventional design; (3) used modern machinery that differs from new versions mainly in price and expected useful life; (4) new or used machinery whose design dates back forty years or more. In analyzing the optimal ex ante technology choice, it is necessary to obtain both current operating productivity and estimates of feasible productivity. If developing country productivity that has been realized with alternative technologies is the only basis for calculation, technology C shown in figure 1-1 is superior to B, as C_1 yields a lower unit cost than B_1; if best-practice coefficients could be realized in the developing country, however, B would yield a lower unit cost. Existing studies utilize either information about best-practice alternatives (aa, bb, cc) or observations from current developing country operations $a'a'$, $b'b'$, $c'c'$).[11]

The above-described analytical framework is also useful for assessing productivity improvement projects. The potential cost reductions to be obtained from improved performance in existing plants are twofold: those arising from a movement from low current productivity levels (for example, $c'c'$) to best practice (cc) as well as from an improved choice of the amount of labor to be employed with machines already installed (the move from C_2 to C_1). (This analysis is developed more fully in chapter 3.) The cost reductions realized do not represent net gains to the firms or the economy, because some costs will typically have to be incurred to realize better practice. Thus the economic optimality of a program to enhance productivity must be established through a careful appraisal of benefits and costs. Such an effort is undertaken in chapter 8.

A Preview

Chapters 2 and 3 present the technical background information needed for the subsequent analysis. Chapter 2 contains the relevant engineering information as well as a discussion of economic issues such as the determinants of ex post factor substitution possibilities. Chapter 3 examines the concept of best practice, derives measures of developing-country plant productivity relative to best practice, and uses the technical information developed in chapter 2 to provide a formal framework for analyzing the sources of the deviation of productivity in developing-country plants from best practice. Chapters 4 and 5 contain two types of analyses of firms in Kenya and the Philippines: first, the current cost structure of plants in each country employing different types of equipment is compared; second, the total-factor productivity of each textile mill is calculated relative to a best-practice counterpart in a developed country, the counterpart being determined by the engineering characteristics of the machinery employed. The sources of the intercountry productivity differentials are then decomposed into the categories set forth in chapter 3.

The presentation in chapters 4 and 5 is largely quantitative and does not include the richness of detail that is one of the benefits of intensive plant interviews. Chapter 6 therefore presents some of the qualitative and anecdotal evidence needed to give the reader a sense of what lies behind measured productivity differentials—the details of how best-practice production relations undergo a deformation in operating plants. Thus chapters 4 and 5 document the hypothesis that technically similar firms within Kenya and the Philippines are not operating on the same production function as their counterparts in the United Kingdom, whereas chapter 6 presents a more concrete sense of the implications. A more formal, quantitative analysis of observed intracountry and international performance differentials is presented in chapter 7, which also places Kenyan and Philippine performance in an international perspective. Chapter 8 uses the insights gained in the preceding chapters to address some questions about the design of industrial projects. In particular, the benefits and costs of establishing additional productive capacity through new investments in plant and equipment are compared with those stemming from efforts to correct existing sources of low productivity.

Chapter 9 summarizes some of the major empirical results and places the question of a program of productivity augmentation within the broader context of trade liberalization. It uses the insights obtained in the preceding analyses of the sources of low productivity to propose some policy options and their desirable temporal phasing.

The individual chapters have been designed to be read in two possible sequences: (1) the reader interested in both the underlying technological issues and methods of analysis may wish to proceed through the volume from start to finish; (2) the reader interested in the study's more general implications for the analysis of economic development and project design may prefer to skip to the introductory sections of chapters 4 and 5, which summarize the significant empirical results in Kenya and the Philippines, respectively, and then proceed to chapters 6–9.

Notes

1. This point was first emphasized by Hirschman (1958), who hypothesized that industrial production methods in which both worker and management effort is determined by the speed

and sequential demands of "machine-paced" operations will exhibit greater productivity than those in which the process can be segmented into individually paced activities. Continuous-process activities, such as most chemical production, would thus exhibit higher relative productivity than metal working, in which individual tasks are subject to considerable latitude in timing. In spinning and weaving, the production process is largely machine paced regardless of technology, so this characteristic of the production process cannot explain observed differences between firms.

2. A comprehensive survey is provided by Kravis (1976).

3. A useful survey and an analysis of what is known about labor productivity in developing countries are provided by Horton and King (1981).

4. Arrow, Chenery, Minhas, and Solow (1961), Daniels (1969), Pack (1984). These and studies of the growth of productivity in developing countries are surveyed in Pack (forthcoming).

5. A review of the use of frontier production functions in analyzing developing country performance is given in Pack (forthcoming).

6. The proper choice should also take into account differences in the reinvestable funds generated by each project if current investment rates in the economy are suboptimal. Little effort has been devoted to empirical work on this aspect of the choice problem. For a complete statement of the theoretical issues, see Sen (1968).

7. There have been two generations of studies of empirical substitution possibilities, beginning with the estimation of the constant elasticity of substitution production functions in the 1960s and continuing with a number of studies based on engineering and microeconomic information. Four extensive survey articles of the second group of studies are Acharya (1974), Stewart (1974), Morawetz (1974), and White (1978). Surveys of the first set include Gaude (1975), Morawetz (1976a), and Nerlove (1967). For a recent and comprehensive set of CES estimates, see Behrman (1982). An estimate of the aggregate quantitative importance of the correct choice of factor proportions is provided in Pack (1982a).

8. Such a prospective move does not provide the basis for infant industry protection; in the presence of perfect capital markets, a firm could finance its own learning, later reaping the rewards. For a full discussion of infant industry arguments, see Corden (1974).

9. As has been noted by Corden (1974), however, this outcome is not necessary. For a complete analysis, see Martin (1978).

10. There is no reason to expect RTFP to be the same for every technology. As noted above, the Hirschman hypothesis that machine-paced operations are more likely to exhibit greater relative productivity is not apposite here, as most of the processes in spinning and weaving are machine paced.

11. For an example of the former, see Pack (1975); for the latter approach, see Rhee and Westphal (1977) and Stewart (1975). A complementary investigation of textile production is also to be found in Ranis and Saxonhouse (1978).

CHAPTER TWO

Technical and Economic Issues in Cotton Textile Production

COTTON TEXTILE PRODUCTION comprises an array of processes that can be characterized broadly as spinning and weaving. A third stage, finishing, which includes the printing or dyeing of woven cloth, is not considered in this book.

Spinning

The production of yarn involves several preparatory processes before the final spinning stage. These processes are opening and cleaning, the formation of laps of clean cotton, carding, drawing, and roving. Each will be described briefly.[1]

Production Processes

The raw cotton used to manufacture yarn arrives at mills in large, tightly packed bales, which contain substantial amounts of dirt and debris. The opening process separates the fiber into smaller particles, or tufts, suitable for cleaning, extracts dirt from the tufts, and combines them into a sheet (or lap) suitable for carding. The initial opening and cleaning is achieved by one or more of the following mechanisms: revolving beaters, revolving saws, or jets of air. The lap of cotton that goes to carding still contains partially unopened fibers as well as some dirt.

Laps from the opening process are fed to cards, which remove the remaining dirt and excessively short or immature fibers. Any unusually hard tufts that failed to open in the previous stage are now broken up. The fibers are then arranged in a roughly parallel disentangled form (called a sliver) that becomes the input for drawing. The drawing process further straightens the fibers and reduces the size of the sliver by passing it between successive sets of rollers, each of which moves more rapidly than

Figure 2-1. *The Elements of a Ring Frame*

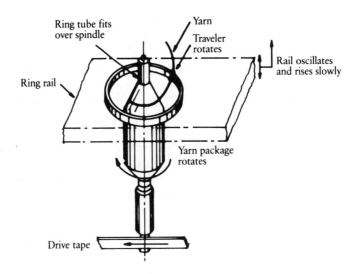

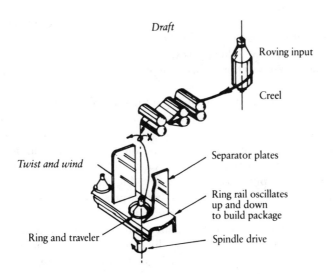

Source: Lord 1981.

the preceding one. The amount of reduction in the weight of the sliver is called the draft; the term is used in a similar way in roving and spinning. The greater the draft, the larger the reduction in weight per yard of the initial sliver.

The roving process takes the sliver from the drawing process and again makes it thinner by the same means of employing increasingly fast rollers. The sliver is simultaneously twisted slightly to strengthen it. Until the 1950s, there were several roving stages, each producing consecutively finer sliver. With the invention of processes that can achieve higher drafts in one stage, roving now generally requires only one passage. The product of the roving process is itself known as roving and provides the material used in spinning, the last step of production.

The purpose of spinning is to obtain a still finer yarn from the roving and to twist previously parallel strands into a spiral so that they adhere together and make yarn strong enough to bear the great stress place on it in succeeding operations. The yarn being spun is twisted as the spindle travels more quickly than the front roller (see figure 2-1), the number of twists per inch being given by the ratio of the number of rotations of the spindle per turn of the front roller. (More precisely, the yarn is taken up by the traveler, a small loop, and is then wound on the bobbin.) Most plants use a standard "twist multiple" to determine the appropriate number of twists per inch, T, the formula being $T = t\sqrt{c}$, where t is the twist multiple and c the yarn count. Two types of yarn are used in weaving, warp and weft; the former are the lengthwise yarns of a woven fabric, the latter the crossing, or filling, yarns. A higher value of t is usually used in warp yarns than in weft yarns because of the greater stress endured by the former.

Spinning is carried out on spinning frames, each of which may have 300 to 500 spindles. Though the spindles are driven by a common motor, each is independent of the others. Labor falls into two major categories in spinning: there are spinners, who set up the supply of roving into creels and mend any breaks that appear in yarn, and doffers, who remove the filled bobbins of spun yarn from the spinning frame.

Over the last two decades an entirely new process—open end, or break, spinning—has been perfected. Rather than rotating an entire bobbin or package of yarn to obtain twist, an open end of the yarn is rotated around the axis of the yarn (see figure 2-2). The major benefits of the process are that yarn formation proceeds at much greater speed than in ring spinning and that the roving process can be entirely skipped.

The thickness of yarn is called its count. Several measures of count are currently used; I will use the nonmetric Anglo-American one, in which a count of 1s indicates that one hank, or length of yarn amounting to 840 yards, weighs one pound. A count of 20s, around which the analysis of the

Figure 2-2. *The Principles of Open-End Spinning*

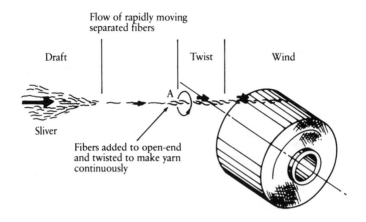

Source: Lord 1981.

following chapters is standardized, thus implies that twenty lengths of 840 yards (16,800 yards) weigh one pound. The higher the count, the finer the yarn, because it weighs less per hank (see Lord 1981, chaps. 9, 13).

To provide an overview of the relative importance of the various preparatory and spinning processes, the shares of total employment and total investment in equipment in a modern best-practice plant are shown in the first two columns in table 2-1, while the third column shows the distribution of employment in a group of Philippine plants. The employment percentage in each section includes only workers directly employed in specific stages. The equipment whose prices form the basis of the calculation is the most modern currently available for ring spinning and includes some accessories, such as automatic chute feeds between picking and carding that are not normally installed in developing country plants; these items are relatively cheap, however. About two-thirds of investment and three-quarters of the labor requirements are concentrated in roving and spinning in best-practice plants. In Philippine mills, about 70 percent of labor hours are used on roving and spinning. Equipment for the preparatory processes is usually of the same vintage as the spindles; the value of the capital stock depends largely on the cost of spinning equipment.

Technical and Economic Issues

A reading of any text on textile engineering will quickly convince a reader that an enormous number of technical and economic decisions are

Table 2-1. *Relative Importance of Spinning Stages*
(percent)

Stage	Share of investment	European share of one-shift factory employment[a]	Philippine share of one-shift factory employment
Opening	5	8	8
Carding	20	11	13
Drawing	8	4	9
Roving	11	13	16
Spinning	56	64	54
Total	100	100	100

a. European best practice.
Source: Manufacturer's information sheets and responses in interviews.

made at every stage in the design of textile machinery and at every step in yarn production (see, for example, Hamby 1965, Lord 1981, and Subramanian and Garde 1974). The discussion here focuses on a small number of issues that are generally agreed to be the most economically signficant (Lord 1981, chaps. 27–30). Many of the engineering choices that arise at each stage in yarn production have already been decided for the textile producer by the manufacturer of textile machinery; only one of the many fiber-cleaning alternatives or drafting systems currently available is embodied in the particular machine purchased, and little significant alteration of the principal machine components is possible without outlays nearly as great as those necessary to purchase an entire new machine.

The output that is physically possible from a given piece of equipment may not be realized in practice, because not all determinants of actual output are embodied in the machine. Inadequate knowledge of textile-processing procedures, such as the blending of fibers, quality control, maintenance, desirable machine settings, and so on, may produce quite different output levels in firms using the same quantities of machines, labor, fiber, electricity, and space. (For a fairly exhaustive list of the required procedures and tests, see Enrick 1980.) This section presents a schematic outline of some of the critical variables in yarn manufacture and considers how variations in them affect total-factor productivity. The more basic question of *why* many developing country plants fail to realize the values achieved in best-practice plants is asked in chapters 6 and 7.

TOTAL-FACTOR PRODUCTIVITY. The following subsections describe some important reasons why total-factor productivity varies among firms that employ the same equipment. They also explain the assumption in succeeding chapters that a shortfall relative to best practice decreases average labor and capital productivity by the same percentage, an assumption that permits differences in productivity among firms to be calculated relatively simply (see chapter 3). In addition, the technical description of selected aspects of the manufacturing processes provides the engineering basis necessary to understand the sources of potential variations in factor proportions in equipment that has already been installed. The procedures used to establish numerical measures of the sources of productivity variation are set forth in chapter 3.

A simplified description of the spinning process shows output per spindle hour for a given count of yarn, Q, depending on the speed, R, at which spindles rotate per minute, the numbers of twists, T, inserted per inch, and the hourly rate of spindle utilization, e, known among textile technologists as machine, or spindle, efficiency. The functional relation is

$$(2\text{-}1) \qquad\qquad Q = \frac{R}{T} e.$$

Three operating characteristics may result in downward shifts of the production function, namely, failure to operate spindles at rated speed, insertion of a greater number of twists per inch than is standard ($T = t\sqrt{c}$) for a given count, and inability to operate spindles for the same percentage of each hour that best-practice plants do. Each characteristic is discussed in turn.

It is important to distinguish between those alterations in the variables that produce shifts in the production function through pure efficiency changes and those that reflect a movement along it; although these differences are simple to articulate in principle, they are fairly difficult to distinguish in practice. The speed at which spindles rotate, for example, may be lower than the maximum physically achievable. The first level of analysis of this fact may reveal that it results from inadequate maintenance or a decision to economize on electricity. In the former case the lower speed is attributed to technical inefficiency, in the latter to cost minimization. We could, however, step further back to inquire about the source of inadequate maintenance, if this is indeed the problem. At this second level it might be established that the firm allocated most of its limited quantity of technical personnel to improving the mixing process rather than to establishing maintenance routines. At this more disaggregated level, the observed insufficient maintenance would more appropriately be classified as the outcome of a cost-minimizing strategy rather than as x-inefficiency.

Thus whether a particular observed deficiency should be assigned to the category of technical inefficiency or to cost minimizing often depends on the number of stages through which one traces back the decision process of the firm. Indeed, all measured *x*-inefficiency may have as its source allocative inefficiency at some higher level. The categories used in the following chapters stop at the first level and do not inquire into more basic allocation decisions within firms, such as the division of managerial effort between the improvement of mixing and the establishment of more adequate maintenance procedures. This decision was made for pragmatic reasons; it is possible, and tempting, to pursue ever more disaggregated inquiries, but such a process can become an infinite regression that precludes even partial understanding of the issues involved.

A major development in conventional ring spinning has been the realization of greater potential spindle speeds. For ring frames of a given vintage, however, the actual speed employed can differ from the maximum achievable physical speed. The conditions leading to such a divergence include inadequate maintenance, an insufficient supply of spare parts, and efforts to economize on power or labor (because the requirements of both these inputs per unit of output rise with the speed used for a given count). The growth in labor usage results from higher breakage rates as spindle speed is raised. The potential for carefully discriminating among these alternative sources of divergence is one of the benefits of the interview process undertaken as part of this study, although it remains necessary to check answers for consistency and to avoid accepting the occasional glib response at face value.

If the quality of roving used in spinning is not sufficiently high—for example, as a result of insufficient blending of fibers in the opening process or because of deficiencies in the preceding processing stages—a stronger yarn can nevertheless be manufactured by imparting a higher than normal twist to the sliver as it is spun. (For a discussion of these and related issues, see Hance 1965 and Lord 1981, chap. 8). A larger number of twists per inch is obtained by slowing the speed of the front roller of the drafting system that supplies yarn to the spindle, which itself continues to operate at a fixed speed. The slowing of the roller reduces output in proportion to the increase in the number of twists per inch (see equation 2-1) and is here considered an *x*-inefficient practice if it is attributable to deficient blending. There is an optimal level of twist, however, beyond which yarn strength actually declines and thus sets limits on the correction possible at this stage.

Higher-than-usual levels of *T* may reflect factor substitution rather than *x*-inefficiency. A decrease in the average length of the cotton fiber used, for example, from one and one-quarter inches to one inch, normally reduces the strength of the yarn produced. It is possible, however, to offset this effect partly by increasing the twist multiple.[2] Because an increase in the number of twists per inch reduces output proportionally, the purchase of less expensive short fibers represents a substitution of labor and capital for (quality-adjusted) fiber. When this practice increases the average cost of production, it is allocatively inefficient. In the few cases in the empirical work described in the following chapters in which excessive twist multiples are found, only a small part of the excess is due to poor fiber; it is generally attributable to deficient practices in other respects—for example, to inadequate blending.[3]

Spindle, or machine, efficiency indicates the percentage of each hour during which the spindles are actually spinning and not stopped for repair of a broken end or for some other reason.[4] An increase in the rate at which yarns break will, at a given labor-spindle ratio, result in an equal percentage decrease in the average product of labor and equipment; most often the output per spindle is partly restored by increasing the labor-spindle ratio. Other reasons why efficiency may fall below 100 percent include the stopping of the spindle when the filled bobbin needs to be removed (doffed), replacement of the doffed bobbin, unscheduled maintenance, and alteration of ring-frame settings. Although the time taken for doffing and replacing bobbins is usually quite small and is an inherent part of the production process, unscheduled maintenance and frequent alteration of machine settings (for example, to change the tension to which yarn is subjected) can significantly affect spindle efficiency and constitute one source of interfirm and intercountry variation in total-factor productivity.

The productivity losses from lower spindle efficiency just discussed are unrelated to those stemming from more twists per inch and from speeds lower than the standard. Equation 2-1 shows that the three factors act multiplicatively to reduce total-factor productivity.

FACTOR SUBSTITUTION. As breakage rates rise above a desired level, firms may attempt to maintain spindle efficiency by adding spinners to existing frames, a practice that reduces the time it takes to notice and repair a broken yarn.[5] When an end breaks, the affected spindle is automatically stopped by a sensing device and (unlike others on the same frame) remains idle until the spinner, who is patrolling perhaps a thousand spindles along thirty or forty yards of ring frame, notices it, repairs the break with a simple knot, and restarts it. The time during which a spindle is stopped pending attention from the spinner is called machine interference.

Achievable levels of efficiency (the percentage of time during which a spindle is spinning) can be calculated from standard machine interference tables; they depend on the number of end breaks, b, the machine-worker ratio, k, patrol speed, p (the time it takes the spinner to walk around the set of frames he or she is tending), and rest time. Given the spindle-labor ratio initially adopted, and b and p, the potential level of spindle efficiency can be calculated. In this book, observed efficiency rates below this potential are attributed to x-inefficient practices. The relationship between k, b, p, and e permits choices to be made about factor proportions even after a specific type of equipment has been installed. Efficiency is partly a function of the machine-worker ratio and is an endogenous economic variable, ultimately depending on factor prices and engineering substitution possibilities. Speed is also partly endogenous; firms facing low wage rates may operate at high speeds and may employ additional workers to repair the excessive breaks occasioned by high speeds.

The expression for the optimal spindle assignment per worker $(K/L) = k$ that a cost-minimizing firm would choose can be shown to be

$$(2-2) \qquad\qquad k = \sqrt{2w/rbp}$$

where w is the hourly wage and r the hourly user cost of a spindle.[6]

This rule is derived by expressing unit cost in terms of the cost of capital, labor, and material waste as well as technical parameters such as the breakage rate and patrol time and then determining the value of k that minimizes unit cost. An increase in the breakage rate thus provides an incentive for raising the labor-capital ratio. The optimal level of efficiency implied in equation 2-2 can then be found from

$$(2-3) \qquad\qquad e = h - bkp$$

where h is a constant depending on a number of technical parameters. The cost-minimizing level of efficiency falls with an increase in k as $\partial e/\partial k = -bp(b, p > 0)$ and with an increase in b as $\partial e/\partial b = -kp$ $(k, p > 0)$.[7] In interfirm comparisons in Kenya and the Philippines, firms not achieving their lowest cost factor proportion according to equation 2-2 are considered to be allocatively inefficient.

OTHER CONSIDERATIONS. The discussion so far has implied that, given the speed of spindles, the rate of end breaks (and yarn quality more generally) is a given for the firm. This is too simple a view. Yarn characteristics, such as the number of thick and thin spots, affect the breakage rate and can be altered: greater expenditures on the quality of raw fiber, maintenance, humidity control, the determination of proper machine settings, and quality control can all improve the attributes of yarn produced.[8] If lower end breakage rates can be achieved, productivity will rise, particularly in spinning proper. Indeed, almost all deficiencies in activities affecting yarn quality manifest themselves in shortfalls in spinning productivity rather than in the preparatory processes from opening through roving.

Thus the decision on the optimal level of spindles per spinner is more adequately understood as one part of what should be a simultaneous decision problem, namely, the joint determination of optimal yarn quality and the cost-minimizing capital-labor ratio. The analysis in the following chapters takes the quality level as a given and attributes to it part of the deviation from best-practice TFP. Whether firms have made correct decisions that minimize firmwide costs is left open—I do not inquire into whether additional outlays on maintenance or quality control would raise or lower average production costs. The discussions that follow do indicate some opportunities of this kind, but as I indicated earlier, analyzing them would require a degree of disaggregation that is beyond the scope of this study. The issue is of considerable importance, however, and I will return to it in chapter 7.

THE PRODUCTION FUNCTION. The preceding discussion can be summarized in a simplified engineering relationship describing the output of the spinning process as

(2-4) $$Q = A \frac{R}{T} qe \, (b, L)$$

where Q is output per hour per set of ring frames, A is a set of engineering constants, R is spindle speed, T is twists per inch, e is "normal" efficiency (see equation 2-3) achievable, given b end breaks per hour and the use of a given quantity of labor (L being determined through equation 2-2), and q measures the impact of all procedures that reduce operating efficiency to less than normal levels. The better the technological practice, the greater the value of q. The observed value of e, namely, e^*, will thus be equal to qe. The thoroughness of fiber blending and quality control, for example, are determinants of b and T, whereas maintenance, the availability of spare parts and initial design, are important factors affecting R and q. The relevant partial derivatives are

(2-4a)
$$\frac{\partial Q}{\partial R}, \frac{\partial Q}{\partial L}, \frac{\partial Q}{\partial q} > 0$$
$$\frac{\partial Q}{\partial T}, \frac{\partial Q}{\partial b} < 0.$$

Note that $\partial e/\partial L > 0$ and $\partial e/\partial b < 0$.

Poor yarn quality, maintenance, and other x-inefficient practices have three multiplicative effects: decreasing R, increasing T, and, for a given level of labor, decreasing efficiency as $\partial e / \partial b < 0$. Technical problems affecting R, T, or b (before any movement along the production function according to equation 2-2) reduce the average product of labor and capital in equal proportions—that is, they are factor neutral.

Weaving

Weaving involves interlacing lengthwise yarns (warp) and crosswise filling yarns (weft) and is carried out on a loom. The weft yarns undergo little stress during this process, whereas warp yarns (or ends) sustain considerable strain and thus require greater strength than is provided solely by a higher twist multiple. The additional strength is obtained by the sizing (or slashing) process, in which a chemical coating is added to the warp yarns.

Production Processes

The simplest weaving is accomplished by raising alternate warp yarns and inserting one length of weft (a pick) through the "shed" formed by raised and lowered ends and then reversing the pattern of raised and lowered warp yarns and inserting a second pick. The product of this pattern is called plain weave. The raising of ends is done by the heddles through which they are threaded, the heddles being raised and lowered by the loom-driving mechanism. To produce a simple pattern such as plain weave (in which weft is interlaced among alternate ends rather than, say, between two ends at a time), a plain, or cam, loom is adequate. Where complex interlacing patterns are desired, dolby, or Jacquard, devices are used to move the heddles in the required manner.[9]

The weft is usually placed on a small cylinder, or pirn, which is itself inserted in a larger cylindrical conveyor, or shuttle.[10] The shuttle may be propelled through the shed by a number of mechanisms including a simple mechanical arm, a jet of air (air jet loom) or stream of water (water jet loom), a gripping mechanism on each side of the loom (Sulzer loom), or a number of variants of the latter.[11] As cloth is woven, it is wound on a cloth beam, the process being known as taking up. Simultaneously, more warp must be released by the roll or warp beam on which it is wound, the process being called letting off. Among the important characteristics of a loom are the speed of weft insertion, described by picks per minute (PPM), the effective weaving width, and the strain the shuttle places on warp yarns as it moves between the raised and lowered warp yarns; the greater the strain, the greater the number of broken ends.

The analysis of weaving in the following chapters skips the stages between spinning and weaving (in which yarn is transferred from the bobbins on which it is spun to smaller ones used in weft supply or to larger ones used to form warp supplies). Also omitted are sizing and beaming (the placing of warp yarns on a large roller). The reason for omitting these stages is the large number of separate operations, the very large number of alternative processes, the importance of chemical skills in some activities (for example, in sizing), and, most important, the relatively small percentage of total production costs accounted for by the steps of weaving preparation. For a typical fabric the combined costs of the preparatory processes, such as sizing and beaming, amount to less than 20 percent of the cost of weaving itself.

Finally, this book leaves open the question of the proper degree of integration of spinning and weaving operations. With the exception of a few plants, notably those employing open-end spinning to produce large bobbins of low-count yarn for denim production, most textile mills in Kenya and the Philippines are vertically integrated, including not only spinning and weaving but finishing as well. A substantial body of opinion asserts that integrated plants in developed countries are less efficient than specialized spinners or weavers; some of the arguments are presented in Textile Council (1969). Whether specialist spinning and weaving mills lead to a lower unit cost in weaving will obviously depend, among other things, on the organization and transportation costs of shipping spun yarn between physically separate factories. Although the issue raises some interesting questions that have recently been the basis for imaginative work in economic history (Lazonick 1981), the present book omits it because of space limitations.

Technical and Economic Issues

A simple formula for calculating the production of cloth per loom hour is given by

$$(2\text{-}5) \qquad\qquad Q = \frac{\text{PPM}}{\text{PPI}} e$$

where Q is linear production per hour,[12] PPM is the number of picks per minute, PPI is the number of pick or weft insertions per inch (a characteristic of the final product), and e is efficiency. The term e gives the percentage of each hour during which the loom is actually weaving (inserting picks) rather than stopped for pirn transfer, mending of broken warp ends (the pressure exerted by the shuttle usually breaks warp rather than weft threads), and other nonroutine maintenance such as the removal of dust. PPM for a given weft insertion mechanism will be lower the greater the width of the loom.

Loom efficiency will fall, other things being equal, with a greater number of ends, whether this results from a construction with more warps per inch or from greater width with a given number of warp yarns per inch—more ends present a greater opportunity for breakage to occur and increase repair time. Finally, efficiency will fall when higher yarn counts are used in either warp or weft, as finer yarn is more likely to break.

The other-things-being-equal qualification about the determinants of efficiency is important. It will be remembered from the discussion of spinning that an important factor influencing efficiency is machine interference—the time it takes for a stopped machine, in this case the loom, to be noticed. Machine interference falls as the loom assignment per weaver decreases. Thus if breakage rates, the number of ends, or the count is increased, it is possible (in principle) to maintain roughly the same physical efficiency by increasing the weaver-loom ratio; whether it is economically efficient to do so depends on the same features that were discussed in spinning, suitably expanded (see equations 2-2 and 2-3). Best-practice plants show very little variation in loom efficiency when the same loom is used to make cloths with different characteristics (ends and picks per inch, yarn count, and type of weave); it is not clear whether this similarity results from cost minimization or from the use of rules of thumb to determine desired efficiency levels.

TOTAL-FACTOR PRODUCTIVITY. The preceding discussion of weaving indicates that there are two major intraplant determinants of productivity, given the characteristics of the loom (primarily PPM) and the product; these are the quality of yarn (as measured by the rate at which warp and weft yarns break) and the level of loom efficiency. In turn, loom efficiency depends, among other things, on the level of maintenance and the availability of spare parts. As the rate of yarn breakage rises, output per unit of labor and loom fall by equal percentages because looms stop when a break occurs. In addition to the downward shift in the production function, there may be a movement along it as the labor-loom ratio is increased to restore the level of loom utilization partially. The same set of factors as in spinning determines the optimal magnitude of the move along the production function. Even if firms do not follow the rule described by equation 2-2 (appropriately modified for weaving), given whatever labor-loom ratio they do choose, together with the observed rate of yarn breakage and patrol time, the physically achievable level of loom efficiency can be calculated. Any shortfall below this rate is attributable to deficiencies in maintenance, a shortage of spare parts, or x-inefficient practices. Calculations of the effect of both excessive breakage rates and lower-than-achievable levels of loom efficiency are used in later chapters to explain the discrepancy between actual productivity and best-practice productivity in operating plants. The effects of observed changes in the capital-labor ratio engendered by both differential breakage rates and wage-rental ratios are incorporated as movements along the production function. If firms do not follow this rule, the calculations attribute part of their excess cost to allocative inefficiency.

OUTPUT QUALITY AND FACTOR SUBSTITUTION. Several of the technical features of the weaving process need to be examined if we are to understand issues other than those directly affecting TFP. Of the myriad technical questions that arise, those selected for consideration here are generally acknowledged to be critical in determining economic efficiency, including the question of appropriate factor proportions.

When a pirn containing weft yarn is exhausted, the loom stops, and the weft is replenished manually on a semiautomatic loom; in an automatic loom, a sensing device called a feeler determines the need to move a new, full pirn into weaving position. Automatic pirn changing can significantly reduce unit labor requirements and can raise quality. Automatic looms have been available since the early part of the twentieth century and have largely displaced semiautomatic looms in developed countries except in the production of some special cloths. In some developing countries, such as the Republic of Korea and India, semiautomatics remain in use and are even made locally.[13] The two types of looms present well-defined technologies with different capital-labor ratios.

A critical issue in evaluating the economic merit of different types of looms is the effect of starting marks that may occur when an empty pirn is changed. In automatic looms, it is possible to avoid any starting marks when a depleted pirn is replaced by a full one, as the feeler senses the imminent exhaustion of the weft and orders the shuttle transfer mechanism to move a replacement pirn into place. If an automatic loom's feeler is incorrectly connected, it may leave a starting mark when a replacement is needed. Even where a correctly functioning changing mechanism exists, there will still be a flaw (a mispick) when a break in yarn occurs; thus automatic looms do not guarantee cloth of better quality unless mispicks are kept low, which in turn requires high-quality yarn.

In contrast, each time a pirn runs out of yarn in a semiautomatic loom there is the potential for a flaw as the shuttle crosses the shed once without inserting any weft while the woven fabric on the cloth beam is moved up one pick and the let-off roll also moves one pick. Experienced weaving managers claim that defects are not inevitable when semiautomatic looms are being used; a skilled weaver will generally anticipate actual pirn depletion, stop the loom, and replace the almost empty pirn. Even if the pirn does run out, it is possible for an able weaver to adjust the let-off and take-up rolls so that the pick with an empty pirn will not cause a starting flaw. Nevertheless, it is acknowledged that these operations (sensing a nearby empty pirn and adjusting the warp or cloth beams) require substantial experience, diligence, and dexterity. Thus an automatic loom may substitute capital (in the form of a somewhat higher price for the feelers and automatic changing mechanism) for skilled labor, and the competitiveness of the semiautomatic loom, at least in producing high-quality cloth, will be contingent on the availability of inexpensive, highly skilled labor.

More generally, the relevance of concern about starting places is questionable: starting places may be noticeable where a single color finishing is used but are not readily discernible in a printed pattern. In many developing countries, printed goods constitute the overwhelming majority of products destined for the domestic market, and printed fabrics with weaving starting marks are not normally lower in price.[14] If semiautomatic looms yielded lower-cost fabric production, there would be a prima facie, static efficiency case for using them, though questions about the development of the quality consciousness necessary for successful exporting might still arise in a dynamic framework. Even here, however, if the only defects associated with semiautomatic looms were starting places, a marketing program for printed cloth might yield substantial sales and might permit expanded use of labor-intensive technology.

THE PRODUCTION FUNCTION. The above description can be summarized with an explicit production function for weaving:

$$(2\text{-}6) \qquad Q = \frac{\text{PPM}(W)}{\text{PPI}} \, qe(W, E, c, b, L)$$

where Q is the output per set of looms per hour and the other symbols are: W, loom width; E, ends per inch; c, count of yarn; b, end breakage rates; L, the number of operatives; and q, the impact of procedures that reduce operating efficiency below the level achievable, given other variables. In particular, the inability to procure spare parts may be a significant determinant of q. Equation 2-6 has the following characteristics:

$$(2\text{-}6a) \qquad \frac{\partial Q}{\partial \text{PPM}}, \frac{\partial Q}{\partial L}, \frac{\partial Q}{\partial q} > 0, \ \frac{\partial \text{PPM}}{\partial W} < 0$$

$$\frac{\partial Q}{\partial \text{PPI}}, \frac{\partial Q}{\partial W}, \frac{\partial Q}{\partial E}, \frac{\partial Q}{\partial c}, \frac{\partial Q}{\partial b} < 0.$$

Labor requirements per linear yard of output, z, are implied by the foregoing and can be written explicitly as

(2-7) $$z = g(\text{PPM}, \text{PPI}, E, W, c, b)$$

with partial derivatives

(2-7a)
$$\frac{\partial z}{\partial \text{PPM}} < 0$$
$$\frac{\partial z}{\partial \text{PPI}}, \frac{\partial z}{\partial W}, \frac{\partial z}{\partial E}, \frac{\partial z}{\partial b}, \frac{\partial z}{\partial c} < 0.$$

The expression $\partial z / \partial \text{PPM} < 0$ captures the fact that, for a given level of output, the faster the loom, the smaller the labor requirements. Net changes in z are the outcome of several simultaneous changes in specific skill requirements. As the count is increased, for example, fewer weft carriers are needed to bring filled pirns to the loom, as each pirn contains a longer-lasting supply of weft and each yard of production requires fewer pirns. When finer counts are used, however, more breaks occur, increasing the requirement per unit of output of skilled weavers (assuming it is economic to restore machine efficiency partly). Evidence based on best practice indicates that the net effect of higher counts on labor requirements will be positive. Thus an increase in product quality in the form of finer yarns could lead to a net increase in the total demand for labor and a substitution among workers of different skills. This is a more complex picture than has emerged in recent discussions of the interaction between product and factor choice; the best statement of the issues appears in Stewart (1977).

Product Specialization and Productivity

Thus far I have focused on the engineering determinants of productivity, specifically noting the critical machine parameters and the process by which potential performance may be reduced if certain technical, firm-specific capabilities are unavailable. In practice, however, plant productivity may also be penalized by the economic environment in which the plant operates.

The adverse effect of short production runs is a staple of much of the causal discussion among plant managers and textile technologists about the determinants of productivity in textiles. Production costs are said to rise with product variety even when output is such that each plant is fully utilized. Average and marginal cost curves shift upward because of shorter average production runs as variety increases even though, for a given product mix and for a given plant and labor force, average cost may decline as fuller utilization occurs. Conversely, longer average production runs shift the cost curves downward. The precise engineering bases for postulating these upward shifts are rarely specified, but they appear to be a combination of optimal batch size and the cost of attaining routinized production.

Part of the upward shift in cost curves is attributable to increased setup times. If a count is to be changed in spinning, roller speeds, which determine the amount of draft (sliver attenuation), must be adjusted from drawframes through ring spindles. Even with good mechanics, the process can be time consuming; meanwhile operatives and equipment are idle. Setup time assumes even greater importance in weaving, where an entire warp beam may be changed when a new pattern is to be woven and the ends of the new beam must be tied through the heddles. If frequent product changes occur, setup time significantly reduces productivity relative to best practice. There is an irreducible level of setup costs, however, even without frequent pattern changes, for example when an exhausted warp beam must be changed. Short production runs are viewed as a major source of the lower productivity of U.K. plants relative to their counterparts in the United States (Textile Council 1969) and are clearly an important cause of lower productivity in plants in Kenya and the Philippines relative to plants in the United Kingdom.

Despite the importance of setup costs, it seems likely that the higher costs associated with short production runs arise mainly from the need to be almost continually learning about, and reacting to, processing problems that would become routine in longer production runs. Consider spinning. It will be shown in chapter 6 that many mills are careless with respect to the blending of fibers and have limited proficiency in quality control. Under these conditions, switching to a new count will reduce productivity even more than it would in the presence of greater skills in these areas. Problems with strength and uniformity, which would be noted immediately in a plant with good quality control, will be noticed only with a lag, and correcting them will therefore take longer. Before the correction occurs, the productivity-depressing effects will have been felt in the form of a greater number of end breaks. When longer production runs prevail, however, a larger percentage of output is produced after the necessary corrections have been made, and this output is manufactured under routine conditions that permit higher productivity. Similar arguments hold for weaving.

These problems undoubtedly explain the attempt by many U.S. textile mills to produce no more than two or three yarn counts and a similar number of fabric types over the course of a year. In contrast, it was not uncommon for the firms that I visited to have ten or twelve yarn counts (a problem worsened by constantly changing mixtures of cotton and synthetic fibers) and forty to sixty cloth types.

The following statement explains why U.K. firms are less productive than those in the United States and aptly summarizes the discussion so far:

> Such changes (in count or cloth) present technical and organizational problems which strain the ability of the staff and work people to cope with them. When staff at all levels can concentrate on the production of a very limited number of products, the smallest details can receive attention and be brought to near perfection. Production planning becomes relatively easy. Time and effort which would be widely uneconomic in normal circumstances can be justified if the volume of production is sufficiently great. (Textile Council 1969, vol. 1, p. 72.)

This remark suggests that an improvement in technical management that provides better quality control (faster identification and correction of problems) could offset some of the adverse effects of product diversity.[15] Hence plants in two economies might have differing levels of total-factor productivity—even though they had the same domestic market size and similar levels of protection—if one of them had expended more effort than the other on augmenting firm-level technological capabilities.

Saxonhouse and Wright (1984) have shown that Japanese textile firms put considerable effort into mixing, operative training, and supervision in the early stages of their development and thus obtained higher productivity with low-quality domestic cotton fiber than would otherwise have been possible. Such care throughout the production cycle can reduce the problems arising from constant changes in product specification but will not eliminate them.

Product Specification and Factor Proportions

Much attention has recently focused on how the choice of product characteristics affects optimal factor proportions (Stewart 1977). This topic is not addressed systematically in subsequent chapters, but some of the relevant issues are considered here. In both spinning and weaving, different product specifications lead to variations in the best-practice capital-labor ratio for a given technology, such as a conventional automatic loom. Factor proportions may also vary when different technologies are used to make an identical product, the conventional issue in the choice of technology debate. The magnitude of the range in factor proportions that arises from choices in these two areas—product specification and technology—has elicited some empirical research in recent years. For attempts to evaluate these questions in an econometric framework, see Rhee and Westphal (1977) and Ranis and Saxonhouse (1978).

Of the several sets of data from which such comparisons may be made, I have utilized figures gathered in a comprehensive analysis of U.K. textile production in the late 1960s (Textile Council 1969). There is no reason to believe that recent developments have altered the picture significantly.

In spinning, six different yarns constitute the products compared: they differ in both thickness (count) and raw material (cotton, cotton-polyester, rayon). The technologies used in the comparison are a modern ring-spinning plant and an open-end, or break, spinning plant employing a revolutionary breakthrough in spinning. Table 2-2 shows the substantial variation, up to 60 percent in conventional and up to 200 percent in open-end spinning, in the capital-labor ratios needed to produce different yarns using the same technology.[16] The variation in capital intensity, however, between the two technologies (column 3) for the identical product typically exceeds 300 percent. Thus although both product and technology choice offer substantial scope for achieving variations in factor proportions, the latter is of greater quantitative significance in spinning.

Table 2-2. *Variation in Capital-Labor Ratio in Spinning by Product and Technology*
(thousands of pounds sterling)

Count	Fiber product	Ring spinning (1)	Open-end spinning (2)	(2) ÷ (1)
12	Cotton	7.1	18.9	2.6
20	Cotton	8.4	37.0	4.4
30	Cotton	9.6	48.8	5.1
32	Rayon	8.3	45.2	5.4
40	Cotton-polyester	9.9	41.7	4.2
50	Cotton	10.8	56.1	5.2

Source: Textile Council (1969), vol. 2.

A related conjecture often put forth, that products consumed by upper-income groups are more capital-intensive than those consumed by lower-income groups, also merits attention. Relatively coarse yarns (12s) have a lower capital-labor ratio than 50s cotton or 40s cotton-polyester.

The latter two are indirectly consumed in the products purchased by higher-income families, as they are used in finer and no-iron cloths. A full evaluation of the hypothesis requires information on other processing stages as well, however—particularly weaving, the most costly stage.

In weaving, five different products are compared. Their specifications appear in table 2-3. The capital-labor ratios associated with looms based on four different weft insertion principles are shown in table 2-4; they reveal variation as great as 50 percent but generally less than 25 percent between products when all are produced with the same loom.[17] The variations between different kinds of looms making identical fabrics are much greater, being at least 100 percent and reaching multiples of ten to eighteen when the semiautomatic and Sulzer looms are compared.

To return to a question briefly touched on above, there is no simple association between better cloth quality (in the same sense of more picks

Table 2-3. *Characteristics of Woven Fabric*

Fabric	Count Warp	Weft	Ends per inch	Picks per inch	Finished width (inches)	Weave	Yarn
Sheeting	20	20	60	60	90	Plain	Cotton
Printer	30	30	80	80	36	Plain	Cotton
Shirting	40	40	123	66	42	Plain	Cotton-polyester
Zephyr	50	50	100	100	36	Plain	Cotton
Rayon	32	32	88	60	38	Plain	Spun

Source: Textile Council (1969), vol. 2.

Table 2-4. *Variation in Capital-Labor Ratios in Weaving by Type of Loom*
(thousands of pounds sterling)

Fabric	Semi-automatic loom	Automatic loom	Automatic loom with unifil attachment	Air jet loom	Sulzer loom
Sheeting	3.1	10.1	15.0	—	55.8
Printer	5.1	13.0	16.9	17.3	59.2
Shirting	4.6	9.7	12.2	14.7	44.4
Zephyr	4.8	11.4	13.7	13.2	40.5
Rayon	5.3	10.8	13.4	16.8	49.8

— not applicable.
Source: Textile Council (1969), vol. 2.

and ends per inch and finer yarn count) and greater capital intensity. If, for example, zephyr and printer cloths are compared, zephyr (the higher-quality cloth) is typically produced with a capital-labor ratio ranging from 68 percent to 95 percent of that associated with printer.[18] In addition to the direct capital intensity of the weaving process, the indirect require-ments of the spinning stage must also be considered: the capital-labor ratio for the yarn used in zephyr is 13 percent greater than it is for that used in printer. Taking direct and indirect input requirements together, the total capital intensity for spinning and weaving combined is consider-ably greater for printer. The total capital intensity by cloth type depends on both the type of loom used (because the capital-labor ratio varies among looms) and the required weight of yarn per square meter of cloth. The ultimate labor and capital requirements for the finished product also depend on the finishing process employed; however, because spinning and weaving constitute the two major cost components in textile manufactur-ing, the finishing process will not much alter the results obtaining after the first two. In sum, it is difficult to discern any simple relation between total-factor intensity and the importance of particular goods in the con-sumption baskets of different income groups. At the same time, however, the choice of technology, at least in spinning and weaving, significantly affects the direct employment generated by a given investment.

Two additional observations may be made. First, the capital and labor coefficients that form the basis for the figures in table 2-4 are those of best-practice plants in a developed country. Operational differences be-tween plants could alter the relationship between factor intensity and such product characteristics as count and picks per inch if operations that were important in producing one or another characteristic were poorly carried out. Second, the introduction of still other product charac-teristics, such as more complex weaves that require Jacquard, or dolby, looms, could alter the weaving results, though it is not clear that the pattern described above would be reversed.

Notes

1. For elaboration of the technical activities in spinning, the interested reader may consult Hamby (1966), vol. 1, chaps. 6–10, and Lord (1981), chaps. 11 and 12.

2. Lord (1981). In India it is apparently common practice to increase the number of twists per inch to compensate for poor fiber.

3. The length of fiber and other fiber attributes were among the data collected in the plant interviews. The attribution of excessive twist multiples to causes other than poor fiber reflects partly the results of standard quality-control tests at each stage where these are performed and, where they were not available, the judgment of R. Grills, a textile engineer from the

Shirley Institute who accompanied me on all plant visits. Thus the basis for the attribution between x-inefficiency and cost-minimizing responses is partly subjective. It is worth emphasizing that no matter how "micro" the research strategy employed, some minimum subjective judgment will always be required. The leap of faith in this respect is, I would claim, considerably smaller than that required in econometric modeling of secondary data collected on an industrywide basis.

4. The variations in the rate of machine utilization per hour should not be confused with variations in the number of hours per week or per year during which a factory utilizes its plant and equipment; the latter may reflect a set of factors different from those discussed here (Betancourt and Clague 1981; Winston 1973). The productivity measures presented throughout this book are based on hourly production data, and fluctuations in capacity utilization over the year do not affect the comparison with best practice discussed in chapter 3.

5. High breakage rates may be encountered as spindle speed is increased for a given count or for a variety of other reasons. The most complete account of the phenomenon in developing country mills is that of Subramanian and Garde (1974).

6. Whether firms in fact follow the dictates of this cost-minimizing rule is a question addressed in chapter 7. The normative rule is introduced here to indicate the behavioral and technical basis of postinstallation variability in factor proportions.

7. For a derivation and discussion of these formulas, see Lord (1981), pp. 532–34, for spinning, and Lord and Mohamed (1976), pp. 319–23, for weaving. Also see Ormerod (1979), chap. 2, and Enrick (1978).

8. Among the best discussions of the relevant issues is that of Subramanian and Garde (1974).

9. For a very clear and detailed account of the weaving process, see Marks and Robinson (1976); also Aitken (1964) and Lord and Mohamed (1976). The best discussion of some of the economic issues appears in Ormerod (1979).

10. Exceptions occur in some of the newer looms, in which the weft is not wound onto pirns.

11. For good technical discussions of the various looms, see Aitken (1964) and Duxbury and Wray (1962).

12. The greater the width of the loom, the larger the area of fabric woven. This is an important economic consideration, price being a function of total area. Moreover, for some items, such as sheeting, only wide widths can provide an acceptable product. Loom prices rise with width, though not proportionally. Shuttle speed and picks per minute fall with width, but not proportionally. In calculations reported in later chapters, differences in the widths of looms and products have been taken into account so that all inputs are stated on a common basis.

13. The semiautomatic loom should not be confused with a hand loom: the former is electrically powered, and its shuttle speed is quite high. In hand looms, all operations, such as propelling the shuttle, are done manually. A useful technical discussion of the weft replenishment process can be found in Marks and Robinson (1976), chap. 9.

14. There are no durability problems associated with starting places as there are with other defects.

15. The effect of increasing product specialization continues to be realized even when quite substantial specialization has already occurred, as indicated by the following: "Recently the Rendall Company of the USA, for example, announced that it had split one large shed into two sheds of 690 and 550 looms, reduced warp counts from four to two and weft counts from ten to three. As a result of these changes, overall productivity increased by 40 percent. This example is no exception. A recent survey of seven of the most modern mills in the United States, five modernized and two newly built, showed that the trend to fewer yarn counts and

fewer fabrics continues. Of the seven plants, only two had more than two warp and weft counts and they are concentrating on a basic fabric with few changes. In the seven plants, groupings of 500–600 looms have become the norm" (Textile Council 1969, vol. 1, p. 73).

16. The greater capital-labor ratio as the count increases reflects the need for a larger number of spindles to produce a pound of yarn of higher count. Although the increase in the number of spindles per pound is partly offset by the increase in labor requirements occasioned by the higher breakage rate as count increases, the net effect is the measured increase in the capital-labor ratio.

17. Some of the variation between products is not relevant; for example, sheeting material is not very suitable for clothing.

18. The lower capital-labor ratio of the finer cloth arises from the fact that the use of higher yarn counts generates more broken ends, so that additional labor is used as firms attempt in part to restore loom efficiency. The implication is that the requirement for additional weavers outweighs the negative employment effect of the reduced frequency of weft replenishment. Rhee and Westphal (1977) also find that labor requirements increase with the specifications usually associated with high-income consumption.

CHAPTER THREE

Best Practice
and the Source of Deviations
from It

THIS CHAPTER discusses the concept of best practice as opposed to "pure" engineering standards and then presents best-practice coefficients for spinning and weaving in a developed country environment. The data I have collected on input requirements in developing country textile plants show that, for plants that are technically similar in terms of the type of equipment used, developing country operators typically use more of most inputs per unit of output, that is, they are less physically productive than their developed country counterparts. The sources of this difference in productivity, as we shall see, include factors arising from shortcomings in the national economy, aspects of industrywide phenomena, features specific to individual firms, and, finally, poor task-level performance of individual operatives. Unfortunately, there are no independent measures of the last item; it is calculated as a residual that may include other possible sources of low productivity, such as poor measurements of the other factors or sources of low productivity that have been totally omitted.

I subsequently present the algebra involved in the actual calculation of total-factor productivity of developing country firms relative to their developed country counterparts as well as the decomposition of the difference into its various sources. Both Cobb-Douglas and constant elasticity of substitution (CES) production functions are used as weighting functions to make possible some quantification of the relative total-factor productivity of firms in developed and developing countries.

In addition to international differences in productivity and its sources, I analyze the varying production costs of firms using different technologies within Kenya and the Philippines, present the conceptual framework that forms the basis of the interfirm comparisons presented in chapters 4 and 5, and set forth the actual empirical procedures used to calculate each of the productivity-depressing factors. An appendix addresses the measurement of inputs and the determination of parameter values used in the calculations. Both the last section and the appendix may be omitted by the reader not interested in detail.

The Technical Frontier and Best Practice

An isoquant represents an efficient set of technologies. A range of machinery is currently available from equipment manufacturers for each stage of the production process in cotton textiles; each machine or set of machines is operated by a group of workers using specific amounts of raw materials. The amount of machines, materials, and labor per unit of output for a specific technology as envisaged by the equipment producers may be described as an engineering standard or norm and represents the current technical frontier. Some of the anticipated input-output ratios primarily reflect physical laws governing the process; others are also affected by economic and social variables such as relative factor prices and the state of management-labor relations. As will be seen in the following chapters, the best-practice ratio of machines to output is more nearly realized than the analogous labor-output standard. The quanity of output per card per minute specified in operating manuals by a card manufacturer, for example, is usually fairly close to its actual productivity on the factory floor: the wastage rate, required floor space, and kilowatt hours of electricity are also generally close to the manufacturer's specifications.

The manning levels suggested by machinery manufacturers are derived from a variety of sources, including their own experimental workshops and extrapolations of the experience of current users of earlier versions of their equipment. Labor-output ratios generated by these observations are, however, not purely technical data reflecting underlying physical imperatives. Labor productivity in manufacturers' own experimental plants or the high-productivity plants of their purchasers may reflect the rigor of the hiring process, incentive pay systems, supervisory quality, the ability of management to provide high-quality raw materials, and workers' and managers' awareness that they are being observed. Unlike the case of the well-known Chenery engineering production functions for gas flow (Chenery 1953), derivable from the laws of chemistry, observed input-output coefficients in textiles will reflect these nonmachine behavioral relations as well as the physically feasible engineering coefficients. Thus the concept of best practice rather than that of engineering norms seems appropriate as the standard against which to compare operating firms. Best practice reflects the realized performance of the best (or better) firms in an industry, and the relevant input coefficients will be inferior to those physical maxima achievable under ideal conditions.

The evolution of best practice over time largely reflects the development of the more basic engineering production function. At any given moment, however, the product per worker or machine in even the best-managed plant will be inferior to the then-known maximum engineering standard, the degree of the shortfall being related to the extent to which plant operations fall short of ideal practice in activities ranging from blending to humidity control to personnel relations.[1] The best-practice input-output coefficients presented below have been calculated from

Table 3-1. *Best-Practice Coefficients in Cotton Spinning*

| | Input[a] | | Cost per spindle |
Item	Operative hours	Spindles[b]	(U.S. dollars)[c]
Ring spinning			
1950	0.1722	0.0071	n.a.
1960	0.1128	0.0060	n.a.
1965	0.0815	0.0056	n.a.
1977	0.0512	0.0054	116
Open end	0.0370	0.0015	776
Average annual compound rate of decrease			
1950–60	4.14	1.67	—
1960–65	6.29	1.37	—
1965–77	3.80	0.30	—

n.a. not available.

— not applicable.

Note: All of the coefficients have been derived by assuming a common product, namely, 20s count according to the English system. Where the original data were given for other counts, interpolations were made using standard adjustment factors. The count measure, *s*, indicates the number of lengths of 840 yards per pound of cotton. Throughout the volume, this count measure, known as English count, is used rather than the alternative metric measure or the newer tex measure.

a. Per kilogram of 20s yarn.

b. Rotors for open end. The number shown is the inverse of the annual output per spindle or rotor, assuming 7,200 hours of utilization.

c. Per spindle or rotor.

Sources: 1950 and 1960: Textile Council (1969); 1965: UNIDO (1967b); 1977 and open end: Grills (1978) and unpublished manufacturer's data sheets.

Table 3-2. *Best-Practice Coefficients in Cotton Weaving*

Item	Semiautomatic Lancashire	Automatic battery	Air jet	Sulzer
Operative hours per yard	0.0436	0.0222	0.0163	0.0101
Loom hours per yard	0.249	0.201	0.133	0.070
Price per loom (U.S. dollars)				
1968	n.a.	2,665	4,493	11,963
1979[a]	3,500	10,000	21,000	66,000
		8,200		
		7,200		
		6,800		
Index of loom purchase price				
(1979) per unit of output	100	157[b]	370	530

n.a. not available.

a. Prices for conventional battery looms vary substantially among suppliers, and four quotations are provided for looms with very similar specifications.

b. Based on loom price of US$6,800.

Source: Textile Council (1969) and information provided by loom manufacturers.

plants in the United Kingdom whose productivity places them at the upper quartile of British textile mills. Data available for firms at the upper quartile in other Western European countries show similar coefficients. The data for the United Kingdom constitute the most carefully done empirical description of best practice; they provide an enormous amount of production engineering information that is critical for the analysis of the sources of low productivity given below. The less detailed information available for other countries is much less useful in this respect. In chapter 7, the U.K. coefficients will be placed in an international context so that the results reported in this study can be embedded within a cross-country context.

Each input vector represents one technology along the ex ante isoquant *EABCE'* in figure 1-1. The continuous nature of the isoquant as depicted there reflects the large number of choices available from each textile equipment manufacturer at any point in time. In spinning, for example, ring frames capable of similar speeds may be ordered with or without automatic cleaning devices. If the option is not chosen, more unskilled workers are needed to clean the spinning room. Variation in technique once a technology is chosen is also possible, for example, by altering spindle efficiency, thus moving along *aa* or *a'a'* in figure 1-1.

The Evolution of Best-Practice Standards

Spinning

Table 3-1 presents measures of best-practice unit input requirements in the United Kingdom for cotton spinning with equipment manufactured in four different years, 1950, 1960, 1965, and 1977. There are a number of other sources of data for the first three years, and all provide similar estimates of output per spindle and output per man-hour (for example, see UNIDO 1967a and b; ECLA 1951 and 1965). The 1977 norms are those presented to prospective purchasers by the engineering department of one major producer of textile equipment and are not corroborated by other evidence. These estimates are consistent with earlier trends, however, and the norms are considered accurate by textile engineers. The 1965 data are based on the same company's estimate and thus provide consistency in intertemporal comparisons.

The unit labor requirements (operative hours per kilogram of 20s cotton) measure the labor input for the entire spinning process from the opening of bales of cotton fiber to the removal from ring frames of bobbins of spun yarn; they do not reflect labor used in processes subsequent to spinning, such as preparation of yarn for weaving. The (physical) capital-output measure, spindles per kilogram, describes only the spinning process proper, omitting opening, cleaning, carding, drawing, and roving. Productivity per machine in these activities has roughly increased at the same rate as in spinning, though some variation exists. The emphasis on spinning proper focuses attention on the essential features of technical change while avoiding excessive detail.[2]

The coefficients shown in table 3-1 are the best-practice norms against which the actual coefficients in developing country spinning plants can be compared. They also provide a capsule summary of the nature of technological change in spinning.

Over the 1950–77 period, operative hours per kilogram in best-practice plants fell by 70 percent and spindles per kilogram by 23 percent. This growth in productivity was achieved by continuing progress within a basically unchanged technology and resulted from increased speed, changes in the physical dimensions of some machine components (ring size) and accessories (cans collecting slivers), and a number of devices that turned the production sequence into one approaching continuous processing, thus eliminating workers whose job had been the transfer of material from one stage to the next. Table 3-1 shows the compound rates of decrease in the coefficients for various subperiods. It is noteworthy that the labor coefficient continued to fall rapidly throughout the twenty-seven years, though with some variation. Despite the halving of the labor coefficient between 1950 and 1965, opportunities for further declines were hardly exhausted even with the conventional technology. In contrast, the rate of decline in the physical capital coefficient for ring spinning has decelerated over the period.

The process of rapid technical innovation characterizing the cotton spinning process did not come to an end, or even slow down, after the remarkable productivity increases in ring spinning in the third quarter of the century. A completely new process, developed in the 1960s and known as open-end (or break) spinning, is now being diffused to operating plants. This process requires a quarter less labor than the 1977 ring-spinning norms and reduces the number of spindles (more precisely, rotors) per unit of output by three-quarters, though at a 570 percent increase in cost per rotor (table 3-1). Whereas the improved performance levels between 1950 and 1977 reflect the results of steady advances in a process whose basic features would be recognizable to a nineteenth-century mill owner, open-end spinning initiates an essentially new process. The unit capital requirement should not be compared with those for ring spinning; the change in technology is so radical that the comparison of spindles and rotors per unit of output is not meaningful in analyzing technical evolution. Nevertheless, the almost sixfold difference between cost per rotor and cost per ring spindle implies that, despite the dramatic change in technology, the least-cost decision facing textile producers choosing between the two remains a meaningful one. As with earlier technical evolution, this innovation does not necessarily yield lower production costs in developing countries, given their low wages and the high opportunity cost of capital.

Weaving

The major technical developments in weaving, it will be recalled, have been in how the weft is replenished as the supply on the pirn currently in use is exhausted (chapter 2) and the technique of weft insertion. The best-practice input coefficients for shirting are shown in table 3-2 for looms ranging from the Lancashire semiautomatic (electric-powered weft insertion but manual replacement of weft supply), to the gripper, or Sulzer, loom. These coefficients capture much of the technical development of the last forty years, though this evolution has not been temporally sequential, and new innovations have occurred simultaneously in some cases. As in spinning, the major quantitative change has been the decrease in labor requirements, though loom hours per unit of output have also fallen significantly, mainly because of a faster rate of weft insertion, measured by picks per minute. Nevertheless, the greater price of the physically more productive looms implies that the least-cost technology choice depends on relative factor prices. The input coefficients in table 3-2 and comparable ones for woven products with other characteristics are employed as the best-practice norms. Although input requirements differ for alternative versions of the various looms, the differences are typically small.

More recent (1976) data on input coefficients in weaving presented in a careful study by Pickett and Robinson indicate that little change has occurred in best-practice coefficients except in a few cases, notably air jet looms, which are slightly faster than 1968 models.[3] Moreover, more recent information collected for the present volume by the Shirley Institute of Manchester also suggests relatively little change in best practice since the date of the earlier study (the Textile Council 1969), upon which many of the detailed calculations are based. These issues are also discussed below in the present chapter.

A Decomposition of Cross-Country Productivity Differentials

A recurrent feature in the data collected in Kenya and the Philippines for this study, as well as in earlier published data on Latin America, is the lower productivity in developing country plants compared with the best-practice ones in developed countries. The difference between productivity (labor productivity is usually emphasized) in developed and developing countries has often been noted, and several explanations have been offered for it.[4] These often rely on descriptions of the cultural background or educational characteristics of industrial workers but almost never consider the nature of the manufacturing process or economic factors such as the rationality of using greater labor-capital ratios when lower wage-rental ratios prevail. They emphasize one major obstacle (absence of "modernity") in an occasionally tautological way, and the implicit hypotheses are largely incapable of being tested or quantified. A more fruitful approach involves the identification of the most likely major sources of deviation from best-practice productivity and the quantification of each of them where possible.

A descriptive schema that I have found useful in other industrial analyses can also be utilized here (Pack 1981). A firm's productivity may be affected by (1) conditions determined at the national and industry levels, (2) the managerial capacities of the firm, and (3) the task-level productivity of individual workers. The empirical implementation of the decomposition is discussed below. Productivity is calculated on an hourly basis, and fluctuations in capacity utilization because of seasonal, cyclical, or random phenomena such as interruption in electricity supply do not affect measured productivity.

The National Economy

If productivity is evaluated for a given period such as a month, some features of the national economy will affect the plant: breakdowns in the transportation system, failures in electricity supply, and other intermittent sources of production delays will lead to fluctuations in capacity utilization. Even if transient disturbances are omitted and productivity per hour of actual production is calculated, the national economy will impinge on individual plants. Inadequacies in the educational system, for example, will increase the training costs of firms; this in turn may lead firms to provide less instruction than they would otherwise and may lower the productivity of operatives or managers.[5]

The success of the economy in providing jobs may affect the willingness of workers to accept rationalization of the production process in terms of both general plant reorganization and individual work loads. National labor legislation that limits the ability of firms to fire excess workers, for example, may adversely affect productivity, whereas management's commitment to raising it may be influenced by the structure of existing incentives, ranging from those affecting international and domestic competition to those determining the terms of loans from the financial system.

Despite their number and potential importance, I do not try to quantify the impact of features of the national economy that affect measured productivity for individual firms. Some of them ought not to enter into the calculations as formulated for this study: for example, the impact of intermittent interruptions is not relevant, because all comparisons involve output per hour and inputs per hour when equipment is in fact operating; annual productivity may be affected significantly by such stoppages but is not at issue here. Other characteristics of the national economic environment, such as the impact of the protection afforded by trade barriers on the intensity of worker and managerial effort, are difficult to model, and no attempt has been made to model them. Such omissions may lead to an unexplained difference in productivity between developing country and developed country best-practice plants, which is included in the measured residual task-level productivity.

The Industry

Among the industrywide features that can affect plant productivity are the number of firms in the industry and the resulting intensity of competition. Competitive imports are largely excluded and do not affect the level of internal competition in either Kenya or the Philippines. If an industry has been encouraged by high rates of effective protection to expand its productive capacity beyond the requirements of the domestic market but remains unable to produce cheaply enough to export its output, it will operate at higher than necessary average cost. In Kenya and the Philippines, most firms are producing a sufficiently large volume of output that excess costs are not attributable to economies of scale in the conventional sense that average costs decline with increasingly intensive use of fixed facilities. An important source of high cost, however, is the small scale of individual production runs in weaving and the range of yarn counts in spinning. For any given percentage of capacity utilization, unit costs could be reduced if the variety of yarns or fabrics produced were decreased.[6]

ECONOMIES OF SPECIALIZATION. The prevalence of short production runs, with each firm producing a broad spectrum of products that duplicates those of others, presents a puzzle. Any firm that moved toward specializing in a small range of products would enjoy a cost advantage that would provide it with a competitive edge.[7] If we assume that it lowered its price, it would attract sales away from nonspecializing mills, which would then have an incentive to reduce the diversity of their own output.[8] In both Kenya and the Philippines, the domestic market is large enough relative to the minimum efficient scale of an individual firm's operations to permit greater intraindustry specialization, yet this has not occurred. Moreover, even the failure to specialize does not necessarily imply the short production runs that currently prevail. There are two key questions. (1) Why do firms typically produce a large range of products, given the decrease in unit production costs obtainable by greater specialization? (2) Given a decision to manufacture a wide spectrum of products, why do firms not attempt to realize longer production runs by producing for inventory? Each question is addressed in turn.[9]

Several answers to the first question can be posited, including the role of risk aversion and the effect of vertical integration and historical links to particular distribution channels. If specialization existed, shifts in demand among products could lead to excess capacity for any individual product. An attempt by the producer to diversify into other areas would probably not succeed, given the lower costs of firms already specializing in these goods. To avoid this unattractive scenario, individual firms may maintain a broad product line as a strategy of risk reduction, if it is assumed that fluctuations in their individual markets are not positively correlated. This interpretation requires an explanation of the willingness of firms in more developed countries to specialize more narrowly. The possible reasons include a lower degree of risk aversion, given higher profit levels, a lower probability of dramatic shifts in large markets with stable past histories, an ability to export and thus to offset domestic demand fluctuations (if it is assumed that identical shifts do not occur throughout the world), and a greater ability to alter product specifications efficiently and quickly because of the generally higher quality and breadth of experience of management and technical personnel.

Most textile mills in the Philippines, and to a lesser extent in Kenya, are closely linked to specific wholesalers or retailers and have often been established by the latter during the period of growing import substitution. There is substantial evidence that the wholesalers and retailers prefer to have their own mills manufacture the entire range of products, fearing monopolistic behavior on the part of unaffiliated mills should the retailer require a good not produced by its own subsidiary. Shifts in demand and the attendant risks will intensify any preference for internal production of the complete spectrum of products. If historical ties and the avoidance of potential high prices are a major motivation for product diversification, the ability to purchase inputs such as yarn at world prices would constitute an incentive to abandon the current structure.

Insofar as the establishment of new plants is possible, new entrants could lower their costs by increasing their specialization. But the new firms would have difficulty in domestic markets, given the vertical integration of the textile sector. If the new mills were oriented to export markets and specialized in a narrow range of products, they could realize lower unit costs, which might also induce greater specialization among existing firms. These issues are discussed further in chapters 8 and 9.

Given the fact that each firm has decided, for the above-mentioned reasons, to produce a large range of products, it is nevertheless possible that production for inventory would permit a significant proportion of the benefit from large individual lot sizes to be realized. The determination of the optimal size of an individual production run has been a staple of the operations research literature.[10] The optimal lot size is determined by minimizing the joint cost of production and the cost of holding inventories and yields the following decision rule:

$$(3\text{-}1) \qquad\qquad Q^* = \sqrt{2FD/hV}$$

where F is the fixed cost incurred in setting up an individual production run, D is the firm's demand per unit of time, h is the cost of carrying inventory (including interest, charges for storage space, and obsolescence or spoilage costs) as a percentage of variable costs, V, which is assumed to be constant. For the individual firm, D is determined by the size of the market and the factors affecting the degree of specialization among products.

The formulation contained in equation 3-1 does not explicitly recognize the possibility that variable cost declines with the length of production run, for reasons discussed in the preceding chapter. Assume that variable cost takes the simple form $V = A + B/Q$, where A is the asymptote approached as Q becomes large. In this case, the optimum-lot formula changes slightly and becomes

$$(3\text{-}2) \qquad\qquad Q^* = \sqrt{2(F + B)D/hV}.$$

The reluctance of firms to produce for inventory rather than for current orders might result from very high values of h, caused by rapid shifts in tastes that lead to a reduced value of inventory at the time of sale. This does not appear to be a plausible description of the overall textile market. Nor are high interest or storage costs plausible explanations of observed behavior. An absence of a cost calculus similar to that applicable in other instances (which will be discussed in chapter 6) needs to be invoked to explain the failure to produce systematically for inventory.

OTHER INDUSTRY CHARACTERISTICS. Other industry activities that may affect productivity include the financing of research institutes, the diffusion of their findings, and the establishment of central education facilities for operatives and technicians.[11] In Kenya and the Philippines, however, the potential benefits of these activities are dwarfed by those of product specialization.

The Firm

Managerial and technical skills in production engineering can have a major influence on productivity at the firm level.[12] Important factors include adequate blending of raw fiber at the beginning of the production process in spinning (inadequate blending produces imperfect yarn that causes high breakage rates in both spinning and weaving); good humidity control in spinning and weaving; appropriate quality of sizing, the liquid used to add strength to yarn before it is woven; and the use of quality-control tests throughout the process to obtain quick identification and correction of production errors accounting for defects. Inadequate knowledge of or ability to implement these and other aspects of production engineering may lower capital, labor, or material productivity. Frequent breaks in spinning caused by poor blending and weak roving, for example, will lower average output per spindle and per worker.

Knowledge of these and other technical requirements of production is unevenly distributed among firms.[13] The most efficient firms are usually in command of almost all of the relevant skills. The less capable are aware of the general issues and make some attempt to achieve technical mastery of the production process but often do not understand the precise methods for achieving it. Others may be aware of the required changes in managerial practice but have decided that they are too expensive relative to expected benefits.

Although an explicit effort is needed by individual firms to obtain most elements of technical knowledge, it might plausibly be argued that operating practices depend partly on the industry; with a well-developed sector (a large number of competent firms) possessing substantial technical knowledge, informal contacts and interfirm mobility of workers and managers will diffuse technical information.[14] It could also be argued that, although the immediate locus of inadequate training is the firm, the latter's own cost would be decreased and its instruction improved if a large number of other firms also provided such education; when employees trained at one's own expense moved to other firms, the loss would be at least partly compensated by a reverse flow. These and other possible interactions suggest that the focus of the decomposition procedure on single stages of a process can yield only proximate results that do not capture potentially important interdependencies.

Task-Level Productivity

Task-level productivity (TLP) will depend on worker skills and motivation. These in turn may be affected by the care with which workers are recruited, the quality and extent of firm-level instruction, the incentive structure, and the quality and intensity of supervision. Most efforts to explain low industrial productivity in developing countries emphasize task-level productivity.[15]

Unfortunately, TLP cannot be measured directly, for example, by using time and motion studies that firms have already carried out; the plants visited have not undertaken such analyses. Thus TLP is calculated as a residual, and any errors or omissions in assessments of productivity depressants in the preceding stages will be reflected in TLP. Given the omission of national economy productivity depressants and the inclusion of only a subset of possible industry- and firm-level factors, measured TLP of developing country plants relative to best-practice plants is probably understated for the Kenyan and Philippine firms. Surprisingly, in light of this probable understatement, measured TLP relative to best practice is not a major source of low relative total-factor productivity in the numerical results presented in chapters 4 and 5.

The four levels in the explanation of productivity differences are conceptual categories and are not mutually exclusive. A decomposition of the sources of productive inefficiency using these categories can identify only proximate causes and not the fundamental sources of industrial inefficiency. Thus the adverse incentive effects of a protectionist trade system may be the underlying problem, manifesting itself at the industry and firm levels in the form of excessive product differentiation, inadequate technical knowledge, and a low intensity of managerial and labor work effort. An economy characterized by slow growth in total job opportunities may prompt workers to withhold achievable productivity gains—a behavior pattern that may show up, as a residual, in low task-level productivity. Nevertheless, the kind of decomposition discussed here can be useful in policy discussions, by indicating, for example, possible fruitful loci of government intervention even where national policies such as a protectionist regime continue to prevail.

Just as social cost-benefit analysis attempts to develop social prices that permit the correct evaluation of individual projects within an interventionist milieu, some of the results developed here indicate economically desirable technological policies to employ in a second-best world; moreover, it is arguable that many industry- and firm-level deficiencies would not simply disappear within a liberalized trade environment and would have to be addressed by more direct means.

A finding of low productivity does not imply that "excess" labor or capital can or should be removed. The normative question for the private firm is whether such a reduction would raise or lower its total profits, given that the effort to achieve increased productivity will require at least some expenditures. From a social viewpoint, the guiding principle must also be a benefit-cost calculus. Thus public provision of better vocational education may increase labor productivity in textiles, but the social rate of return on such expenditures may fall short of that obtainable from other investments. Some of these issues are discussed in chapters 8 and 9.

Formalization of the Decomposition

To implement the decomposition, a production-theoretic framework is employed that has been extensively used at the aggregate level. Assume that plant A is being compared with a best-practice developed country plant, B. Both possess the same types and quantities of machines.

Postinstallation variations in the labor-equipment ratio are assumed to be possible in both the best-practice and developing country plants, according to the production functions[16]

$$(3\text{-}1a) \qquad Q = \pi_i P_i K^\alpha L^{1-\alpha}$$

or

$$(3\text{-}1b) \qquad Q = \pi_i P_i [(1-\delta)L^{\frac{\sigma-1}{\sigma}} + \delta K^{\frac{\sigma-1}{\sigma}}]^{\frac{\sigma}{\sigma-1}}$$

and labor productivity is given by

$$(3\text{-}2a) \qquad Q/L = \pi_i P_i (K/L)^\alpha$$

or

$$(3\text{-}2b) \qquad Q/L = \pi_i P_i[(1-\delta)+\delta(K/L)^{\frac{\sigma-1}{\sigma}}]^{\frac{\sigma}{\sigma-1}}$$

where the terms P_i are neutral productivity indexes reflecting national, industry, firm, and task-level productivity. (The empirical counterparts of the P_i terms are discussed in the next section.)

The difference between best-practice and observed labor productivity depends on differences in the productivity index and in capital intensity,[17] or on

$$(3\text{-}3a) \qquad \frac{(Q/L)_A}{(Q/L)_{BP}} = \pi_i \left(\frac{P_A}{P_{BP}}\right)_i \left[\frac{(K/L)_A}{(K/L)_{BP}}\right]^\alpha$$

or

$$(3\text{-}3b) \qquad \frac{(Q/L)_A}{(Q/L)_{BP}} = \frac{\pi_i P_A \left[(1-\delta)+\delta(K/L)_A^{\frac{\sigma-1}{\sigma}}\right]^{\frac{\sigma-1}{\sigma}}}{\pi_i P_{BP} \left[(1-\delta)+\delta(K/L)_{BP}^{\frac{\sigma-1}{\sigma}}\right]^{\frac{\sigma-1}{\sigma}}}$$

and $\pi_i P_A/\pi_i P_{BP}$ equals relative total factor productivity (RTFP). If the predicted ratio of actual to best-practice labor productivity after adjustment for differences in capital intensity and $\pi_i P_i$ is denoted by q^*, task-level productivity can be calculated as

$$(3\text{-}4) \qquad \left(\frac{P_A}{P_{BP}}\right)_{TLP} = \frac{(Q/L)_A/(Q/L)_{BP}}{q^*}$$

where TLP denotes task-level productivity.[18] TLP thus calculated is a residual and is sensitive to any errors in the other P_i and to the assumed value of the elasticity of substitution (σ) and the distribution parameter, δ.

Though neoclassical in appearance, the role of the production function in this analysis is simply to permit the weighting of observed input-output coefficients to obtain a measure of RTFP. I do not believe, nor does the evidence show, that firms are in fact operating within a well-understood neoclassical production environment in which all share freely available, identical technical knowledge. Rather firms using similar equipment obtain widely varying levels of output, the variations being considerably larger than can be explained by differences in employment. Indeed, the various sources of productivity differentials enumerated above have been introduced precisely to obtain a better understanding of why firms achieve such disparate results with similar levels of productive inputs. Thus the spirit in which RTFP values are calculated and in which observed differentials are decomposed into a number of components much more closely approaches the recent articulation of production theory in Nelson and Winter (1982) than the standard neoclassical production framework in which all firms are able to move along the same freely available, fully understood production frontier. Much of what follows is closer to the growing literature on econometric estimation of production frontiers than to conventional analysis of sources of growth.[19] Insofar as the former is largely concerned with estimating the intracountry production frontier rather than with comparing this frontier to the international one, however, its main focus differs from that of the present study, though the results are complementary.

One useful interpretation of the numerical decomposition results is to view them as indicative of the achievable growth of short-term productivity over, say, one to three years. The estimates of industry, firm, and task-level deficiencies indicate the upper limits of potential gains in total-factor productivity from selective interventions, which could involve reorganization of the industry to rationalize the production structure and avoid short production runs, assignment of a group of foreign technicians to a firm, or introduction of incentive payment systems. These estimates are maximum ones, because some of the potential productivity growth may not be realized unless complementary action occurs simultaneously at the national level. In the absence of sufficient domestic competition, a liberalized trade regime may be necessary to provide incentives to utilize such help as becomes available. Policies designed to foster the growth of modern sector employment may be needed to allay workers' fears that improved task-level productivity may lead to job losses. Less restrictive policies on technology licensing or payments to consultants may be an important component of a productivity enhancement program.

The Choice of Best-Practice Coefficients

Of interest are not only the several sources of low productivity but also the product of all of them, $\pi_i(P_A/P_{BP})_i$, or relative total-factor productivity, RTFP. Three issues related to its measurement, and more generally to the empirical implementation of equation 3-3b, warrant attention. These are the choice of best-practice production coefficients; the particular functional form used, including the effect of differing values of the elasticity of substitution; and the role of economies of scale.

The values of $(K/L)_A$ are obtained from the operating performance of plants in Kenya and the Philippines. Data have been collected in each plant about the specific equipment employed as well as about labor, raw materials, space, and power at each stage of production. Given this information, a technologically matched developed country best-practice plant employing essentially identical equipment is used for comparison. The values of the best-practice variables are largely obtained from those shown in tables 3-1 and 3-2 (the latter adjusted to other product specifications as necessary), which show the performance of mills at the upper quartile of the U.K. textile plant distribution.

For some purposes, particularly those related to questions of international trade, it would be preferable to employ production coefficients for countries that are important international exporters of textile products. The data from the United Kingdom, however, have an important advantage; they include a large amount of detailed technical information that conforms to the data needs of the decomposition undertaken here—such as spindle speed, twists per inch in spinning, loom efficiency, and so on. Given the critical importance of these variables, the employment of the U.K. best-practice coefficients would be indicated by the requirements of the analysis even where other best-practice data were available but were unaccompanied by such detail.

Two factors suggest that the use of the U.K. data does not limit the usefulness of the analysis. First, the better U.K. firms are, in fact, fairly efficient (see the international comparisons in chapter 7), particularly in weaving, and careful inference permits deductions about the potential competitiveness of firms of Kenya and the Philippines, given their performance relative to U.K. best practice. The United Kingdom's lack of competitiveness in some products reflects its factor prices rather than its technical inefficiency. Second, the best-practice capital and labor coefficients are available from the same source for the other major textile-producing nations as well (Textile Council 1969). Thus the sensitivity of the particular set of results presented in chapters 4 and 5 to the choice of the United Kingdom as a standard of comparison can be explicitly determined by use of the cross-country results presented in chapter 7. Finally, 1976 evidence carefully collected by Pickett and Robinson (1981) permits comparisons with the data I have employed for best practice. There is very little difference between their 1976 figures and the input coefficients employed in this study to reflect best practice, even where the latter pertain to 1968 (as in weaving); the only differences occur where equipment specifications such as picks per minute of some looms have increased. Such changes, however, have in any event been taken into account in my calculations.

The Elasticity of Substitution

The developing country plants typically manifest lower total-factor productivity than their best-practice counterparts in developed countries, for example operating with technique A in figure 3-1 at A_3 along the unit isoquant $a'a'$, the radial projection of aa. The typical developing country firm also exhibits a different (usually lower) capital-labor ratio than its best-practice twin, and some weighting function is necessary to obtain a measure of relative total-factor productivity. The functions 3-1 and 3-2 are two of many functional forms that could be used. The engineering basis, particularly the relationship between spindle or loom efficiency, the labor-output ratio, and the machine-output ratio, suggests that the major phenomenon that should be captured is a short-run elasticity of substitution, σ, of about 0.5 (see equation 2-2, the appendix and note 31 to this chapter). Although a variety of functional forms could be used to capture

Figure 3-1. *The Effect of the Elasticity of Substitution on Measured Productivity*

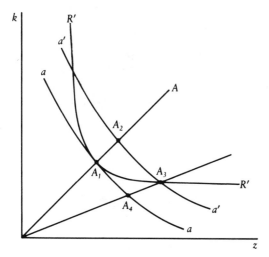

this fact, the increased complexity of the exposition when they are employed does not appear to me to be offset by any increase in the verisimilitude with which it represents the underlying engineering reality. A Cobb-Douglas function is used to capture the upper-bound results that would occur with $\sigma = 1.0$, and a CES with $\sigma = 0.2$ is used to obtain lower-bound results.

The critical assumption made to permit the comparison is that the ex post elasticity of substitution along aa and $a'a'$ in figure 3-1 is identical.[20] This assumption is plausible because knowledge of the possible ways of varying the amount of labor used in conjunction with a given set of machines is quite widely diffused. Likely to be less well known, for example, between firms in different countries, are those aspects of technological mastery that determine the height or level of the production function.

To determine the sensitivity of the productivity calculations to possible differences in the ex post elasticity of substitution, I will present calculations using the three values of the parameter. Although it would be possible to estimate conventional (average) production functions or frontier production functions and to use the parameter estimates thus obtained in the calculation of relative total productivity, there are several problems with such estimates that reduce their reliability, and this approach will not be attempted here.

In the calculations in chapters 4 and 5, it will be seen that a lower value of the ex post substitution elasticity results in greater relative productivity of developing country plants. The reason can be seen in figure 3-1, where aa and $a'a'$ are the ex post unit isoquants exhibiting greater values of σ than $R'R'$. Assume that the best-practice technique is OA and the plant is producing at A_1, whereas the developing country plant has adopted the same equipment but uses it with more labor (point A_3). If the "true" ex post unit isoquants are aa and $a'a'$, then the developing country plant's relative productivity will be OA_1/OA_2 (or OA_4/OA_3), less than unity. In contrast, if the "true" elasticity of substitution is lower, and $R'R'$ is the relevant isoquant, then A_1 and A_3 lie on the same isoquant, and total-factor productivity is the same in both plants.

Returns to Scale

The use of Cobb-Douglas and CES production functions does not, of course, preclude the introduction of increasing returns to scale. The role of increasing returns is not taken into account in the various analyses, however, as a number of studies using detailed engineering and economic information have concluded that economies of scale have been exhausted at the plant sizes considered in this study (ECLA 1951, 1965). A reduction in unit cost is not obtainable simply by increasing the hourly rate of output, but a decrease in the range of products made could lower unit costs.

Intracountry Cost Comparisons

Until now only international comparisons of total-factor productivity have been considered. The other major concern of this book, however, is the analysis of the costs of production that result from employing various types of equipment within one country, in particular Kenya or the Philippines.

There are three potential sources of cost differences: technical or productive inefficiency, incorrect choice of technology, and incorrect choice of technique once a technology has been chosen. Firms with identical machinery may operate it at different levels of total-factor productivity, for example, at C_1 and C_2 in figure 3-2, which amplifies figure 1-1. The cost incurred at these two points is TC_1 and TC_2, the difference between them representing the cost of technical inefficiency. Some firms may also

Figure 3-2. *Intracountry Cost Comparisons*

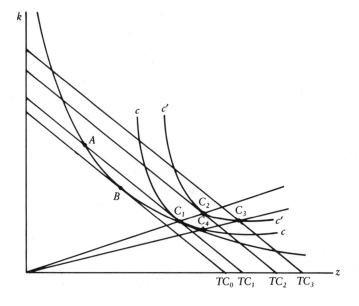

be characterized by inefficient choice of technique, operating at C_3 along $c'c'$, whereas the cost-minimizing capital-labor ratio occurs at C_2; this error raises cost further, from TC_2 to TC_3. Thus if a technology is operated at less than best-practice productivity and with an incorrect choice of technique, the excess cost relative to a firm that is efficient in both dimensions is $TC_3 - TC_1 = (TC_2 - TC_1) + (TC_3 - TC_2)$.

Nevertheless, TC_1 may not be the lowest cost obtainable at the given wage-rental ratio. In particular, the choice of technology B, if it were operated at B, would lower costs to TC_0. Usually allocative efficiency is used to denote the cost reduction stemming from the move from C_1 to B. It will also be used in the following chapters, however, to denote cost reductions stemming from improved choice of technique. The context will make clear which type of allocative gain is of concern.

This framework implies three potential routes by which a firm could lower its cost: greater technical efficiency, an improved choice of technique with a given technology already in place, and a different choice of technology. The first two are obtainable by improving the firm's performance with existing equipment, but better technology can be obtained only by selling the firm's current machinery and purchasing the more appropriate type.

Two broad choices of technology are considered in the following chapters: first, that between currently produced conventional equipment and recently introduced machinery of radically new design; second, that between older equipment still available in used machinery markets and new equipment (whether of conventional or newly introduced design). The context will make it clear which choices are involved. Although extensive discussions exist about the uncertainties associated with the employment of used equipment (Cooper and Kaplinsky 1975), many of them pertain to the difficulty of purchasing it in an imperfect market; this difficulty is irrelevant to the problems considered in the succeeding chapters, insofar as firms already possess the machinery. In this case, the major issues revolve about the effectiveness with which equipment is employed. As will be seen, older machinery is, on the average, more efficiently employed than new equipment.

The actual cost comparisons involve the calculation of each firm's transformation cost, defined as the sum of capital, labor, fuel, and waste. (See the appendix to this chapter for details regarding the factor prices used.) The information employed could be transformed from conventional unit cost of individual firms to a measure of social optimality such as the domestic resource cost (DRC).[21] This has not been done because much of what follows is concerned with investigating the determinants of private behavior. Nevertheless, firms exhibiting lower private unit production cost are likely to have a lower DRC, given that the costs used in the calculations are uniform and probably differ little from social costs. The correlation will not be perfect, however, because of the differing productivity with which firms use primary and intermediate inputs. Chapter 8 analyzes both private and social benefit-cost ratios of programs to enhance productivity. In view of the considerable scope for improvement, the calculation of existing static DRC levels has limited interest.

Details of the Calculation of Productivity-Depressing Factors

The empirical measurement of each of the terms P_i is explained in this section. Four productivity-depressing factors are calculated for spinning and three for weaving. In addition, task-level productivity is calculated as a residual depressant in both manufacturing processes. The specific factors considered are tabulated in table 3-3.

The basis for the decomposition is obtained from the engineering production relations for spinning and weaving set forth in equations 2-4 and 2-6.[22] The product of the deviations from best practice in each variable in the operating plants taken together accounts for the failure to realize best-practice total-factor productivity. The shortcomings accounting for a particular deviation vary from plant to plant. One firm may fail to run its spindles at the speed of which they are capable because of a shortage of "traveler" replacements that can withstand the heat generated by high-speed operation. In another, poor maintenance procedures may have caused the deterioration of critical components affecting speed. In the following chapters, these and other deficiencies are presented in terms of their impact on the variables shown in table 3-3. In chapter 6, the problems are illustrated and their proximate origins are analyzed.

Table 3-3. *Productivity-Depressing Factors*

Factor	Type	Spinning	Weaving
P_1	Industry effect	Specialization	Specialization
P_2	Firm specific	Speed (breakage rate)	Yarn quality
P_3	Firm specific	Twists per inch	—
P_4	Firm specific	Spindle efficiency	Loom efficiency
P_5	Labor performance	Task-level productivity	Task-level productivity

— not applicable.

Spinning

INDUSTRY EFFECT. It will be recalled from the earlier discussion that economywide, or national, determinants of relative total-factor productivity are not calculated, factors having an impact at the industry level being the most macroscopic considered. Of the potential industry-level sources of low productivity, excessive product variety receives attention here. Executives concerned with profitability and technicians dealing with productivity agree that inadequate specialization and the consequent short production runs raise unit cost. Other sources of low productivity relating to insufficiently developed industrywide institutions (such as training institutes) are generally thought to have considerably lower quantitative importance.

It is difficult to obtain precise quantitative assessments of the impact on productivity of short production runs. Estimates of these effects have been made for both spinning and weaving; production engineers with experience in developing countries agree that these have roughly the correct order of magnitude.

Improved productivity from specialization in spinning depends on (1) reducing the output of counts that diverge widely from those for which the plant was designed (such counts will be manufactured inefficiently as a result of machine imbalances and the use of less appropriate equipment) and (2) decreasing the number of yarn sorts produced where each sort is described by its count, twists per inch, and the fiber mix (for example, cotton-polyester). Because such rationalization of production involves changing several output characteristics simultaneously, establishing the impact on productivity of a decrease in count range and in the number of sorts requires a carefully controlled multiplant experiment. A study of this type being impossible to locate in the textile engineering literature, I have used the description in an internal World Bank report of one effort at rationalization to establish orders of magnitude. Although only rough estimates, they permit some quantitative assessment of a phenomenon that is widely acknowledged to be of considerable importance in the economics of textile production.

Using the discussion in the World Bank document, I have estimated the effect on productivity when a plant produces counts different from those for which it was designed. This procedure provides a conservative estimate of the true cost involved, as it omits the impact of excessive yarn sorts, which is generally believed to be an important potential source of low productivity. The relationship used to describe the interdependence of best practice and actual productivity resulting from variation in the range of counts is illustrated by the following figures (in percent):

Variation from the
mean count for which

the plant was designed	$(P_A/P_{BP})_{SPC}$
± 20	95
± 40	85
± 60	77

P denotes the productivity factor and BP and A best practice and actual practice, respectively, and SPC denotes specialization. Thus a firm whose plant is designed to produce a mean count of 20s but is producing a range from 8s to 32s (a 60 percent variation) will exhibit 77 percent of the productivity of a plant with a range of 18s and 22s if we assume that the 10 percent variation in the latter does not affect productivity.[23]

SPEED. For each spinning mill the speed in revolutions per minute (RPM) at which the spindles are operated is compared with the speed at which the ring frames of the given vintage and design are operated in best-practice plants. The ratio of the speed, $(P_A/P_{BP})_{SPD}$, appears in the decomposition using equation 3-3b. In principle, speed is an endogenous variable that should be chosen to minimize average production cost. Several production inputs such as power vary positively with speed; if their costs differ between actual and best-practice plants, it is possible that the observed discrepancy represents efficient substitution along a multifactor isoquant rather than an x-inefficient practice (see chapter 2). Both careful questioning during the plant interviews and calculation of the probable quantitative impact of power cost on the choice of speed, however, suggest that the observed differences represent a shift in the production function rather than a movement along it.

It is also possible that the observed differentials between actual and best-practice speed represent a substitution between labor and capital in which alteration of speed changes the breakage rate, thus permitting a change in the spindle-labor ratio. Ranis (1973) has suggested that Japanese spinning plants achieved a "capital-stretching" effect by operating at high speed and using additional workers to maintain spindle efficiency. For most plants in Kenya and the Philippines, observation indicates that speeds lie below best-practice levels. Although this difference may be attributable to an effort to decrease breakage rates and hence avoid the use of still more labor, the spindle-labor ratio in these plants is sufficiently low that an increase in the breakage rate from current levels would exert a very small quantitative effect on spindle efficiency (see below); increased speeds would thus raise both labor and spindle productivity.[24] Nevertheless, procedures such as blending and weight control are sufficiently bad in some firms to make it likely that past efforts to increase speed resulted in a significant growth in end breakages and a decrease in spindle efficiency even at the low prevailing spindle-labor ratio. In these firms, primarily in the Philippines, below-normal speed is attributable to lack of mastery of the early stages of processing as well as to deficient maintenance and housekeeping.

Those firms exhibiting speeds higher than best practice do not appear to be substituting labor for capital in a capital-stretching fashion, as they also exhibit spindle-labor ratios in a range in which increased breakage rates have little impact on spindle efficiency (see below). Hence it seems reasonable to infer that high speed permits these firms to increase both capital and labor productivity, an inference supported by their typically high capital-labor ratios and TFP as compared with those of other firms using similar equipment.

TWISTS PER INCH. As seen in chapter 2, the number of twists or turns per inch inserted into yarn in best-practice plants is determined by use of the rule $\tau = t\sqrt{c}$, where t equals the twist multiple and c the yarn count. For any given count of yarn, the twist multiple, and hence τ, will differ slightly according to variations in the properties of the yarn up through roving, but the range in t is usually quite small. Nevertheless, in a few of the firms in the sample, deviation in the twist multiple (and hence in τ) from best practice constitutes an important source of the difference between actual and best-practice productivity. Although a high value of τ might reflect practices designed to redress the undesirable properties of very cheap fiber, evidence from interviews (particularly with regard to characteristics of the type of fiber currently employed), and also the feasible technical substitution of greater τ for shorter fibers, suggest that the observed ratio of $(P_A/P_{BP})_\tau$ in these firms largely represents x-inefficiency, not factor substitution. In other words, large numbers of twists per inch are introduced to correct weaknesses resulting from inadequate command of the earlier stages of processing.

SPINDLE EFFICIENCY. In chapter 2 it was shown that the observed level of efficiency, e^*, equals $qe(b,L)$ and depends on three variables: the amount of labor used in conjunction with the ring frame, the rate of yarn breakage, and other factors reflected in q, such as the frequency and quality of maintenance. It was noted in chapter 2 that an increase in breakage rates, the spindle-worker ratio being constant, leads to a downward shift in the production function, whereas any response in the capital-labor ratio to differential breakage rates constitutes a movement along the isoquant. There are thus three effects that need to be considered: (1) differences between actual and best-practice breakage rates and their impact on labor and spindle productivity; (2) given b and the labor-spindle ratio, the expected level of efficiency, e; and (3) the difference between expected efficiency, e, and observed efficiency, e^*, where $e^* = qe$. Given the calculated value of attainable or normal efficiency, q is calculated as e^*/e and provides an estimate of $(P_A/P_{BP})_{EF}$, where EF denotes efficiency.

Although the breakage rates in all of the Kenyan plants and a few of the Philippine plants exceed those found in best-practice mills, no productivity-depressing correction is introduced for breaks per se or for the effect noted under (1) in the preceding paragraph. The reasoning is as follows. At observed spindle-spinner ratios in both countries, about 600–800 spindles, end breakage rates of even eighteen per 100 spindle hours (which considerably exceed that of most plants in the sample) permit a spindle efficiency of over 99 percent.[25] Efficiency can remain high because spinners with a relatively small number of spindles to check are able to identify and repair any breaks quickly, thus keeping machine interference quite low; the only loss in efficiency arises from creeling and doffing time. Once the efficiency that should be achieved (given observed breakage and capital-labor ratios) has been calculated, the effect of other productivity depressants is obtained as $q = e^*/e$. Values less than unity are due to defective maintenance, inadequate supplies of spare parts, and so on.

TASK-LEVEL PRODUCTIVITY. Task-level productivity is calculated as a residual according to equation 3-4. Given the nature of the calculation, any error in estimates of other P_i or the use of a value for the elasticity of substitution that differs from the true value will lead to an incorrect estimate of P_5.

Weaving

INDUSTRY EFFECT. To establish the effect of product diversity in weaving, I have used the results of a study of the British textile sector that measured the impact on labor and loom productivity of the number of warp beam changes per 10,000 loom shifts.[26] Some warp beam changes are inherent in the process, as the initial warp supply is exhausted and must be replaced even if no alteration in product is planned. More frequent replacements occur when the product is altered before a given beam has been completely exhausted. A firm that can halve the number of its warp changes per 10,000 loom shifts from eighty (approximately the bottom quartile in the U.K. sample of plants) to twenty (roughly the top-quartile value) for example, can increase its total-factor productivity by 59 percent, so that $P_A/P_{BP} = 1/1.59 = 0.63$. Given difficulties in establishing precisely how many different fabrics are produced, 0.63 will be used as a standard for the ratio of actual to best-practice productivity in the Kenyan plants and 0.70 in the Philippine plants, with mills in the Philippines reporting slightly longer production runs than their Kenyan counterparts.[27]

YARN QUALITY. The impact of breakage is greater in weaving than in spinning. The difference arises from the fact that, when a warp or weft yarn breaks, the entire loom is shut down, whereas in spinning only the spindle on which the break occurs is halted, and the rest of the spindles on the ring frame continue to spin. The impact of increased breakage rates on TFP will be smaller in weaving mills in which the loom-labor ratio is lower, for reasons similar to those set forth in the discussion of spindle efficiency. In both Kenya and the Philippines, the ratio of looms to weavers is low. In the Philippines, for example, the mean ratio is 6.5, the range being 3 to 14, whereas 24 to 36 looms per worker is the norm in best-practice plants, depending on the particular product. Nevertheless, because the entire loom stops when a break occurs, each break entails the loss of some small percentage of potential production.

The impact on total-factor productivity of higher stoppage rates occasioned by excessive breaks is calculated by means of the expression $(1 - br/60)$, where b is the breakage rate per hour and r is average repair time. If we use the values of b and r in best-practice and actual mills, the expression provides an estimate of the maximum number of minutes per hour that a loom could run in each mill if repairs occurred immediately, that is, if machine interference were zero. This is the maximum efficiency level, given the limitations imposed by existing breakage rates. The estimate thus obtained yields the value of $(P_A/P_{BP})_{YQ}$, where YQ denotes yarn quality.

LOOM EFFICIENCY. In practice, loom interference is not zero, as assumed in the preceding paragraph, though it is very small, given the existing loom-weaver ratios. The (high) potential level of loom efficiency, e, that could be realized, given the current levels of breakage rates and looms per weaver, is calculated and compared with the observed value, e^*. The value P_3, or $(P_A/P_{BP})_{LE}$, where LE denotes loom efficiency, is calculated as e^*/e.[28]

Appendix

The data obtained from visits to firms include the manufacturer of the machinery used at each step in the production process, together with information on its labor, raw materials, space, and power requirements. Knowledge of the manufacturer also allows identification of the performance capabilities embodied in equipment according to the manufacturer's estimates. Finally, critical engineering variables such as speed, breakage rates, and twists per inch were collected.

This appendix presents a brief discussion of the measurement of capital and labor inputs and the choice of values used for the parameters of equations 3-3a and 3-3b.

Labor and Capital Inputs

SPINNING. Two calculations are frequently carried out in the chapters that follow: measurement of the difference in total-factor productivity between plants in two countries and estimation of the variation in cost of production between different firms in the same country. In both calculations the measured labor input is the unweighted labor hours per kilogram of yarn; the time of operatives, mechanics, and auxiliary workers (such as cleaners) in all processes from opening through spinning is included, whereas that of supervisory labor is excluded. Unweighted labor hours are used because wage differences between the various categories of labor are minor and based largely on seniority.

In international productivity comparisons, the quantity measure of capital input is spindle hours per kilogram of yarn in each plant; all comparisons involve mills employing physically similar equipment of roughly the same age. Use of this variable may somewhat understate the efficiency of developing country spinning plants, as their machine-output ratios in the earlier stages (opening through carding) are closer to those of developed country plants than is the ratio in spinning; the main difference in machine-output ratios, particularly in the Philippine mills, is in roving and spinning. Sensitivity tests embodying various assumptions, however, suggest that, for the plants with the worst spinning performance, the overstatement of the capital-output ratio resulting from omission of equipment from earlier stages is about 10 percent. The ensuing understatement of total-factor productivity for these spinning mills compared with best-practice mills is about 3–4 percent. Given measured RTFP differentials of 30–40 percent, the effect of potential misestimates of the capital stock in the productivity calculations is relatively small.

In calculations of production cost variations among firms in Kenya and the Philippines with different types of equipment, new machines are priced at current market prices provided by equipment manufacturers. The value of all equipment, from opening machines to ring frames, is included in the cost measure. Older equipment is employed by many firms. The price of used equipment in a competitive market should ideally reflect the market evaluation of the quasi-rents to be earned from its employment. Neither Kenya nor the Philippines, however, has an active used equipment market. The second-best solution employed here relies on estimates of potential resale value provided by textile manufacturers in each country and on informed guesses by textile engineers.[29] The procedure followed is to use the same price for spinning equipment of each vintage rather than trying to establish different estimates of the value of each plant's equipment, depending on its actual condition. Firms are thus charged with the opportunity cost of using machinery of a given vintage even if the value of their own machinery is not equal to that of the average firm. This procedure may lead to some biases, for example overstating the capital cost of production in plants that have ignored maintenance and whose equipment reflects such neglect. Such firms are likely, however, to face greater current costs for maintenance and spare parts in order to compensate for past laxness. Although current maintenance costs are not explicitly considered (most firms having limited and unreliable information), the overstatement of opportunity cost and the understatement of maintenance should partially cancel each other.

In the cost calculations, the hourly user cost of capital is derived by using the capital recovery factor and assuming an interest rate of 10 percent. The number of years remaining for each type of equipment depends on its vintage and is uniform for each vintage rather than varying with past or future maintenance.[30] It is assumed that every firm operates its plant for 7,200 hours per year. The hourly wage used in the cost calculations is the current market wage in Kenya or the Philippines, inclusive of standard fringe benefits.

WEAVING. The capital input in weaving for international comparisons of productivity is loom hours per meter of woven cloth. Comparisons are made between mills employing looms with similar operating principles and of similar vintages. Cost comparisons between firms within each developing country use loom prices that are derived on the same principles as equipment prices in spinning. Labor input is measured as the number of hours per meter of cloth and includes the hours of operatives, cleaners, and mechanics in weaving, excluding preparatory processes such as sizing.

Capital and labor input per unit of output have been adjusted to a common product specification in both spinning and weaving. In spinning, all inputs have been adjusted to those that would hold if a plant were producing an average 20s count yarn rather than its current mean count. In weaving, the standardization is to a cloth with the same number of ends and picks per inch, width, yarn count in both warp and weft, and type of weave. Such adjustments are necessary, as unit inputs differ significantly with product characteristics; for example, higher-count yarns in spinning and fabrics using higher-count yarns in weaving are subject to greater breakage rates that raise both labor and equipment inputs per unit of output.

Power costs reflect the current charges for electricity in Kenya and the Philippines, whereas the cost of floor space reflects the same charge for plants in each country, based on current reproduction costs and a capital recovery factor that presupposes a thirty-year life and a 10 percent interest rate.

Parameter Values

To obtain a measure of total-factor productivity, it is assumed that after installation the ratio in which workers and machines can be combined is described either by a Cobb-Douglas function or by a constant elasticity of substitution production function, with σ alternatively equal to 0.5 and 0.2 in the latter case.[31] Our assumption is thus that knowledge of the production process is sufficiently diffused that the postinstallation factor substitution possibilities for developed and developing country producers are similar, even though the efficiency of production may differ among countries. If, in fact, the substitution possibilities in Kenya and the Philippines differ from those in the United Kingdom, even when similar equipment is in use, the correct procedure for deriving relative productivity indexes is the use of mean values (across countries) of the elasticity of substitution and other relevant production parameters (see Caves, Christensen, and Diewert 1982; Christensen, Cummings, and Jorgenson 1980). There is little reason, however, to believe that the simple technological knowledge reflected in the substitution parameters (as opposed to those determining efficiency levels) is not well diffused.[32]

To perform the calculation, it is necessary to obtain factor shares for the Cobb-Douglas function and their analogues, the distribution parameters for the CES. The factor shares are obtained from best-practice plant profiles and reflect only the costs incurred in manufacturing operations. These differ from the national accounts data that are normally used (which include remuneration of factors not directly involved in plant operations). There is only a small discrepancy, however, between the two sets of estimates of factor shares. When the CES is employed, a value for δ, the distribution parameter, is calculated, and the same value is used for both the developing country plants and the U.K. plants.[33]

Notes

1. A detailed description of some of the procedures needed to achieve best practice is provided in chapter 6.

2. This focus on the spindle-output ratio is also justified by the substantial share of roving and ring-frame costs in total spinning, as shown in chapter 2. Technical advances in roving have generally reflected those in spinning.

3. Pickett and Robinson (1981). On questions of the optimal choice of technology, their study is a useful complement to the present volume, as is Amsalem (1978).

4. For a summary, see Hagen (1975), chap. 6; see also Leibenstein (1976, 1978). The most thorough attempt to measure micro-level sources of productivity differences between operating and best-practice firms is that of ECLA (1951). I have recast some of its findings into the framework outlined below; see Pack (1982b). The ECLA study was extremely imaginative and careful. Unfortunately, the results it obtained cannot be directly compared with those in the two following chapters; not surprisingly, given the date of the study, the theoretical framework did not reflect concepts that have since become standard. In particular, the effects of downward shifts in the production function and movements along it are lumped together, and given the presentation of the data, the two cannot be separated with certainty.

5. Saxonhouse (1978) emphasizes the role of the national education system in Japan in providing a basic education upon which firm-specific technical training could build.

6. The implications of this statement in terms of average and marginal cost curves of the firm are extensively discussed in Alchian (1959) and Hirschleifer (1962).

7. Economies of specialization imply that, with full utilization of fixed equipment, increased product diversity results in higher unit cost because, for example, setup time increases. This finding contrasts with recent discussions of economies of scope, which see unit cost as falling and *total* output as rising when more products are manufactured and each type of machinery is utilized more intensively because all of the products use the same equipment. In the typical textile mill, all equipment is already fully utilized on three daily shifts. There are no cost reductions obtainable from economies of scope, but substantial decreases in unit cost may be realized from greater specialization.

8. The extensive literature on intraindustry trade considers a number of related issues at the national level but does not explore the origin or stability of the initial nonspecializing equilibrium in the case in which identical products are produced by all firms. See, for example, Grubel and Lloyd (1975) and Krugman (1981).

9. These issues, in the context of multiplant firms in developed countries, are carefully explored by Scherer and others (1975), particularly chaps. 2 and 7, which also contain references to much of the literature. The problems posed by insufficient specialization within small domestic markets have been a dominant theme in analyses of industrial performance in Australia and Canada. See Caves (1984) on Australia and the references therein to the literature on both countries.

10. A good discussion is provided by Hillier and Lieberman (1967). Scherer and others (1975) also discuss the issue of lot size within the context of specialization.

11. Saxonhouse (1976) provides a fascinating account of the Japanese spinners' association's collection and dissemination of information on the performance of its member firms. Several industry-financed textile research institutes pursue similar objectives in India and produce high-quality research germane to the industry (ATIRA 1977). Nevertheless, results have been disappointing in terms of industry performance.

12. For a survey and an excellent synthesis of the many types of analyses purporting to explain the productivity of individual firms, see Nelson (1981), particularly sec. 2. Other useful

summaries and analyses include Freeman and Jucker (1981), Marsh and Mannari (1976), and Horton and King (1981).

13. See the discussion of uneven diffusion of technical knowledge by Nelson and Winter (1982).

14. The dependence of a firm's productivity level on the size of the industry underlies the concept of irreversible dynamic-scale economies developed by Marshall as well as the great faith in the external effects of industrialization embodied in many early development plans.

15. See, for example, Hagen (1975) and Moore (1951). Leibenstein's work on x-efficiency (1978) applies to firm- and task-level determinants of productivity but does not take into account the influences of the industry and national contexts.

16. The productivity comparisons could also be carried out with superlative index numbers, as suggested by Caves, Christensen, and Diewert (1982). Their work assumes that the underlying production function is translogarithmic, whereas the textile engineering literature implies that a simpler CES form is appropriate.

17. It is necessary to analyze the technology carefully to discriminate between shifts in the production function and movements along it. Thus low-quality yarn that leads to high breakage rates will, other things being equal, decrease labor and machine productivity by roughly the same percentages. Though a firm may react to this phenomenon by increasing the labor-machine ratio to restore the initial machine-output ratio, this substitution effect is separable from the initial neutral downward shift in the production function and constitutes a movement along the production function. See chapter 2 and the next section in this chapter.

18. The term q^* is the right-hand side of equations 3-3a and 3-3b after the inclusion of national, industry, and firm-level effects and differences in capital intensity.

19. For an early and interesting application of the production frontier approach, see Timmer (1971). The most original recent application of the method is that of Nishimizu and Page (1982). A recent survey of the literature appears in Forsund, Knox-Lovell, and Schmidt (1980).

20. It is also assumed that efficiency differences are factor neutral and that the distribution parameter in the CES function or its analogue, the elasticity of output with respect to each factor, is the same for both firms in the comparison. The neutrality assumption is justified by the nature of the production process (see chapter 2, where it is noted that most production problems such as excessive end breaks reduce the productivity of labor and equipment by equal percentages). There may also be a movement along the production function if an attempt is made to maintain machine efficiency rates.

21. For a recent review of alternative definitions, see Lucas (1984). On the relation between allocative and technical efficiency and the DRC, see Page (1980).

22. The omission of the impact of breakage rates in spinning is discussed below.

23. Most plants do not exhibit a range count that is symmetrical about the mean count. I have used the smaller deviation as if it were symmetrical, thus introducing a conservative bias into the calculation. A simple functional form is used to derive actual values of P_A/P_{BP}.

24. In cost comparisons across firms within Kenya and the Philippines, low spindle-labor rates are treated as allocatively inefficient. In the international productivity comparisons, only technical efficiency is considered.

25. See tables 1.2–1.4 in Subramanian and Garde (1974). Firms' decision to operate with a low capital-labor ratio to begin with is explainable in terms of differential relative factor prices; in the decomposition the effect of the difference in capital-labor ratios is captured by the capital-labor terms in equations 3-3a and 3-3b.

26. Textile Council (1969), vol. 1, p. 73. The figures have been adjusted to measure the downward shift in the production function before any changes occur in factor proportions.

27. A limited sample of the nature of product variety appears in table 2-3. Among the differing properties of fabrics are the yarn count of the warp and weft, the number of yarns (ends and picks) per inch, and the type of weave (plain, twill, satin, and so on).

28. The Kemp-Mack tables of machine interference are used to calculate e. See Ormerod (1979), chap. 2.

29. One alternative considered for valuing used equipment was the amount for which machinery, but not the plant, was insured. It was not possible to obtain sufficiently detailed information to pursue this idea, however.

30. For an endogenous determination of the remaining life of equipment, see Rhee and Westphal (1977).

31. Recall that the optimum machine assignment per worker is $(K/L)^* = (wC/r)^{1/2}$, where C is a constant (equation 2-2). Then if we define σ as d $\log(K/L)/$d $\log(w/r)$, $\sigma = 0.5$. This is a measure of the ex post elasticity of substitution and establishes a presumptive case for using 0.5 as the best approximation for the desired parameter.

32. For an explanation of the sources of technical substitution possibilities, see the discussion in chapter 2 of the determinants of machine efficiency.

33. The calculations that follow are insensitive to 10–20 percent variations in δ.

CHAPTER FOUR

The Kenyan Textile Sector

THIS CHAPTER presents a detailed analysis of the data collected for Kenya. After reading the following brief summary, some individuals may want to skip to the summary section on the Philippines at the beginning of chapter 5 and afterward to resume reading with chapter 6, in which an attempt is made to analyze the behavioral reality that generates the numerical results.

Comparisons between plants using different vintages of spinning equipment show that current unit production costs are fairly similar, with no pattern emerging to indicate which type of technology is cheaper at current productivity levels. If total-factor productivity were improved to a high but not best-practice standard, new spinning mills would realize an average 11 percent reduction in unit costs; at this higher productivity level, newer equipment could achieve costs about 8 percent below those of used equipment.

Current unit costs of weaving vary widely, reflecting productivity differences between firms using essentially identical automatic looms and the much lower productivity with which semiautomatic looms are employed. Average unit cost reductions of 20 percent on automatic looms and 42 percent on semiautomatic looms could be realized from higher TFP, the gains from improved choice of technology and technique being smaller. The two weaving sheds using both automatic and semiautomatic looms have much higher costs with the latter, mainly because of their lower productivity. Even if both types of loom were operated at a higher and uniform productivity, however, automatic looms would still produce cloth at a lower unit cost; this result suggests that there is no effective choice of technology in the current Kenyan environment.

Productivity calculations indicate that RTFP for both spinning and weaving in Kenyan mills reaches about 70 percent of its level in best-practice plants in the United Kingdom. The absence of specialization is a major source of lower productivity. On the other hand, task-level productivity, despite qualifications about its precise measurement, is fairly high.

The last section of the chapter speculates on the international competitiveness of Kenyan textile production and concludes that, if inputs were
available at international prices, both spun and woven products could
probably be exported. Even if this assessment is correct, chapter 8 will
demonstrate that specific technology policy interventions are likely to be
desirable in addition to a reform of international trade policies.

All of the larger textile-producing plants in Kenya were visited, and data
were obtained from all but one of them. Of the plants visited, four manufactured only spun yarn and textile cloth, whereas others also produced
large amounts of knitted fabric or clothing. These mixed factories have
been excluded from the analysis, as different processes share some of the
facilities and workers. A relatively small spinning mill that produces
mainly sewing thread has also been omitted from the following analysis,
given the somewhat different production process it employs and the difficulty of obtaining a reference plant in a developed country.

Spinning

The four firms analyzed in the following sections are all managed by
expatriates: two by Indian nationals, one by Western Europeans, and one
by Japanese. All of the higher-level managers have considerable experience
in textile production in other countries.

The vintage of equipment and other relevant data on physical inputs
and unit costs are shown in table 4-1, all data being expressed as ratios of

Table 4-1. *Indexes of Inputs and Unit Cost per Kilogram*
of Spun Yarn (20s)

Plant	Vintage	Operative hours (1)	Spindle hours (2)	Waste (3)	Power (4)	Space (5)	Current unit cost (6)	Unit cost with RTFP = 0.85[a] (7)
A	Mid-1970s	68	70	81	128	84	101	90
B	Mid-1970s	67	85	95	105	81	108	89
C	Late 1940s	100	100	100	100	100	100	99
D	Mid-1950s	136	108	102	101	133	112	95

Note: All underlying figures have been expressed relative to those of plant C, the plant
with the lowest unit cost, and multiplied by 100. Yarn count is a measure of the thickness of
yarn expressed in terms of the number of lengths of 840 yards per pound. Thus 20s count
indicates that a pound of yarn contains 16,800 yards.

a. Unit cost if a firm achieves 85 percent of the total factor productivity of a best-practice
plant expressed as a percentage of the initial cost of plant A.

plant C's figures multiplied by 100. (For a discussion of the input prices employed see the appendix to chapter 3.) For the moment the reader should ignore column 7. There are two pairs of roughly matching plants, (A, B) and (C, D). The machines used by each pair are technically comparable, and subjective judgment suggests that each pair also shares a distinctive kind of management experience. Plants A and B are managed by expatriates whose background is primarily in modern textile plants, whereas the managers of plants C and D have worked mainly in older plants in other developing countries. The newer plants, A and B, exhibit greater physical productivity: spindle hours, labor, raw material waste, and space per unit of output are all lower than in the older plants; only electricity input is greater. The slightly lower unit cost of plant C (column 6) relative to plants A and B, despite the latter pair's better performance in most physical input-output coefficients, reflects the lower cost of plant C's used machinery. Firm-specific differentials that are not solely dependent on equipment vintage are clearly important. Firm D, for example, operating a mid-1950s plant, has greater unit cost than plant C, which uses a modernized mid-1940s plant. Moreover, plant D has higher unit requirements for every input. The other pair of firms, A and B, use almost identical machinery, but the former's unit cost is lower.

The determinants of unit cost are discussed further below, in terms of the variables used in chapter 3—technical efficiency, choice of technique, and choice of technology. Later in this chapter I present estimates of each firm's relative total-factor productivity. Assume that, whatever its current RTFP, each firm could move to a level of 85 percent and thus eliminate much of its current technical inefficiency relative to its best-practice counterpart.[1] The unit cost that would be realized at an RTFP of 85 percent is shown in column 7 of table 4-1.[2] The average unit cost reduction for the four plants from improved technical efficiency is 11 percent; individual reductions of 1–18 percent reflect current differences in RTFP. Once a technology has been chosen, variations in the choice of technique are of smaller importance. These can be read directly as the unit cost differences between firms once productivity differentials have been eliminated.[3] They are 1 percent between plants A and B and 4 percent between plants C and D, a sectoral average of 2 percent.

Finally, the cost reduction to be obtained from superior choice of technology A or B rather than technology C or D, at identical RTFP, averages 8 percent, with the newer technology exhibiting the lower cost.[4] Where capacity is to be expanded, more modern equipment has a lower expected unit cost than older equipment, provided that reasonably high RTFP can be achieved with the former. Otherwise, it may in fact be cheaper to use older equipment: compare the current unit cost of plants B and C, despite the latter's disadvantage at uniformly high productivity. That plants A and B during the mid 1970s chose machinery of recent vintage is thus consistent with ex ante cost minimization; in the event, however, plant B exhibited higher costs than plant C because of its failure to realize sufficiently high total-factor productivity.

Weaving

The data needed to analyze the cost performance of Kenyan weaving sheds are shown in table 4-2. All figures are expressed relative to those of plant A. The input coefficients reflect the adjustment of each firm's actual unit inputs to those that would result if all were producing an identical fabric (see chapter 3 appendix). Interfirm variation in both labor and loom requirements per unit of output is much larger than in spinning because of the less routinized production process involved. The power and space variations per unit of output largely reflect those in the loom-output ratio, power and space per loom hour varying much less.[5] Firm-specific abilities again show themselves to be important. All of the firms operate technically similar automatic looms but differ substantially in unit input levels. Two firms, B and C, operate both automatic and semiautomatic looms. The latter have significantly higher unit costs in both mills, a result analyzed below. It is again useful to analyze the figures in terms of technical and allocative efficiency. The last column of table 4-2 shows the adjustment of current unit costs to those that would be realized at RTFP of 85 percent.

Consider first the performance of automatic looms. The average reduction in unit cost stemming from a movement from current productivity

Table 4-2. *Indexes of Inputs and Unit Cost per Meter of Woven Cloth*

Plant	Loom type	Operative hours (1)	Loom hours (2)	Space (3)	Power (4)	Current unit cost (5)	Unit cost with RTFP = 0.85[a] (6)
A	Automatic	100	100	100	100	100	99
B	Automatic	109	115	100	100	135	114
	Semiautomatic	565	144	95	73	219	146
C	Automatic	210	198	25	53	122	80
	Semiautomatic	446	338	25	50	217	106
D	Automatic	187	129	100	100	175	127

Note: All underlying data have been expressed relative to the figures obtained from plant A, the plant with the lowest current unit cost, and multiplied by 100.

a. Unit cost if a firm achieves 85 percent of the total-factor productivity of a best-practice plant expressed as a percentage of the initial cost of plant A.

levels to the higher one is 20 percent. There is also a reversal in the unit cost ranking of sheds A and C, the former employing an automatic European-made loom, the latter a similar loom of Japanese manufacture. The current disparity in unit cost is not inherent in the properties of the looms but reflects the difference in RTFP achieved by each firm. Except in the case of shed D, little of the cost differential remaining after the uniform productivity adjustment (column 6) reflects variation in the choice of technique; A, B, and C all exhibit similar labor-loom ratios (column 1 divided by column 2). Rather it stems mainly from differences between sheds A and B in the acquisition cost of essentially identical looms and from shed C's gain from the lower capital charge of its used looms.[6] Some of shed C's cost advantage is also a result of the lower power requirements of its Japanese looms. Finally, shed D's high cost relative to that of the other three firms even at RTFP of 85 percent mainly reflects its excessive labor-loom ratio relative to that of the others. The reason for this discrepancy cannot easily be identified.

Consider now the performance of the semiautomatic looms. The average reduction in unit cost obtainable from an improvement in technical efficiency is 42 percent, considerably larger than that obtainable with automatics. Thus part of the current cost advantage enjoyed by automatic looms stems from their operation at productivity levels closer to best practice than those attained by semiautomatic looms. Furthermore, although firm C's unit cost when employing semiautomatics at 85 percent RTFP would be lower than that realized by firms B and D with automatic looms at the same RTFP level, it remains true that firm C's own cost at the higher productivity level would be about 25 percent less than with semiautomatics.

The implications of the choice of technique with a given technology also appear clearly in a comparison of the results from the use of semiautomatic looms in two firms. At the uniform 85 percent RTFP level, plant C's unit cost is 27 percent below plant B's, mainly reflecting the former's much lower labor-capital ratio (column 1 divided by column 2). Even at low Kenyan wages, too much substitution of labor for capital can occur. It is difficult to determine why firm B used so much more labor per unit of capital.

Performance Relative to Best Practice

Spinning

The two older Kenyan plants, C and D, are compared with best-practice firms of 1950 and 1955.[7] The newer plants, A and B, established in the mid-1970s, are compared with 1977 best-practice standards. As firms A and B have not systematically adopted some of the newest labor-saving devices (such as chute feeds from opening to carding) that are reflected in the 1977 norms, there may be some slight downward bias in the calculation of their productivity relative to best practice.

Table 4-3 shows the mean value, relative to best practice, of unit labor and spindle requirements, the capital-labor ratio, and total-factor productivity (which depends on the assumed elasticity of substitution). The unit capital requirements in Kenyan plants are close to best practice, whereas relative unit labor requirements considerably exceed best-practice norms, being worse in the modern plants (A and B) than in the older pair. Although labor-saving technical progress enables best-practice firms to reduce unit labor input 70 percent by switching from 1950 to 1977 machinery (see table 3-1), the modern Kenyan firms realize on average only a 50 percent reduction in labor input, relative to the older Kenyan plants, from the equivalent change in spindle vintage.[8]

A measure of total-factor productivity is necessary to obtain an assessment of overall performance. There is no simple pattern in relative total-factor productivity. Differences between plants decline at lower assumed elasticities of substitution as a result of the substantial variation in spindle-labor ratios relative to best practice. For the plausible value of σ, 0.5 (see chapter 3), the two newer plants exhibit RTFP levels of 0.71 and 0.61, the older plants 0.80 and 0.64.

The data in table 4-3 suggest two interesting features of Kenyan plants that should be addressed by a full explanation of productivity differentials: the generally low values of RTFP and the fairly close conformity of

Table 4-3. *Unit Labor and Capital Requirements and Total-Factor Productivity Relative to Best Practice: Spinning*

Item	Plant A (mid-1970s)	Plant B (mid-1970s)	Plant C (late 1940s)	Plant D (mid-1950s)	Mean, all plants
Labor	4.57	4.45	1.99	3.26	3.57
Capital	0.96	1.15	1.00	1.17	1.07
Capital-labor ratio	0.21	0.26	0.50	0.36	0.33
Relative total-factor productivity					
$\sigma = 1.0$	0.56	0.51	0.76	0.57	0.60
$\sigma = 0.5$	0.71	0.61	0.80	0.64	0.69
$\sigma = 0.2$	0.92	0.77	0.89	0.75	0.83

Note: Each of the figures in the upper half of the table shows the unit input in the Kenyan plant relative to its best-practice counterpart.

unit capital requirements in all plants to that of best practice. The second of these topics is discussed in a more general context in chapter 7; the sources of low Kenyan productivity are analyzed below.

The decomposition of productivity differentials follows the approach discussed in chapter 3, and the numerical results are set forth in table 4-4. The industry variable reflecting the absence of specialization is considerably more significant for the newer plants than are the firm-specific productivity-decreasing factors—speed, the twist multiple, and machine efficiency. It seems likely, if hard to prove, that the difference in specialization between the two sets of mills arose as the newer firms accepted even very small orders in order to increase utilization rates, given their recent establishment and very high fixed capital costs. Nevertheless, as noted in chapter 3, the failure to achieve greater average specialization requires explanation. The plants considered here, the four largest in Kenya, are all vertically integrated, and the demand for yarns of various counts derives from the demand for woven fabric. Even if each weaving shed manufactured a large range of products, independently owned spinning plants with the same total capacity could specialize in a narrow range of counts, assuming that total final demand for each count was relatively large and stable. In integrated plants, however, changing demand for fabric requires production to switch from one count of yarn to another, thus limiting the gains from specialization. Although production for inventory in the integrated plants might mitigate some of the fluctuations, storage of spun yarn is expensive. In principle there could be trade in yarns among the integrated mills, but they would then forgo the main benefit of inte-

Table 4-4. *Factors Reducing Total-Factor Productivity: Spinning*

Factor	Plant A (mid-1970s)	Plant B (mid-1970s)	Plant C (late 1940s)	Plant D (mid-1950s)	Mean, all plants
P_1, specialization	0.73	0.76	1.00	0.88	0.84
P_2, speed	1.05	0.96	1.15	1.19	1.09
P_3, twists per inch	0.95	0.99	0.91	0.71	0.89
P_4, machine efficiency	0.96	0.94	1.03	0.91	0.96
πP_{1-4}	0.70	0.68	1.08	0.68	0.79
P_5, task-level productivity					
$\sigma = 1.0$	0.79	0.74	0.71	0.83	0.77
$\sigma = 0.5$	1.01	0.90	0.75	0.93	0.90
$\sigma = 0.2$	1.30	1.12	0.83	1.10	1.09

Note: The lower the value for a given entry, the lower the relative performance in this dimension of the Kenyan firm relative to the best-practice standard, each of the P_i being defined as $(P_A/P_{BP})_i$.

gration, namely, low transportation cost between spinning and weaving sheds. More important, in an oligopolistic market, competitors might be reluctant to supply each other with yarn that would ultimately permit other mills to compete with them.

These results demonstrate that nothing in the technology itself prevents the modern plants from obtaining the higher RTFP of plant C (table 4-3, $\sigma = 0.5$). Rather the decomposition shows that the newer plants' poorer performance stems from their lack of product specialization.

One result of particular interest is that firms operating older spindles not only ran them at a greater speed (relative to best practice) than did newer firms but also imparted a greater number of twists per inch, tending to offset some of the greater spindle speed. The higher speed of spindles confirms empirical findings in other countries that developing country firms may attempt to "stretch" their capital and achieve lower capital-output ratios (Ranis, 1973). The concomitant higher twist multiple, however, shows that such capital-augmenting activity may be partly offset by the firms' inability to master the preparatory processes (see chapter 6 for details) and that the capital-stretching achievement implied by focusing solely on speed may seem less important with fuller documentation of all of a firm's production parameters.[9]

Firms C and D use a smaller percentage of longer staple yarns than do firms A and B, and their use of a high twist multiple reflects, to a quantitatively small extent, a lower-quality fiber mix. Both firms attribute their behavior to quotas on imports of non-Kenyan cotton, though plants A and B deny the significance of quotas. The difference in the fiber mix, however, cannot alone account for the particularly high twist multiple used by plant D: other deficiencies, such as inadequate blending, are present.

Task-level productivity is quite close to unity for three of the firms, with values of 0.90, 0.93, and 1.01, assuming that 0.5 is the correct value for the elasticity of substitution. Even the remaining firm's value of 0.75 is higher than might be inferred from the literature on labor inefficiency in developing countries (see chapter 3). Are these relatively high values an artifact owing to the decomposition procedure, or do they capture the reality of the production process? Here it is important to recall that task-level productivity is calculated as a residual. If one or more productivity-depressing factors whose value relative to best practice is less than unity have been omitted, Kenyan relative task-level productivity will be understated in the computations. Similarly, if any of the P_A/P_{BP} terms that are included have a mistakenly high value, then measured TLP will again be too low. Both of these errors, particularly the first, are more likely than their opposites. It is thus probable that any misestimate of task-level productivity understates it and that the calculated figure represents a lower bound of its actual value; this in turn suggests that performance gaps in individual tasks are not major sources of low productivity in Kenyan spinning.

A related question is whether high TLP would continue to hold if machine loads per worker were increased or whether the current result obtains precisely because of the low capital-labor ratio chosen by the plants.[10] One weak test of the last hypothesis is the relationship between observed values of the capital-labor ratio and task-level productivity. There is no systematic relationship in spinning, although the plants with the highest and lowest TLP exhibit the lowest and highest relative capital-labor ratios; in weaving, no relationship exists despite the greater operative skills required. More generally, given the simple nature of the individual operative's tasks in cotton textile manufacturing, there is little reason to expect nonneutral productivity differences such that TLP decreases with an increase in machine load per worker.[11] Although the possibility of overestimating task-level productivity cannot be ruled out, the more extensive evidence from the Philippines shows no relationship between the equipment-worker ratio in individual plants and their measured task-level productivity, despite 100 percent variations in the spindle-labor ratio.

The high measured value of TLP is partly attributable to the careful education programs that have been instituted by the Kenyan firms. These include training for up to four years in other developing country subsidiaries of the controlling company and intensive year-long programs within the local mills. The regional isolation of each firm within Kenya has the interesting effect of reducing its fear of losing locally trained workers, while education at more advanced mills in other developing countries, rather than in Western Europe, increases the probability that trainees will return to Kenya.

Consider now the question of the optimal choice of technology. In table 4-1 it was shown that, when all firms achieve RTFP of 85 percent, plant B realizes the lowest cost. Table 4-4 sheds light on the possibilities for such uniform moves toward best practice and the varieties of capabilities needed if these gains are to be realized. Firm C, using older equipment, is already close to or above best practice in all dimensions of performance except task-level productivity. Indeed, one sees that its successful performance is linked to a high degree of specialization as well as its specifically technological capacities measured by relative performance in speed (P_2) and spindle efficiency (P_4). The main potential source of still greater productivity is task-level productivity, which is likely to be the most difficult activity to improve because it requires changes in management style, including the introduction of wage incentive systems and training and recruiting programs.

In contrast, firms A and B suffer mainly from inadequate specialization, which could be remedied by industrywide coordination to rationalize production combined with a liberalized trade regime to prevent monopoly profits (chapter 9 discusses these issues). For these firms, a move toward best practice from current productivity levels and the resultant change in unit cost rankings is unlikely without some policy intervention that would encourage greater specialization.[12]

Weaving

In weaving, both single-input requirements relative to best practice are higher than they are in spinning, the mean relative labor requirement in all sheds is 5.15, the mean relative capital requirement is 1.21, and the relative total-factor productivity for all sheds is 0.62, if we assume that $\sigma = 0.5$ (table 4-5). Both the single-input requirements and total-factor productivity are worse for semiautomatic looms than for automatic ones.

The decomposition of the differences in total-factor productivity shown in table 4-6 provides some insight into the nature of low productivity in the Kenyan weaving sector. A major source is the typically very small size of production runs. The particular result shown, that total-factor productivity in all sheds decreases by 37 percent on average, reflects the assumption that Kenyan plants exhibit an average length of run (measured by the number of warp changes per 10,000 hours) that would place them at the lower quartile of British firms.[13] Clearly, the precise magnitude, firm by firm, is open to some degree of uncertainty.

The second potential source of low productivity is below-norm machine efficiency (see table 4-6). It will be remembered that the measure of inefficiency is deviation from achievable utilization rates, given the current loom assignment per worker, breakage rates, and patrol and relaxation time. The automatic looms in all sheds except shed C are operated at efficiency rates relatively close to best practice. In contrast, nonautomatic sheds in plants B and C realize efficiency levels that are 82 percent and 54 percent of best practice. Poor performance in these sheds is partly attributable to the failure to use warp stop mechanisms to detect broken ends, a puzzling deficiency, given good general performance in maintenance. Moreover, this difficulty did not reflect a temporary shortage but represented a long-term decision not to introduce warp stop mechanisms.

The relatively high efficiency levels in the automatic loom sheds of plants A, B, and D are achieved by devoting considerable effort to both maintenance and inventory control. The general manager of plant A, for

Table 4-5. *Unit Labor and Capital Requirements and Total-Factor Productivity Relative to Best Practice: Weaving*

Item	Plant A	Plant B		Plant C		Plant D	Mean		
	A	A	SA	A	SA	A	All sheds	A	SA
Labor	3.25	3.68	8.00	5.31	4.39	6.25	5.15	4.62	6.20
Capital	0.84	1.00	1.18	1.27	1.86	1.09	1.21	1.05	1.52
Capital-labor ratio	0.26	0.27	0.15	0.24	0.42	0.17	0.25	0.24	0.29
Relative total-factor productivity									
$\sigma = 1.0$	0.69	0.59	0.39	0.44	0.38	0.46	0.49	0.55	0.39
$\sigma = 0.5$	0.84	0.71	0.56	0.55	0.41	0.61	0.62	0.68	0.49
$\sigma = 0.2$	1.05	0.88	0.75	0.69	0.48	0.81	0.78	0.86	0.62

A = automatic loom.
SA = semiautomatic loom.
Note: Each of the figures in the upper half of the table shows the unit input in the Kenyan plant relative to its best-practice counterpart.

Table 4-6. *Total-Factor-Productivity-Reducing Factors: Weaving*

Item	Plant A	Plant B		Plant C		Plant D	Mean		
	A	A	SA	A	SA	A	All sheds	A	SA
P_1, specialization	0.63	0.63	0.63	0.63	0.63	0.63	0.63	0.63	0.63
P_2, loom efficiency	0.98	0.98	0.82	0.83	0.54	0.96	0.85	0.94	0.68
P_3, yarn quality	1.00	1.00	1.00	0.94	0.94	0.97	0.98	0.98	0.97
πP_{1-3}	0.62	0.62	0.52	0.50	0.32	0.59	0.52	0.58	0.42
P_5, task-level productivity									
$\sigma = 1.0$	1.12	0.96	0.76	0.89	1.20	0.77	0.95	0.94	0.98
$\sigma = 0.5$	1.35	1.15	1.07	1.10	1.31	1.04	1.17	1.16	1.19
$\sigma = 0.2$	1.69	1.43	1.42	1.40	1.51	1.38	1.47	1.48	1.46

A = automatic loom.
SA = semiautomatic loom.
Note: The lower the value for a given entry, the lower the relative performance in the dimension of the Kenyan firm relative to the best-practice standard, each of the P_i being defined as $(P_A / P_{BP})_i$.

example, reports that 50 percent of his work week is devoted to ensuring that supplies of raw materials and spare parts are adequate; the firm employs twenty-three expatriates, including a large number of technicians who provide the basic preventive maintenance program. In contrast, plant C trains and employs domestic maintenance personnel who are frequently lured away by firms in other sectors. For this reason it applied for work permits for foreign technicians, requests not acted upon with alacrity, given the government's interest in ensuring that technical skills were transferred to Kenyan residents. The resulting inability to provide continuous maintenance and to service defective equipment is one source of the lower relative productivity in plant C. The problem also provides one example of a nationwide shortcoming, inadequate vocational training, that is difficult to remedy for individual firms.

Finally, although plant C, unlike the other firms, has encouraged local machine shops to produce simple spare parts, more complicated parts are obtained abroad. It reports delays in obtaining foreign-made spares because of the existence of quantitative restrictions on imports, although this difficulty would not hamper production if sufficient inventories were maintained. Assuming that the firm could finance higher inventory levels, its failure to do so in the face of the substantial costs implied by lower than technically feasible equipment utilization suggests a failure of rational calculation.[14] This may in turn reflect the difficulty, particularly in very complex and shifting economic environments, of scanning the whole range of desirable actions and choosing among them. Even in more stable circumstances, bounded rationality clearly limits the set of actions that can reasonably be evaluated (see Nelson and Winter 1982).

To ascertain the impact on unit cost of equalizing relative loom efficiency in both automatic and nonautomatic sheds, the level of unit costs that would be realized if loom efficiency relative to best practice were the same in each shed has been calculated.[15] Thus the value of P_2 (in table 4-6) for semiautomatic looms is set equal to that for automatic looms operated by the same firm. The relative unit costs (automatic versus semiautomatic) before and after this change in machine efficiency levels are:

	Plant B	Plant C
Current loom efficiency	0.62	0.56
Equalized relative loom efficiency	0.74	0.87

The difference in unit costs is narrowed. The results indicate, however, that, given existing firm and worker abilities, semiautomatic looms do not currently provide an efficient technological alternative to conventional automatic looms. It is equally clear from other evidence, however, that this result is not inherent in the physical equipment but is decisively affected by changeable features of the economic environment, including both managerial and labor skills.[16]

Potential Competitiveness

Despite the lower total-factor productivity exhibited in Kenyan plants relative to best practice, most of them could probably export cloth if their purchased inputs were available at international prices and were not subject to tariffs, quotas, and the uncertain availability of specific qualities of fibers. Because each of the plants is integrated, the potential for cloth exports depends on efficiency not only in weaving but also in spinning.[17] The potential costs of each process in 1980 had liberalization occurred are considered in turn.

In spinning, the input coefficients used are those prevailing in Kenya in 1980 and those characterizing U.K. best practice in the late 1970s; in weaving, the comparisons are between input coefficients for Kenya in 1980 and U.K. best-practice coefficients in 1968. As noted in chapter 3, however, more recent estimates of U.K. performance for 1976 by Pickett and Robinson indicate relatively little difference between the 1968 and 1976 coefficients. Thus the rough cost estimates are a guide to competitiveness relative to the better U.K. firms that do export, although as noted below a more relevant market test requires comparisons with low-cost exporters of East Asia.

The comparison of Kenyan spinning plants using equipment of 1970s vintage with best-practice British plants of the late 1970s allows a fairly good approximation of comparative yarn production costs then prevailing and permits a generalization to the two other older mills. In the late 1970s, British textile wages for operatives were roughly nine times those of Kenya, while labor productivity was at most 450 percent greater (table 4-3). Capital productivity was comparable, as were market rates of interest in the two countries. Power costs per unit were also similar, although space was somewhat cheaper in Kenya. Hence apart from raw material costs, unit production cost was less in Kenya despite lower total-factor productivity. Competitiveness in relation to British plants cannot be advanced as a demonstration of the ability to export, though the better British plants do meet international competition. Information on the costs of East Asian producers is clearly more germane.

Wages in the major exporting nations of East Asia were considerably above those in Kenya, their shipping costs to most of the countries of the Organization for Economic Co-operation and Development (OECD) were greater, and it is likely that their fiber costs were also higher for geographical reasons. Unless the productivity of the Asian mills was markedly superior to that of the better British firms, it seems likely that the two modern Kenyan firms could, in fact, have matched the cost of yarn if inputs had been freely available at international prices. This statement is true of the two older plants as well, insofar as table 4-1 reports costs resembling those of the newer plants. Moreover, the admittedly rough cost calculations in this section are purely static, with no allowance for the benefits likely to accrue from the specialization made possible by a shift to exports. These would be particularly large for the two modern plants that exhibited relatively low degrees of specialization (table 4-4). Other productivity gains could also be expected; for example, to the extent that the use of inferior fiber requires a higher twist multiple than is technically desirable, a small decrease in twists per inch—a possibility if lowered trade barriers made better fiber available—would decrease unit cost. More generally, a growing body of literature attests to the importance of learning from technical advice provided by foreign purchasers (Morawetz 1981; Westphal, Rhee, and Pursell 1981) and these would presumably accrue in Kenya as well if foreign firms became significant purchasers of cloth. As the analysis of the sources of productivity differentials demonstrates, there is considerable scope for such learning in yarn production.[18]

In the case of weaving, even the largest labor productivity differentials shown in table 4-5 for automatic looms would have yielded lower labor cost in Kenyan plants.[19] Moreover, British weaving plants had relatively good comparative labor productivity in the late 1960s (chapter 7). Given the similarity of 1968 and 1976 best-practice coefficients, the Kenyan firms, even at actual 1980 levels of productivity, should have been able to export if their yarn costs were similar to those prevailing internationally. Furthermore, as in the case of spinning, the dynamic cost picture could well change if firms were to export, and the potential benefits of specialization would loom quite large.

Although these questions of current and potential international cost comparisons are of great interest, it is impossible to pursue them further without comparably detailed data from the major producer countries. Unfortunately obtaining such data is a major project in its own right.[20]

Notes

1. Some uniform figure is necessary to carry out the analysis; 85 percent is often used in ex ante project appraisal. The assumed change in productivity affects all input requirements uniformly (except for waste, which is close to best-practice levels in all plants). Both electricity and space requirements are affected, as they vary directly with the spindle-output ratio. The

feasibility of the postulated change in productivity is discussed below. The shift to RTFP $= 0.85$ corresponds to a move from C_2 to C_1 or C_3 to C_4 in figure 3-2, if we assume, to keep the geometry simple, that CC represents RTFP of 0.85 rather than best practice itself, as it does in the discussion of that figure.

2. The precise value of the decrease in unit cost depends on the initial value of RTFP, which itself varies with the size of the elasticity of substitution. See table 4-3 and the discussion of the role of the elasticity of substitution in chapter 3. The calculation of unit cost in the last column of table 3-1 is based on the improvement from the current RTFP with $\sigma = 0.5$, the most plausible value of the parameter, given the technological basis of short-run factor substitution. See the discussion in chapter 2 and chapter 3.

3. The cost differences correspond to those incurred in producing at C_4 and C_1 in figure 3-2.

4. Some of firm B's equipment is manufactured in India under license from a European manufacturer. If the lower price of this Indian-produced equipment had been employed in the cost calculation rather than the price of European-manufactured equipment, firm B would exhibit still lower cost. The European price is employed, as it was not possible to obtain price quotations from the Indian supplier, although the firm using the equipment indicated that the price was considerably below that of the European licenser.

5. The lower use of power in firm C despite its greater loom-output ratio reflects the design of its Japanese loom. The smaller space requirement arises because much smaller aisles separate looms in this plant rather than because the dimensions of the looms themselves differ.

6. See the appendix to chapter 3 for a brief discussion of equipment prices. It could be argued that the failure to obtain the lowest available price for equipment of a given design constitutes still another form of inefficiency that merits a separate category, perhaps search inefficiency. I think this argument would overextend the benefits of the existing taxonomy. In the categories suggested in chapter 2, disparities in equipment prices may reflect one of those second-level allocational decisions that I do not pursue in the current book.

7. The comparison presents some problems for plant C. The basic equipment in plant C is of 1930–50 vintage. The slight improvement embodied in 1950 best-practice relative to this somewhat older machinery may lead to an overstatement of unit labor requirements relative to best practice. Some of C's equipment has been modernized, however, and thus unit labor inputs have been reduced. Although the net result of these two factors is not easily quantified, textile engineers claim that the use of 1950 best practice for comparisons with plant C is not biased.

8. This result uses the absolute level of labor input per unit of output for each firm and cannot be calculated from table 4-3.

9. Analyses of international data presented in chapter 7 indicate that the East Asian countries, but not other developing countries, have been able to increase speed without sustaining offsetting reductions in twists per inch or efficiency.

10. This is the same question as whether task-level productivity is neutral with respect to the capital-labor ratio, an assumption that underlies the calculations. The plausibility of this assumption is also suggested by the analysis of the spinning process in chapter 2. This assumption has been a staple of the econometric production function literature, and many tests, including the original Arrow, Chenery, Minhas, and Solow (1961) article, have confirmed it.

11. See, for example, ILO (1972).

12. As will be noted below, access to inputs at world market prices would allow at least some of the manufacturers to realize profitable exports, thus also promoting specialization.

13. The reason for using a uniform assumption about the length of runs is the inability of some of the firms to provide an estimate of either the number of warp changes per period or the average length of run. Most firms reported that they were willing to produce a batch as small as 2,000 yards; the two newest firms reported weaving thirty-eight and forty fabric types

(different yarn count and construction combinations). Even if the minimum acceptable order were 6,000 yards, and if twenty looms were devoted to weaving a given style, only three days of three-shift production would be needed to complete the order. Thus the assumption of a uniform 37 percent reduction in productivity may well be conservative. Although it is impossible to discriminate between firms in this dimension, all of the statements indicate so much variation in product that the uniform approximation is unlikely to be grossly in error.

14. As noted in chapter 2, it is difficult to explore the rationality of such second-level intrafirm decisions. For some numerical results regarding the benefits and costs of different inventory policies, see chapter 6.

15. The implication is still that semiautomatic looms are operated at a lower level of absolute efficiency, given that best-practice machine efficiency is greater on automatic looms.

16. Rhee and Westphal (1977); also see chapter 2 above.

17. It is occasionally argued that the textile sector should not have integrated factories; that is, spinning and weaving should be done in physically separate plants so that management can concentrate on one process or the other. As noted in chapter 2, evaluation of the organization of the sector requires detailed information on transport and other costs that are beyond the scope of this study.

18. As shown in chapter 7, international differences in total-factor productivity among the developed countries are substantial in spinning and are most likely attributable to variations in levels of specialization.

19. Unless there were radical changes in the productivity of semiautomatic looms, they would not be relevant for the production of exports as they were in the case of Korea analyzed by Rhee and Westphal (1977).

20. For a sample of the information needed and the extensive organizational requirements for obtaining it, see Textile Council (1969), vols. 1 and 2, especially chaps. 5 and 8 and relevant appendixes. These studies were carried out by a large international textile consulting firm and rely extensively on closely guarded commercial information.

CHAPTER FIVE

The Philippine Textile Sector

ELEVEN COMPANIES were visited; with one exception, all were integrated mills operating both spinning and weaving plants. Several had two related but separate spinning mills. Fifteen spinning plants were examined, including two that used open-end spinning. All firms were owned and largely managed by Philippine nationals; in a few instances, important managerial personnel came from other countries in East Asia.

Unit costs vary considerably in spinning, the interfirm differentials being much larger than they are in Kenya. The plant with the lowest unit cost employs equipment of mid-1950s vintage, although its competitors generally use newer machinery. At a uniformly high level of productivity for all firms, the current lowest-cost plant maintains its rank, but the size of its advantage is considerably diminished. At the assumed high level of productivity, both very old equipment and very new open-end equipment manifest greater costs than recently made conventional ring frames. Unit cost could be reduced by an average of 15 percent if all firms were able to achieve a uniform level of 85 percent relative total-factor productivity.

Unit cost also varies widely in weaving, despite the fact that most firms use similar looms. A 65 percent average cost reduction could be obtained from a combination of improved technical efficiency and an alteration in the labor-loom ratio, with the former accounting for three-fifths of the gain.

In spinning, average productivity performance as measured by relative total-factor productivity exhibits a mean of 73 percent, fairly similar to that in Kenya. The average level realized in weaving is considerably lower, however, at 55 percent. In both activities, the inability to realize productivity gains from greater specialization accounts for a major part of the shortfall in productivity, although in weaving a considerable fraction is also attributable to low loom efficiency—some of which stems from a lack of spare parts. As in Kenya, in neither spinning nor weaving is poor task-level productivity a principal source of low total-factor productivity.

Spinning

Interfirm Cost Comparisons within the Philippines

Summary data for spinning plants by vintage, all expressed relative to the lowest-cost mid-1950s mill (plant L) are shown in table 5-1. For one vintage group the coefficient of variation of the relevant characteristics is also shown.[1]

It is striking that the plant with the lowest unit cost is of mid-1950s vintage. Mills with much more modern ring spindles as well as ones using open-end spinning incur greater costs (column 7). The characteristics of the low-cost firm that seem to be critical in achieving this success are discussed in chapter 6. The present chapter is largely descriptive and includes only a limited examination of the actions of firms that result in the observed patterns. If we ignore plant L for the moment, comparisons of the three groups employing ring spindles (rows 1, 3, and 5) show that newer conventional equipment permits a reduction in labor and spindles per unit of output. For the only group for which there are several observations (plants with machinery that dates from the period 1960–70), however, there is substantial interfirm variation in performance, and the date of a machine's manufacture within this period is not a good predictor of the productivity that can be obtained from its use. The coefficients of variation of both labor per unit of output and capital per unit of output are fairly large, and some of the older plants exhibit better performance than newer ones.

In production characteristics most often thought to be purely technological—for example, power and space per unit of output—the performance of many newer plants is worse than that of plant L. The reason is that power and space use are defined per unit of output, not per spindle hour. Insofar as the spindle-output ratio varies among firms, the power and space unit input requirements vary along with it. Thus even where new vintages are designed to require less space per spindle, this advantage is partly or totally offset by a greater spindle-output ratio.

Although newer equipment embodies designs that reduce the waste per kilogram of final output, even here there is not a strict correspondence of unit requirements with vintage. Thus the lowest-cost firm, L, has a lower waste percentage than the average of the 1960–70 vintage plants, though the latter's machinery incorporates devices explicitly intended to reduce waste. Such reversals in actual use of the performance characteristics embodied in equipment reflect differing knowledge of the technology not embodied in equipment, such as the ability to choose cotton fibers with

Table 5-1. Inputs and Unit Cost per Kilogram of Spun Yarn (20s): Mean Values by Group

Plant vintage	Number of plants (1)	Operative hours (2)	Spindle hours (3)	Waste (4)	Power (5)	Space (6)	Current unit cost (7)	Unit cost with RTFP = 0.85 (8)
Pre-1950	2	280	203	143	185	214	170	150
1950–59	1[a]	100	100	100	100	100	100	116
1960–70	8	181	124	109	184	129	140	119
Coefficient of variation		0.22	0.24	0.22	0.12	0.21	0.11	0.10
1970–77	3	122	103	88	172	71	154	123
Open end	2	145	20[b]	96	192	148	177	145

Note: Yarn count is a measure of the thickness of yarn expressed in terms of the number of lengths of 840 yards per pound. Thus 20s count indicates that a pound of yarn contains 16,800 yards. L is the plant with lowest cost. Figures in the last two columns are expressed relative to plant L's current unit cost.

a. Plant L.

b. Rotors per unit of output.

properties (for example, length) best suited to a particular set of machines.

Most important, consider unit cost. The costs of the open-end plants exceed those of firm L by 77 percent; at the other end of the technology spectrum, the two pre-1950 plants exhibit costs 70 percent above those of firm L. The three ring-spinning plants of mid-1970s vintage exceed firm L's costs by 54 percent. The best group average is achieved by firms employing 1960s equipment. The reason is partly that, like firm L, their cost of using equipment is lower than that for the 1970s or open-end plants, the cost of older equipment being taken as the current market resale value as estimated by plant managers (though the interest rate assumed is the same for all plants); see chapter 3 appendix. With respect to the differences in cost between conventional modern ring spinning (1970s) and the open-end plants, the machinery in both is valued at the current new price, so that the lower unit cost of the ring-spinning plants is not attributable to the use of depreciated values for equipment.

As mentioned immediately above, the lower cost currently obtained with existing equipment of older vintages partly reflects the fact that it is valued at a fraction of the price of new equipment. A firm planning to begin production might not find a given older technology as profitable if the relevant equipment could not be obtained at the prices used in the calculation, though a margin of superiority would remain even at a higher equipment price if the firm could achieve high productivity.[2]

In summary, the evidence in table 5-1 indicates that the rapid changes in best-practice input coefficients shown in chapter 3, though not fully realized in the Philippines, nevertheless have enough effect that each successive vintage of equipment is operated on the average with generally greater physical productivity than its predecessors. Nevertheless, none of the mills employing newer machinery are able to match the cost performance of shed L; this statement is true for 1970s plants embodying quite high speeds and many innovations. These results are explained by the low relative total-factor productivity realized by the newer plants, a characteristic that is examined below. It is not only shed L that does well in comparison with the newest ring frames; several plants in the 1960–70 group also have lower costs than the 1970s firms, including one owned by the same firm as shed L. This plant, with 1960s equipment, exhibits roughly the same unit labor and spindle requirements as the 1970s plants; given the lower opportunity cost of its equipment, its unit costs are lower.

The introduction of the most modern equipment, open-end spinning, achieves no cost reduction relative to new conventional equipment. Labor, waste, and power and space requirements are all greater than on 1970s ring-spinning equipment, although comparisons of best productivity specifications indicate that only power requirements should be greater. It is particularly surprising that neither of the two open-end plants can surpass plant L of mid-1950s vintage in several input dimensions, although the comparisons of best-practice plants (see table 3-1) leave no doubt about the potential differences.

The Effect on Cost of Changes in Productivity and Technology

It is again useful to put the discussion of the determinants of unit cost into the analytical framework set forth in chapter 3. The effect on unit cost if every firm were to achieve RTFP of 85 percent is shown in column 8 of table 5-1, the improvement in productivity being based on the assumption that 0.5 is the correct ex post elasticity of substitution. All cost figures in column 8 are indexed on the initial cost of plant L. Because its current RTFP exceeds 0.85, plant L's own unit cost *increases* when costs are recalculated.[3]

Comparisons of the adjusted unit cost figures in column 8 and the existing ones in column 7 show that significant excess cost is incurred by operating at productivity below best practice. The 1960–70 and 1970–77 plant could, on average, reduce their unit cost by 15 and 20 percent respectively, whereas smaller decreases of 12 and 18 percent could be obtained by the pre-1950 and open-end plants. (See table 5-2 for a summary.)

The reduction in unit cost from correct choice of technology can also be given a numerical value. The benefits from improved choice of technique can be calculated as well, but they are relatively small and are thus disregarded here.[4] Along the "efficient" (85 percent RTFP) isoquants, the cost reduction from choosing an appropriate technology (defined as one that minimizes private costs), in this case the 1950s one, is 22 percent when the comparison involves pre-1950 equipment, 2 percent relative to 1960–70 equipment, and 6 percent relative to machines produced in the 1970s.[5] These results are summarized in table 5.2.

The newest technology, open-end spinning, does not become optimal even when used efficiently, exhibiting a unit cost of 25 percent above that of 1950s equipment (table 5-1, column 8) and 18 percent above that of new 1970s ring-spinning equipment, if it is assumed, as in the other cases, that the relevant value of σ is 0.5. Moreover, a comparison of ring and break spinning makes it clear that the correct elasticity of substitution is lower in the latter. If the relevant elasticity is 0.2, then a further improvement in cost performance could not be achieved by merely moving to RTFP of 0.85, as this level is already being achieved. At Philippine relative factor prices, the new technology will exhibit a quite high unit cost even

Table 5-2. *Gains from Increased Productivity and Improved Choice of Technology: Spinning*

| | | Plant vintage | | | | Mean for |
Source of change in unit cost	Pre-1950	1950–59 (plant L)	1960–70	1970–77	Open end	all plants, except L
Realizing RTFP of 85 percent	−12	16	−15	−20	−18	−15
Move to least-cost technology	−22	0	−2	−6	−20	−8
Total cost change	−34	16	−17	−26	−38	−23

at 100 percent RTFP, and choice of the conventional technology is warranted at both current and high productivity levels.

If we view the above discussion in the framework of figure 3-2 and assume for ease of exposition that the isoquant exhibiting 85 percent RTFP is ABC_1, improved choices of technology among the points of this isoquant (table 5-2, row 2) generally generate smaller cost reductions than do increases in RTFP from currently inefficient points such as C_2 (row 1).[6] The gains from improved choice of technology are largest for the oldest (pre-1950) and the most modern (open-end) spinning plants. The precise numbers presented here are best viewed as orders of magnitude only: I would not want to specify, on the basis of them alone, whether improved allocational or technical efficiency offers larger potential cost reductions, but it is clear that both are quantitatively important.[7] Because the realization of either type of gain requires some expenditures, the choice between raising productivity and achieving a better choice of technology must be viewed as an investment decision. Neither productivity improvements nor better information about the range of production technologies can be obtained without explicit outlays on consultants, trips to foreign plants and trade fairs, and other activities that enhance firms' knowledge. In addition to explicit expenditures, the implicit cost to the firm of the required managerial attention is likely to be substantial. The gains noted in the preceding paragraphs are gross of these costs but, once achieved, will accrue to the firm for a long time. Given the magnitude of the cost reductions, investment undertaken to obtain these improvements is likely to yield a high rate of return. Quantitative estimates of these benefits and costs are provided in chapter 8.

The Rationality of Investment Decisions

Comparison of the figures in the last two columns of table 5-1 suggests a tentative answer to a puzzling phenomenon—did the plants established or expanded in the 1970s knowingly purchase new equipment that would result in an average unit cost (154) above what they presumably knew were the average unit costs (100 and 140) of their existing competitors, who had benefited from the lower opportunity (and accounting) cost of older equipment? The explanation could lie in the unavailability of sufficient amounts of older machinery, the costs of acquiring information about such equipment, and misestimates of the cost saving to be realized by the adoption of older equipment.

Although the hypotheses just mentioned cannot be directly addressed (for example, was sufficient older equipment available to outfit an entire plant?), the evidence here accords with the hypothesis that the purchase of

1970s machinery was consistent with cost minimization. If the 1970s firms assumed that their competitors would continue to realize their current unit cost while they themselves attained RTFP of 85 percent, they would have an anticipated unit cost of 123, below the 1960–70 group's average of 140 and indeed lower than that of all but one firm in that group. Only after the fact, with the realization of RTFP below a plausibly expected level, did the particular choice of technology appear to be inappropriate.

Weaving

The relevant data for analyzing interfirm cost comparisons in the weaving sector are shown in table 5-3. The mill with the lowest unit cost (plant L) used Japanese and American-made automatic looms produced between 1956 and 1961. All of the data are normalized on plant L. All other firms but one also used conventional automatic looms of about the same vintage but achieved widely varying results with them. Thus three mills, group N, used them as semiautomatic looms. The semiautomatic mode of operation was attributed by managers to the absence of spare parts, though the other plants utilizing identical looms had no such problems. One mill, plant O, purchased a water jet loom in the mid-1970s and has achieved quite low cost with it. Recently several companies purchased looms that use newly perfected devices such as rapiers and grippers. The results obtained from the use of these mechanisms (and of a new Chinese automatic loom) are not reported here, because the equipment had not been fully absorbed into the production process and the existing input coefficients were clearly not those that would ultimately be obtained. One of the automatic looms in use was produced in Eastern Europe, although it is based on a Western design. The results obtained with it are reported separately, because performance in the weaving shed that employs it seems to be inferior to performance involving Western European equipment of the same design.

Column 6 presents the standard result of the effect of firms moving to a uniform RTFP level of 85 percent, whereas column 7 shows the cost that would be realized if choice of technique also improved. In terms of figure 3-2, column 5 shows TC_3, and column 7, TC_1. The move from column 5 to column 6 is equivalent to the cost reduction $TC_2 - TC_1$, and that from column 6 to column 7 equals $TC_3 - TC_2$, the sum being $TC_3 - TC_1$. Because all firms use the same technology, differences in unit cost shown in column 6 represent the effects of variations in the choice of technique, whereas this source of difference is eliminated in column 7.

Table 5-3. *Inputs and Unit Cost per Meter of Woven Cloth*

Plant	Loom type	Operative hours (1)	Loom hours (2)	Space (3)	Power (4)	Unit cost (5)	Unit cost with $RTFP = 0.85$[a] (6)	Unit cost $RTFP = 0.85$ and correct labor-equipment ratio (7)
L	Automatic	100	100	100	100	100	61	61
M	Automatic (Western Europe and Japan)	213	79	96	92	147	103	61
M'	Automatic (Eastern Europe)	518	90	66	129	238	146	64
N	Automatic used as semiautomatic	528	110	139	119	242	117	61
O	Water jet	52	29	61	42	106	105	105

Note: All underlying data have been expressed relative to the figures obtained from plant L, the plant with the lowest current unit cost.
a. Unit cost if a firm achieves 85 percent of the total-factor productivity of a best-practice plant, expressed as a percentage of the initial cost of plant L.

Comparison of group M (firms using Western and Japanese automatic looms) with the lowest-cost firm (plant L) employing similar looms shows that the major performance difference is the lower relative unit capital input of the former (79) achieved by a much greater relative labor input (213). At existing relative factor prices, the effect of excessive substitution of labor for capital is to raise unit production cost by 69 percent [(103/61) − 1]. These higher costs occur despite the fact that group M exhibits somewhat greater RTFP, as will be seen below. Unlike the result in spinning, where the lowest cost was associated with considerably greater RTFP, lowest cost in the weaving sheds results not from technical efficiency—that is, not because a firm is closer to the best-practice frontier—but as a result of allocative efficiency in which plant L has chosen a factor mix closer to the cost-minimizing one than that selected by its closest competitors (see figure 5-1).[8]

The poor cost performance of the three firms using automatic looms as semiautomatic (group N) is starkly apparent. These plants could potentially reduce unit cost by 75 percent [1 − (61/242)], two thirds of which

Figure 5-1. *Technical Efficiency and Unit Cost*

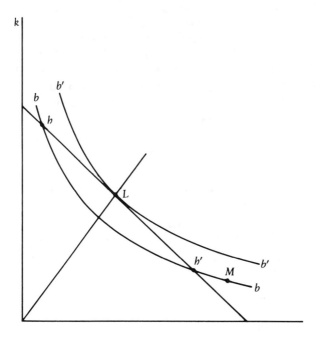

would be obtained by improved productivity and one-third by better choice of technique. The considerably greater space per loom in group N (relative to experience in plants L and M with quite similar looms) contributes to group N's higher cost level; this less economic use of space, together with the inability to obtain spare parts that other firms do manage to acquire, suggests that the high cost of this operation ultimately derives from weak management rather than from any problems inherent in the equipment currently in use.

Perhaps surprisingly to advocates of labor-intensive technology, the shed (plant O) using the most modern of the looms reported on here exhibits almost the same current unit cost as plant L despite the much lower opportunity cost of the latter's 1960 equipment. The firm using the water jet realizes a saving in every input cost except capital, because of the high price of such looms. The small difference in columns 5 and 6 indicates that its good performance relative to plants L and M is largely attributable to its operating closer to best-practice standards than do firms in the other groups. Were plant L able to achieve 85 percent RTFP, plant O's costs would exceed plant L's by 72 percent (column 6); the average cost in group M would also be slightly lower than the average cost in plant O.

Table 5-4 summarizes the potential reductions in cost obtainable from improved productivity and more appropriate factor proportions with existing technology. The percentages shown have been calculated from columns 5–7 in table 5-3. The numbers shown in row 3 correspond to the total cost reduction in figure 3-2 obtained by the move from TC_3 to TC_1; the average for all firms is 65 percent. Of this total, about three-fifths (row 1) is attributable to potential gains in total-factor productivity, the remainder (row 2) to improved choice of technique. Chapter 8 will estimate the costs of achieving such benefits.

Table 5-4. *Gains from Increased Productivity and Improved Choice of Technique: Weaving*

Source of change in unit cost	Plant L	Plant M	Plant M'	Plant N	Average
Realizing RTFP of 85 percent	− 39	− 30	− 39	− 52	− 39
Move to least-cost technique	0	− 29	− 34	− 23	− 26
Total cost change	− 39	− 59	− 73	− 75	− 65

The Choice of Current Textile Technologies

Analysis of the only significant choice of technology, that of water jets versus conventional automatic looms (plant O versus plants L, M, N), demonstrates that the desirability of introducing more advanced machinery depends on the ability of plants using each technology to attain the correct factor mix and productive efficiency. If current performance parameters, including managerial skills, are immutable, the water jet will be close to cost minimizing, at least in terms of current market prices for factors of production. If current firm capabilities can be altered by suitable investment, however, including changing factor proportions to those of plant L, the conventional technology may be optimal; the benefit from adopting it would be a reduction in unit cost of 42 percent $[1 - (61/105)]$ (table 5-3, column 7).

It was shown above that the most modern technology available, open-end spinning, exhibited considerably higher unit costs than the current ring-frame technology if both are purchased at current new equipment prices and are operated at a uniform 85 percent RTFP (table 5-1, column 8). As noted earlier, only one Philippine firm has installed the most modern and highest-cost gripper loom, generally known as the Sulzer loom, and the installation has been too recent to permit comparisons with either best-practice norms or other firms in the Philippines. Nevertheless, it is still possible to compare the firm's unit cost if it were operated at RTFP of 85 percent with that of running a new conventional automatic loom at the same relative productivity.

At the input prices used in the preceding calculations, unit cost for the Sulzer loom is 72 percent greater than that of the conventional loom, reinforcing the conclusion reached in spinning that, at factor prices prevailing in the Philippines, the decision to introduce the most advanced equipment is not based purely on cost.[9] The firm that had purchased the new loom claimed that this was the only way to guarantee the production of export-quality denim under Philippine conditions, although other firms were weaving precisely such denim with considerably less sophisticated machinery. Interestingly enough, the rationalization for adopting open-end spinning equipment is also based on an argument about export-quality yarn to be used for denim. Where cost-increasing technology choices are substitutes for other ways of obtaining competence in production engineering, the potential rate of return on human capital investments designed to develop such competence may be quite high.

Performance Relative to Best Practice

Spinning

In contrast to the previous section, which compared the performance of individual firms within the Philippines, this section compares each plant's productivity with best practice in the United Kingdom. The salient stylized facts (table 5-5) are:

- Unit labor requirements in Philippine plants considerably exceed those in best-practice plants using similar equipment.
- Unit capital requirements also exceed best practice but by a smaller percentage than holds for labor.
- Capital-labor ratios in the Philippine plants are lower than those in best-practice plants.
- Except in the lowest-cost plant, RTFP is less than 75 percent of best practice in conventional ring spinning. If σ is assumed to be 0.5, most plants exhibit about two-thirds of the total-factor productivity of best-practice plants.

Greater unit labor requirements and a lower capital-output ratio are to be expected as a result of the lower wage-rental ratio than in the United Kingdom. The higher capital-output ratio despite the lower capital-labor ratio, however, reflects the lower total-factor productivity in the Philippines. I next consider the values of each of the productivity-reducing factors discussed in chapter 3, which appear in table 5-6.

The largest productivity-depressing factor for all plants (0.79) arises from the inability of firms to realize sufficient product specialization. For all firms (except open end) the combined effect of excessive product diversity, low spindle efficiency, the operation of ring frames at low speeds, and high twist multiples is 0.72. Thus, apart from task-level productivity, total-factor productivity is decreased by an average of 28 percent in Philippine firms relative to best practice. In contrast, task-level productivity—the feature often emphasized in discussions of industrialization and certainly foremost in the minds of plant managers as the source of poor performance—lowers productivity by only 8 percent (on the average) when the Cobb-Douglas is the assumed ex post production function and not at all when $\sigma = 0.5$ and 0.2. Because TLP is a residual, its value depends on the value of total-factor productivity, the magnitude of other productivity depressants, and on factor proportions, hence on σ. As the substitutability of labor for capital falls, more of the shortfall in labor productivity is attributed to the effect of the lower capital-labor ratio and less to the residual task-level productivity (see chapter 3). It will be noted

Table 5-5. *Unit Labor and Capital Requirements and Total-Factor Productivity Relative to Best Practice: Spinning*

| | Plant vintage | | | | All plants, except open end | |
Item	Pre-1950	1950–59 (plant L)	1960–70	1970–77	Open end	Mean	Coefficient of variation
Labor	1.87	0.85	1.99	2.73	5.92	2.05	0.30
Capital	1.28	0.95	1.33	1.30	1.00	1.29	0.26
Capital-labor ratio	0.71	1.12	0.69	0.47	0.17	0.60	0.41
Relative total-factor productivity							
$\sigma = 1.0$	0.66	1.10	0.66	0.61	0.50	0.68	0.25
$\sigma = 0.5$	0.69	1.10	0.69	0.65	0.67	0.73	0.22
$\sigma = 0.2$	0.73	1.11	0.73	0.75	0.88	0.76	0.25

Note: Each of the figures in the upper half of the table shows the unit input in the Philippine plant relative to its best-practice counterpart.

Table 5-6. *Total-Factor-Productivity-Reducing Factors: Spinning*

| | Plant vintage | | | | All plants, except open end | |
Factor	Pre-1950	1950–59 (plant L)	1960–70	1970–77	Open end	Mean	Coefficient of variation
P_1, specialization	0.81	0.78	0.77	0.84	1.00	0.79	0.09
P_2, speed	1.23	1.41	0.94	0.95	1.00	1.00	0.24
P_3, twist multiple	0.98	1.00	1.00	1.00	1.00	1.00	0.01
P_4, machine efficiency	0.85	0.90	0.89	0.99	1.00	0.91	0.10
πP_{1-4}	0.85	0.98	0.65	0.80	1.00	0.72	0.30
P_5, task-level productivity							
$\sigma = 1.0$	0.85	1.12	1.03	0.76	0.50	0.92	0.22
$\sigma = 0.5$	0.86	1.12	1.09	0.82	0.66	1.03	0.26
$\sigma = 0.2$	0.93	1.12	1.16	0.93	0.87	1.11	0.31

that, unlike the small coefficient of variation of the technical productivity-depressing effects (except speed), task-level productivity shows considerable interfirm variation. One interpretation of this feature is that knowledge of production engineering is more uniformly diffused than is the ability to train or manage labor. These questions are discussed extensively in chapter 7. Alternatively, this dispersion may reflect the residual nature of TLP and the variation in the omitted productivity depressants included in it.

The failure of plants to achieve developed country levels of product specialization is a major source of low RTFP, reducing it by about 20 percent; this finding corroborates a criticism often made in the literature about excessive import-substituting industrialization (see chapter 3). Surprisingly, the only mills that realize the best-practice length of run are those using the most modern technology, open-end spinning equipment having been purchased explicitly to produce low-count yarn used in the manufacture of denim for export. Because low-count yarn of the same quality is produced more cheaply by conventional ring spinning, the results merely indicate that firms with some noncompetitive tie to denim exporters have chosen open-end spinning. Given that the Philippine domestic market is large enough to permit considerable product specialization by plants, rationalization of the product mix could, by itself, reduce the operating costs of conventional ring-spinning plants by the aforementioned 20 percent.

The technical capability of firms, as measured by speed and spindle efficiency, varies considerably among the various vintage groups. A major source of the high RTFP of the lowest-cost plant lies in its mastery of these activities. In contrast, the firms using newer vintages of equipment (1960–70 and 1970–77) fall short of best-practice standards. Among the problems producing this result is the failure to use ring spindles at their rated speeds, which in turn reflects difficulties in employing appropriate engineering procedures and quality control early in the spinning process.[10]

The only significant correlation between any one of the P_i and RTFP is that, for speed, $r = 0.56$ (significant at a 95 percent level). The absence of any correlation other than that for speed is consistent with a view that management has many alternatives to increase productivity and profitability. Thus the devotion of scarce managerial time to training, employee relations, or maintenance and upgrading of machines to obtain greater speeds may all improve productivity. The particular path chosen by a firm will depend on the relationship between the marginal cost of managerial effort and the anticipated potential cost reduction in any productivity-enhancing activity.

Both the low-cost firm and the pre-1950 firms run their spindles at speeds exceeding those of the best-practice firms. This additional speed is not offset by a higher twist multiple in the Philippines, as it is in Kenya.

Weaving

Single- and total-factor productivity as compared with best practice are lower in Philippine weaving than in spinning (table 5-7). The values of

Table 5-7. *Unit Labor and Capital Requirements and Total-Factor Productivity Relative to Best Practice: Weaving*

	Loom type					All plants	
Item	Plant L: A[a]	Plants M: A[b]	Plant M': A[c]	Plants N: A[d]	Plant O: Water jet	Mean	Coefficient of variation
Labor	2.26	3.25	6.80	6.66	1.61	4.23	0.54
Capital	1.74	1.34	1.30	1.77	1.02	1.39	0.25
Capital-labor	0.77	0.40	0.19	0.28	0.63	0.40	0.43
Relative total-factor productivity							
$\sigma = 1.0$	0.51	0.54	0.40	0.34	0.82	0.49	0.31
$\sigma = 0.5$	0.52	0.60	0.52	0.41	0.84	0.55	0.25
$\sigma = 0.2$	0.53	0.69	0.68	0.49	0.89	0.68	0.28

A = automatic.

Note: Each of the figures in the upper half of the table shows the unit input in the Philippine plant relative to its best-practice counterpart.

a. Lowest cost.
b. Western Europe and Japan.
c. Eastern European.
d. Automatic used as semiautomatic.

total-factor productivity in weaving are more sensitive to the value of the elasticity of substitution than are those in spinning, because of the lower values of the capital-labor ratio relative to best practice in weaving. Using the Cobb-Douglas production function, the mean value of relative total-factor productivity for all plants is 0.49, increasing to 0.55 when $\sigma = 0.5$. Though most Philippine looms are of the conventional automatic type, plant productivity varies widely; this variation cannot be explained by small differences in loom design or by the type of product made. The major results (assuming that $\sigma = 0.5$) are (1) the slightly greater RTFP of group M relative to group L, (2) the considerably lower single and total factor productivity in group N, which uses automatic looms in a semi-automatic mode, and (3) the quite high RTFP of the shed using water jet looms.

The sources of the differences between actual and best-practice productivity are decomposed in table 5-8. Data were collected on the number of fabrics woven, a given fabric being defined by the type of weave, the count of the yarns, and whether dyed yarns were employed. A typical firm produced between eighteen and twenty-four fabrics, the coefficient of variation among plants being about 15 percent. Unfortunately, the number of fabrics cannot be used as a good measure of the impact of product variety; the technically relevant measure, the average length of production run, may vary substantially for a given number of fabrics, depending on how carefully production is planned and the willingness of

Table 5-8. *Total-Factor-Productivity-Reducing Factors: Weaving*

	Loom type					All plants	
Item	Plant L: A[a]	Plants M: A[b]	Plant M': A[c]	Plants N: A[d]	Plant O: Water jet	Mean	Coefficient of variation
P_1, speciali-							
zation	0.70	0.70	0.70	0.70	0.70	0.70	0.00
P_2, loom							
efficiency	0.72	0.78	0.80	0.72	0.96	0.77	0.09
P_3, yarn							
quality	0.98	0.98	0.99	0.91	1.01	0.96	0.05
πP_{1-3}	0.49	0.53	0.55	0.58	0.68	0.52	0.15
P_5, task-level							
productivity							
$\sigma = 1.0$	1.03	1.00	0.71	0.74	1.19	0.92	0.18
$\sigma = 0.5$	1.03	1.11	0.94	0.88	1.22	1.03	0.14
$\sigma = 0.2$	1.06	1.26	1.22	1.09	1.29	1.19	0.15

A = automatic.
a. Lowest cost.
b. Western Europe and Japan.
c. Eastern European.
d. Automatic used as semiautomatic.

firms to produce for inventory rather than solely for orders received (see also chapter 3). Given the difficulties that firms have in estimating the average length of run in weaving, an assumption is made that productivity is reduced by an average of 30 percent. This figure is based on the conservative assessment that the number of warp changes per 10,000 loom hours is at the median level of British firms. (See chapter 3 for a discussion of the procedure.) The need to use a standard figure to give the effect of variety precludes identification of those firms that are relatively successful in achieving better productivity through long production runs. This drawback is not quite as damaging as it would initially seem to be; in spinning, where one relevant measure of variety (the maximum count range) is easier to obtain, the interfirm variation in product range as measured by the coefficient of variation is relatively low. Philippine weaving managers accept orders as small as a few thousand yards. Thus it is likely that the general order of magnitude of the adverse impact of the absence of specialization in weaving is correct and holds for most firms; deviations by individual firms from the assumed value are probably relatively unimportant.

Yarn quality as measured by breakage rates varies by as much as 20 percent across individual firms, a feature masked by the averages. The breakage rates are not related to the type of equipment that is used in spinning, a result consistent with the finding in the previous section that the major sources of productivity variation are firm-specific differences in know-how. Yarn quality is lowest in firms that use automatic looms as semiautomatics; this characteristic is indicative of a generally low level of technical mastery throughout all processes in these integrated plants. The same spinning equipment that they employ is capable, in the hands of other firms, of producing higher-quality yarn.

The last source of low productivity considered is the level of loom efficiency. In chapter 2, the efficiency of weaving sheds (the percentage of an hour during which looms actually insert weft) was seen to be a critical variable in determining the level of output achievable from a given complement of looms. It was also noted that, when weavers tend a substantial number of looms, any increase in efficiency requires a decrease in the number of looms per weaver. Most Philippine weaving sheds are currently characterized by a very low ratio of looms per weaver, however, the mean ratio for all plants being below 6. Nevertheless, loom efficiency is low, the mean percentage for all plants being 0.63.[11] This low efficiency level is attributable to a number of firm-level deficiencies, ranging from the absence of warp stop mechanisms (see chapter 2), to nonoperating pirn-changing mechanisms (owing to the alleged impossibility of obtaining spare parts), to bad housekeeping that allows dust accumulation (which in turn requires stopping the looms periodically to avoid problems with the quality of the woven fabric). Loom efficiency is also the only one of the productivity-reducing factors exhibiting a significant correlation with RTFP, $r = 0.80$ (significant at the 95 percent level). Increasing average efficiency and bringing all firms up to best practice would largely eliminate the variation in RTFP among plants, although the average level of RTFP would still be considerably below best practice unless greater specialization could be achieved.

If the true elasticity of substitution is in fact 0.5, several firms (plants L and O, and some in group M) exhibit task-level productivity close to or slightly above best-practice levels. (Best practice is defined as the standard of the upper quartile of U.K. firms, and many firms in the United Kingdom will exceed the performance of these better Philippine firms even when the relative TLP of the latter is unity.) The decomposition suggests that the main deficiencies causing low productivity in many Philippine weaving mills stem from the inability to achieve long production runs and technological mastery rather than from the absence of sufficiently skilled workers or other factors included in the residual.

Potential Competitiveness

The argument in the preceding chapter for the potential competitiveness of Kenyan textile mills could be replicated for Philippine plants.

Nevertheless, moving to a situation in which firms faced international prices for their inputs would not enable all of them to compete in the international market, as would be the case in Kenya. Many of the Philippine firms suffer from substantial technical inefficiencies that preclude their attaining internationally competitive production costs. Trade liberalization would have to be accompanied by a program to raise productivity and promote product specialization. These issues are discussed at length in chapter 8.

Notes

1. The coefficient of variation is the standard deviation of the observations for the group divided by the mean of the group.

2. The price at which any two technologies would exhibit identical costs can, of course, be calculated. Because productivity differentials are likely to be more important and are more likely to vary considerably, the calculation is not carried out. For an earlier exercise along these lines, see Pack (1975).

3. Inasmuch as the best-practice coefficients were derived from the performance coefficients of the top quartile of British plants, a firm in the Philippines exhibiting relative total-factor productivity above 100 is not outperforming the very best British plants.

4. The differences between plants of similar vintage in the sum of labor cost and the user cost of machinery are extremely small. For example, for the 1960–70 vintage group, the coefficient of variation is 0.06. The major gains from improved allocation arise from the choice of technology. The same is not true in weaving, as will be seen below.

5. A calculation could also be done at shadow prices to find the social cost reduction. Estimation of shadow prices is a considerable enterprise in its own right, however, and is eschewed here.

6. In principle, gains are also to be obtained from improved choice of technique, that is, the use of varying amounts of labor with the same equipment. See note 4 above.

7. For the different relative importance attached to allocative and technical efficiency in a study of nontextile Ghanaian plants, see Page (1980).

8. This result is illustrated in figure 5-1, in which the ex post substitution possibilities are shown by the unit isoquants bb and $b'b'$, the latter requiring more of both inputs to achieve the same level of output. The low-cost firm L, despite being on the less efficient isoquant, achieves lower costs than the M firms by choosing a more appropriate capital-labor ratio than they do. The fact that greater technical efficiency has not conferred a cost advantage in this case does not, of course, imply that it is irrelevant. If production were to occur along bb, operation at any point between h and h' yields lower cost than that achieved at L.

9. Differences in the productivity with which each loom is operated are unlikely to alter this conclusion. If a shed employing Sulzers were operated at RTFP of 85 percent, then the conventional loom shed could operate at productivity relative to its best-practice counterpart of 58 percent and still match the Sulzer's unit cost. Although many Philippine conventional loom sheds realize levels of RTFP above 58 percent, the mean value (table 5-8) for a group of firms using conventional looms is 60 percent ($\sigma = 0.5$). As will be seen, however, much of this shortfall from best practice is due to the absence of spare parts, a deficiency to which the Sulzer loom is not immune.

10. A Philippine government task force in 1978 also found widespread failure to achieve the speeds of which spindles were capable. See Philippines, Interagency Technical Subcommittee (1978a).

11. This is the average absolute efficiency for all firms, not the average relative to best practice; the latter is shown in table 5-8.

CHAPTER SIX

Behind the Productivity Differentials

CHAPTER 2 provided an overview of many of the important textile engineering relationships. The production functions for spinning and weaving given in that chapter are best regarded as engineering production functions showing the maximum output (of a well-defined product) obtainable with given inputs. As seen in the last two chapters, the total-factor productivity of most Kenyan and Philippine mills falls considerably short of the standard set by best-practice firms. This chapter discusses some of the requirements for realization of the best-practice production function. It then presents descriptive evidence collected in the Philippines and Kenya about the types of failure that prevent the attainment of technically feasible levels of productivity. This chapter may thus be viewed as describing some of the nuts and bolts of the required know-how, the lack or deficiency of which in many factories in developing countries creates the productivity shortfalls measured in the preceding chapters.

This chapter has five sections. The first presents a brief account of some of the production routines that must be mastered before high productivity can be realized. It is meant to illustrate the type of processing knowledge that is critical for achieving the potential output permitted by existing equipment and workers. I then present selected anecdotal evidence about the nature of the inadequacies experienced in contemporary Philippine and Kenyan plants—and, it should be added, in most other developing countries for which such descriptive material is available.[1] There follows a detailed description of some salient characteristics of three Philippine textile mills with greatly varying productivity. A subsequent section examines several failures in technical performance and calculates the benefits and costs to firms of remedying these deficiencies, together with a brief discussion of why such corrective measures have not been undertaken. A final section outlines some issues related to the availability of spare parts.

Selected Issues in Production Engineering

Spinning

Inadequate knowledge about production management and the inability to implement it manifest themselves either as low physical productivity or in a low price for the final product, owing to imperfections in one or more yarn qualities. The following subsections briefly describe some key aspects of three branches of know-how—blending, weight control, and maintenance—in which substantial shortcomings were identified in many of the plants visited. Poor blending and weight-control practices are among the factors giving rise to less than best-practice performance in speed and twist multiple in Philippine spinning, whereas insufficient maintenance contributes to spindle efficiency below best-practice standards. These three areas of technological deficiency are not necessarily those in which firm performance is worst, nor are they the most significant in quantitative terms: many other examples could be provided. The functional problems chosen, however, are representative of others encountered, and the nature of the desirable practice and of likely divergences from it is relatively easy to elucidate.

BLENDING. Before the preparatory processes begin, choices must be made about the length, strength, fineness, trash content, and so on of cotton and other fibers that should be mixed together to obtain specific physical and aesthetic properties[2] in the final output, yarn. In well-run firms, the procedure used to obtain the required properties is based on sampling theory. Given the desired mean and acceptable variance in the desired yarn attributes and the mean and variance of the relevant characteristics obtained from samples of bales of cotton fiber, the necessary number of bales from which raw materials should be mixed in order to obtain the required properties can be determined from readily available tables. Although the procedure sometimes informally considers the cost of various fiber attributes, there is in the literature or in firm practices no reference to the use of a full optimizing procedure such as linear programming to obtain the best mixing pattern. Rather the main concern is with obtaining the necessary physical properties of yarn (within probability limits), the average cost of all inputs being used as a rough check on the reasonableness of the mix.

The task of blending is, however, more complex than simply establishing the correct number of bales from which to feed the opener. The bales of fiber must be tested, labeled correctly, stored in warehouses so that those with the required properties can quickly be located, and so on.

These activities and their coordination require managerial and technical skills. In addition, supervisory ability is necessary to ensure that workers actually doing the feeding follow the preferred mixing pattern and extract only small tufts from each bale. Small tufts are themselves a sample of each bale, which includes the fiber from many individual cotton plants, and, like the use of a large number of bales, prevent a disproportionate concentration of one source of fiber and its properties.[3]

Typical of summaries in textile engineering textbooks of the effect of deficient blending practices is the following:

> Unevenness in blending can cause periodic difficulty in drafting as concentrations of short or overworked fibers pass through the system. [These errors] first show up at the draw frame and then progress through the whole system. At each stage, errors from the prior processes are elongated [because of the introduction of draft] and new errors are added as the short or overworked fibers cause [additional] drafting waves. (Lord 1981, p. 167.)

WEIGHT VARIATION. It is of a major concern to textile technologists at the opening and cleaning stage to obtain laps of uniform weight (see Fiori 1966 and UNIDO 1972a). There may be within-lap variation (often caused by failure to ensure that the feeding of the hopper in the opening machine is continuous and consists of the same weight of fiber at all times) and between-laps variation, which may have a number of causes, including differences in humidity during the working day. Although the opening and scutching (lap-forming) machinery has control mechanisms designed to minimize inter- and intralap variation, these smoothing mechanisms work only over a limited range and cannot control weights outside specified limits.

The concern with a lack of uniformity in lap weights stems from the possibility that laps of inaccurate weight will, when fed to the cards, produce errors in the count. If a lap is underweight, the card may produce a sliver of too low a count, and the problem will be propagated throughout the rest of the production process in drawing, roving, and spinning. There are two possible effects on measured productivity. First, intralap aberrations—leading to count variation, say, every hundred yards in the roving that is fed to spinning—may result in excessive end breaks in spinning. The spinning frame may be set to produce 20s count, and the degree of stress will be appropriate to roving of a given uniform count; with unevenness, there is a possibility of breaking if the count falls below a critical level, although the precise breaking point depends on a variety of factors (Subramanian and Garde 1974). Second, divergence in the weight of different laps may lead to differences in count between spun bobbins that are ostensibly of the same count. This variation in count will show up in weaving, where consecutive pirns should all be of the same count for a specific fabric; divergence in weft count will be noticeable in the finished fabric, particularly if it is dyed rather than printed. It is generally asserted, though often without experimental documentation, that the processes up to and including carding have a limited effect on intrabobbin variation in count, but a substantial one on interbobbin variation (UNIDO 1972a, p. 34).

In principle, "doublings" (the feeding of several laps simultaneously to the card to obtain better blending or evenness and several carded slivers to each drawframe head) should mitigate the problem caused by weight fluctuations. In recent years, however, technical progress in spinning has reduced the number of passages through machines during which doubling occurs, and variations in lap weight have assumed greater importance. Moreover, as spindle speeds have increased, the potential for end breaks resulting from count variation has grown.

Inadequate processing skill in opening, carding, and drawing will not usually manifest itself in lower productivity at these stages but will lead to substantially lower productivity of both labor and spindles in spinning proper. Thus one would expect—and this expectation is confirmed in most of the plants I have visited—disaggregation of productivity by stages to reveal that much of the lower total-factor productivity occurs in spinning, though its sources may be at the beginning of the process. Indeed, the carding or opening sections may produce almost the same total output as the best-practice plant with a given complement of labor and machines. If, however, this is achieved by an averaging of overweight and underweight laps (or slivers, in carding and drawing), little meaning may be attached to the productivity index calculated for this stage alone.

MAINTENANCE AND MACHINE SETTINGS. Blending practices and control of sliver weight are two aspects of the know-how of spinning that are major determinants of the productivity of the entire process. Many discussions of productivity also refer to deficient maintenance routines as a source of substandard performance. Rather than leave the question at the conventional level of generality, the following discussion offers specific examples of maintenance requirements at several processing stages and the consequence of ignoring them.

One imperfection marring the appearance of yarn is a "nep," a ball or knot of fibers. Neps may result from incorrect settings of the card clothing (the sharp wires that clean and orient the fibers), inadequate cleaning of the clothing, or insufficiently sharpened teeth. These short-

comings may also lead to excessive levels of fiber waste and to insufficiently parallel fibers that hamper the drawing process (see, for example,
Enrick 1980, chap. 13; Lord 1981, pp. 140–46, 154; UNIDO 1972a).

In drafting, slippage of the rollers causes variation in the strength of
yarn. In all the stages of spinning in which drafting is an important process, ensuring that the rollers are round and concentric is critical if good
yarn is to be produced (Lord 1981, pp. 59–63).[4] Poor drafting attributable
to defective rollers results in thick and thin spots in the sliver; if this
unevenness occurs in the roving process, it causes subsequent difficulties
in spinning.

In spinning, the production process generates considerable waste that
will have adverse effects if machines are not properly maintained and set:

> The presence of foreign matter or irregular fibers can cause faults. A
> badly arranged or maintained traveling cleaner can blow con-
> centrations of fiber onto the yarn or other strand. Raw material which
> contains an excess of short fiber might lead to a discharge of undesira-
> ble fly into the atmosphere. If the atmosphere is such as to encourage
> fiber electrification, this fly may concentrate into tiny clumps which
> deposit on the yarn during manufacture. Undrawn fibers, particles of
> foreign material and the like can temporarily interfere with the drafting
> process and produce slubs [a yarn imperfection]. Wrong ratch settings,
> worn guides, etc., might cause fiber breakages or other fiber distur-
> bances. Apart from locally irregular drafting, the fiber debris may be
> discharged into the air. Concentration of fly from this or other sources
> may then become wrapped around the yarn to produce faults. Con-
> centrations of fiber finish which accumulate on machine parts and
> then fall into the crucial operating zones of the machines can also cause
> irregular faults. (Lord 1981, p. 449.)

The results of a very careful set of controlled experiments in Indian
textile plants illustrate the quantitative importance of maintenance. The
study was designed to ascertain the causes of the very high rate of end
breakage, five times the developed country standard, in Indian spinning
mills. After experimentally ruling out a large number of potential causes,
the researchers conclude: "The inescapable inference was that the mechanical condition of the machinery was the single major factor of processing that could account for a considerable percentage of the very high
end breakage rate prevalent then in the industry" (Subramanian and
Garde, 1974, pp. 22–23). They found that the breakage rate could be
reduced by 75 percent with proper processing in a pilot mill that used the
same equipment and raw material as other operating mills (Subramanian
and Garde 1974, p. 28). Although the numerical results and the emphasis

on maintenance reflect the specific conditions in Indian plants, deficiencies in other aspects of production such as blending and weight control may have greater explanatory value in other contexts. The quotation, however, is a useful summary of widely held perceptions of textile engineers with experience in developing country plants.[5]

Weaving

Many of the "software" requirements in spinning have analogues in weaving; to avoid repetition, the discussion of weaving will be shorter. One difference between the two processes is that one determinant of productivity in the weaving shed—the quality of yarn available—is often beyond the shed's control. Yarn with an above-average rate of end breakage reduces the efficiency with which looms are used and necessitates the use of more labor per unit of output. Most developing country textile plants are integrated, as are almost all the mills visited in Kenya and the Philippines. The weaving department is a captive of the firm's spinning performance unless internal procedures allow an appeal to a higher management level within the plant when yarn quality is not sufficiently high. Where differences between the sections cannot be settled because of the organizational structure of the firm, a major constraint on the performance of weavers is introduced. With a few exceptions, these internal conflicts have not been important in the plants visited. Processing departments of widely differing abilities do not seem to be able to coexist in one enterprise for long.

The technical knowledge required in weaving includes that determining optimal loom settings, the stocking of an adequate supply of spare parts, and maintenance. Loom settings must be changed with some frequency where short production runs prevail. Although the desirable level of settings is fairly easy to establish and the small number of mechanics required should be relatively easy to train, these points are not always attended to.[6]

Shortages of spare parts are obviously important, particularly when they involve critical devices such as warp protectors, warp stop mechanisms, and "feelers." Warp protectors prevent several ends from simultaneous damage ("smashup," in textile parlance) if the shuttle is obstructed and fails to complete its trajectory across the loom; warp stop mechanisms halt the loom when an end breaks and thus preclude the faults that would otherwise occur if the weaving process continued after the break occurred. Without either of the above devices, weavers must spend more time repairing tangles of yarn, a process that decreases the productivity of both weavers and looms for a given loom assignment per weaver.

The feelers in an automatic loom monitor the pirn to ascertain that sufficient weft remains to allow continued weaving. When the pirn is about to be depleted, a signal is sent to the shuttle box containing filled pirns ordering one to be moved up to the "picker," or shuttle projecting mechanism. If feelers are missing, an automatic loom must be operated as a semiautomatic one; pirns may run out of weft, at which point the loom is stopped, a new pirn is placed into position, and the loom is adjusted to restore the required tension in the cloth and is then restarted. The rate of utilization or machine efficiency will clearly be much lower for a given loom assignment per weaver when the automatic changing mechanisms are not available.

Quality Control

For most of the problems mentioned in spinning (and for innumerable ones not discussed) one quality-control technique or another is available for monitoring production at each stage, for attributing observed defects to specific processing deficiencies, and for altering engineering parameters to eliminate the problem.[7] The last two steps are not a routinized procedure but follow an elaborate decision tree much as medical diagnosis does. Even with good quality-control equipment and competent technicians, there is an art to identifying and remedying production defects, and it is largely a learned art, depending on experience. It does not accrue inevitably as a function of cumulated production, as in simple models of learning by doing. A conscious management policy of insisting on high performance at each stage is necessary to elicit the effort to master the various techniques. But the mere existence of such a policy does not guarantee results. As in most arts, the success of the endeavor seems to depend on the availability of competent instructors; it is unlikely to be learned solely from available published materials, though these may help.[8] Instructors are unlikely to be available domestically and hence must often be brought from abroad for extended periods. Salaries for instructors, usually employees of other firms, are one of the many types of investment to increase output that constitute an alternative to further purchases of equipment.

Summary

Deficiencies in one or more of the procedures discussed in this chapter are fairly common in some of the plants considered in chapters 4 and 5.

What is critical is that some mills have achieved mastery of a large number of the required routines and are thus able efficiently to utilize equipment that other firms insist is not capable of better performance. Such differential ability in production engineering is one of the factors that accounts for the absence of any systematic relationship between the vintage or type of equipment and the unit costs achieved in operating it, particularly in the Philippines. None of the skills required for successful production noted in this section is embodied in machines; rather these skills represent the purposeful accumulation of knowledge, or know-how by individual firms. The managers of a number of mills do not recognize the importance of acquiring such expertise and try to redress current disparities in production costs by purchasing still more modern equipment despite the evidence (see tables 5-6 and 5-8) that the acquisition of such machinery offers no guarantee of improved performance. The differential success in technological mastery forms part of the basis for the suggestions about the nature and desirable phasing of policies to enhance productivity that are discussed in chapters 8 and 9.

Operating Characteristics of Philippine and Kenyan Plants

The following selective description of flaws in production management is designed to convey a more concrete picture of the deviations of actual practice from the desirable procedures described in the previous sections of this chapter. There is no attempt to report the frequency with which any specific practice is found or to establish quantitatively the impact of each deficiency on aggregate plant productivity. Cumulatively, however, these shortcomings must account for most of the firm-specific productivity-depressing factors relative to best-practice counterpart mills. Difficulties occurring in both Kenya and the Philippines are presented together, although where a practice most often appears in factories in one country this is noted. Some mills in both countries were free of most of the problems, but these were exceptions.[9]

Widespread, particularly in the Philippines, are the absence of care in purchasing cotton fiber with appropriate qualities, inadequate (or no) testing and classification of purchased bales, and a casual attitude toward fiber mixing to obtain a desirable set of yarn properties. In some plants only two or three bales of cotton are used at one time as sources of fiber, whereas a well-run spinning mill is likely to use a minimum of thirty or forty bales (Fiori 1966). To compound the harmful effects, in some factories the workers feeding the opening hoppers draw large amounts of fiber from each bale.

There are other problems in the preparatory processes in spinning. Although it is possible to install automatic lap weighers at the end of the opening and cleaning stage, most firms have not done so because weighing is easily done by an unskilled worker. In some plants, however, workers do not reject scutcher laps of incorrect weight. Where a receipt from the scale recording the lap weight must be attached to the lap, a variety of stratagems have been introduced, such as bouncing palpably underweight laps on the scale so that they register the desired weights.[10] The motivation here may be to prevent the detection of defective fiber feeding by coworkers; alternatively, employees may simply not understand the reason for obtaining laps of correct weight and view the requirement as arbitrary, a game with no consequence played against management.

Many mills pay little attention to keeping environments relatively free of waste material. Moreover, the generation of waste is occasionally exacerbated by the use of fibers that are too short. Inadequate cleaning has particularly bad effects in weaving, as some of the waste becomes embedded in fabric and accounts for excessive imperfections.

Despite the high humidity of the Philippines, humidity is often not well controlled by air conditioning, nor are the effects of humidity measured. Although this may be partly a rational response, given the costliness of electricity, few of the inexpensive devices available to measure and mitigate its effects are employed (for example, systematic tests for humidity regain in fiber at the various stages of processing).

In a number of mills, primarily in the Philippines, equipment of recent vintage is operated at much below potential machine efficiency because spare parts have not been stocked in sufficient quantities. The more depressing examples of the problem include quite good automatic looms produced during the mid- to late 1960s that are operated in a semiautomatic mode with assignments of two looms per weaver, in contrast to the thirty- or forty-loom standard in the United States and the eight-to-ten-loom standard in those Philippine firms that are able to obtain spare parts. The most important missing parts are mechanisms sensing broken warp yarns and the imminent emptying of weft pirns.

Examples of worker laxity are less frequent than would be expected, given received wisdom on the sources of inefficiency. Nevertheless, there are some examples. In some plants (particularly in Kenya), pirns containing weft yarns of differing count are incorrectly placed in the shuttle box. As a result cloth produced on new automatic looms shows quite obvious differences in appearance within a meter. Although some managers use color-coded pirns to prevent this, others do not. Stains in the finished cloth produced by the dirty hands of weavers or cloth handlers are also frequent in some Kenyan plants.

Although machine mechanisms were not inspected, there is little reason to doubt the continued applicability in some plants of a description of a technical aid mission to the Philippines in the early 1970s, which noted "shredded drafting aprons, bulging drafting rollers, eccentric rollers and drive drums, worn bearings, shredded gears and wobbly spindles" and a factory with four-year-old Swiss ring frames in which every moving part was worn out (UNIDO 1972b, pp. 21–22). The World Bank found that scheduled maintenance programs are rare and standard loom settings widely ignored. Yet incorrect loom settings can reduce both physical productivity and fabric quality.[11]

In preceding chapters the quantitative impact of excessive product diversity has been shown to play an important role in reducing total-factor productivity. In chapter 2, the absence of long production runs was linked to two phenomena, high setup costs and the inability to correct flaws quickly. Examples of the second phenomenon abound, but only a few will be cited. In some Philippine plants, incorrect loom setting were noted in a number of weaving sheds in 1972 (UNIDO 1972b). These conditions still exist, producing a flaw in the fabric once in ten linear yards, or every two or three hours. By the time the flaws are noted, the loom that produced the defective cloth identified, and the problem with settings understood, a substantial fraction of a given production run has been completed, and much of the fabric produced will fetch a lower price than it would have if it had been perfect. More accurate loom setting has the potential to mitigate some of the adverse effects of short production runs.

Similar difficulties arise in spinning. When too many neps are produced by inaccurate card settings, the absence of quality-control devices (nep-counting templates) does not allow sufficiently rapid correction before production of another fiber combination or yarn count begins. Although quality-control devices exist that would permit faster correction, they have not been introduced despite the relatively small expenditure involved and the knowledge that the instruments are available. Thus short production runs do not present an immutable obstacle to higher productivity; they do, however, place a premium on the firm's capacity to understand its economic environment and on its correct assessment of the value of internationally available technology.

Additional insight into the organizational basis of low productivity can be obtained from a comparison of selected practices and characteristics of three Philippine textile mills. The profiles in table 6-1 provide some observable behavioral characteristics likely to be associated with management interest in (1) obtaining a competent labor force (careful recruiting practices); (2) getting high performance from it (wage incentive plans); (3) improving technical knowledge (the employment of expatriates); and (4)

Table 6-1. *Characteristics of Three Philippine Textile Mills*

Characteristic	Firm A	Firm B	Firm C
Age of equipment			
Spinning	1958	1974	1960
Weaving	1960	1970	1960
Wage incentive plan	yes	no	no
Careful recruitment	yes	no	no
Sustained spare			
parts supply	yes	yes	no
Education of pro-	elementary	high	high
duction workers	school	school	school
Exports	yes	yes	no
Expatriates in tech-			
nical positions	yes	yes	no
Productivity			
Spinning			
Relative total-factor			
productivity ($\sigma = 0.5$)	1.10	0.44	0.55
Productivity-reducing factor			
Specialization	0.78	0.71	0.77
Speed	1.41	0.82	0.76
Machine efficiency	0.90	0.99	0.90
Task-level			
productivity	1.12	0.75	1.06
Weaving			
Relative total-factor			
productivity ($\sigma = 0.5$)	0.57	0.52[a] 0.84[b]	0.47
Productivity-reducing factor			
Specialization	0.70	0.70[a] 0.70[b]	0.70
Yarn quality	1.00	0.99[a] 1.02[b]	0.90
Loom efficiency	0.68	0.79[a] 0.96[b]	0.77
Task-level			
productivity	1.17	0.95[a] 1.21[b]	0.97

a. Conventional automatic loom.
b. Water jet loom.

undertaking some strategic planning (adequate inventories or local production of spare parts). The advantage of the characteristics shown in the
table is their binary nature; other relevant indicators of a firm's capabilities require the use of continuous variables that are difficult both to
measure and to aggregate (for example, the number and capacity of
quality-control instruments, and the skill of laboratory technicians).
Other germane aspects of a firm's pursuit of higher productivity—the
generation of an atmosphere of "belonging" or the extent to which
quality-control reports are acted upon—are both difficult to articulate

and by their very nature hard to measure.[12] My general impression is that firms that perform well on the more easily measured variables are quite good in less easily quantifiable activities.[13]

The three firms are denoted by A, B, and C. Firm A is very efficient (both technically and allocatively) and employs machinery dating to the late 1950s and early 1960s. Firm B operates both conventional automatic and water jet looms at fairly high RTFP. Firm C uses equipment similar to that of firm A but obtains much lower productivity.

Firm A's high RTFP is at least partly explicable in terms of the variables measuring firm effort. Rather than considering its labor pool to consist of anyone who appears at the factory gate, as do firms B and C, the company sends recruiters around the country. It does not require a high school diploma of its production workers—a sensible practice, given the relatively simple and repetitive nature of most production operations. It is one of the few plants to have established a wage incentive program, which it estimates has raised labor productivity by 10 percent. Despite the fact that its equipment is fairly old, it has no problems with spare parts; it has helped to establish a local independent plant to manufacture these items and continues to give this plant substantial technical help.[14] Firm A employes a large number of Japanese expatriates in technical positions; their considerable production and other managerial experience is demonstrated by the relatively high speeds achieved with older ring spindles by slight modifications, including the use of internally produced parts. The higher speed operation is also conditional upon the plant's above-average maintenance record. The mill's success is shown by the fact that most of its output is used by a clothing manufacturer whose production is exported without subsidies.

The main characteristic of firm B that requires explanation is its lower task-level productivity. Firm B also employs a large contingent of foreign technicians who are important in achieving its high technical performance, including a supply of spare parts from other Asian countries. Unlike firm A or other companies in the sector, it employs a large number of college graduates in supervisory positions. Nevertheless, it is much less careful in its recruitment of production workers and does not utilize a wage incentive program; these shortcomings probably explain its inferiority in TLP relative to firm A.

Company C uses equipment that is almost identical to that of firm A. Much of its behavior is inimical to efficient, high-quality production. Planned recruitment and performance-based remuneration are absent, high school graduation being taken as a sign of aptitude. The speed with which its spindles are used is quite low, largely because of an absence of maintenance and spare parts. The firm has done little to initiate its own production of spares, to identify reliable foreign suppliers, or to help establish a local independent machine shop. Significantly, it has no expatriates from countries with a more mature textile industry, and there is an unmistakable sense that the know-how, or tacit production knowledge, enjoyed by the staffs of firms A and B is largely absent in firm C. One measurable consequence is the low quality of its yarn (measured by end breakage rates).

A comparison of the three mills offers some insights into the methods that firms choose to improve their competitiveness with other companies in the industry. Plant B currently possesses some of the newest spinning and weaving equipment in the sector but has the lowest task-level productivity of the three firms (except on its water jet loom). In contrast, measures of its technical proficiency such as yarn quality and machine efficiency imply considerable competence in these areas. Despite the residual nature of calculated TLP, it is likely that the measured differences capture a substantive phenomenon. The implication is that B's difficulty in obtaining high labor productivity, even with its quite new spinning equipment, leads it to seek productivity gains through the use of still more modern equipment that will supposedly lower its costs relative to those of other firms.

The preceding discussion has focused on the determinants of productivity, but interfirm comparisons can also offer insights about the choice of technology. It is often suggested that the absence of sufficiently skilled workers or supervisors may make it economic to substitute more modern equipment for the missing skills (see Baer and Herve 1966). Firm B may, however, exemplify an opposite kind of causality: its hiring of college graduates may have instilled a built-in bias toward the purchase of relatively modern equipment on the grounds that it is hard to meet the expectations of college graduates by hiring them as supervisors in a plant that uses thirty-year-old machinery. The firm's adoption and efficient use of quite modern water jet looms may thus partly reflect the presence of these highly educated supervisors.

The implications of these interfirm contrasts and the more general questions they raise for national governments and international agencies concerned with improving economic performance will be discussed in chapters 8 and 9. Here it can be noted that firms clearly need to work on a wide range of productivity-enhancing activities that conspicuously exclude the purchase of new equipment. To draw a parallel to agricultural development, the necessary policy instruments are more analogous to research on biological and chemical production factors and their dissemination through extension services than to the acquisition of more large tractors.

Performance Gaps

Further comparisons of these and other firms could be made, but it is already clear that the plants visited lack many of the requirements for high productivity and quality. Why this should be so will be discussed in chapter 7 in a more general framework, but some observations may also be appropriate at this point.

The performance gaps noted above may be divided into two types. The first probaby (but not certainly) consists of cost-minimizing responses to the specific economic environment faced by the firm, whereas the second reflects either an absence of knowledge about technically and economically appropriate behavior or an unwillingness to act upon it. As an example of the first type, consider the use of excessively short fibers in Kenyan spinning and the failure to use air conditioning in humid conditions in some Philippine mills. It is difficult to establish whether these factors are responses to tariffs on imported cotton in Kenya or high electricity rates in the Philippines, or whether they reflect gaps in firms' knowledge. If the former, then they are not a true source of difference between actual and best-practice productivity but only appear so when an insufficiently detailed production function is used. In particular, if the production function employed to calculate RTFP were expanded to include cotton fiber qualities such as length or the quantity of air-conditioning equipment, measured RTFP would be greater, and some of the productivity differences attributed to firm-specific technical abilities or to task-level productivity would be lower. The technical literature suggests, however, that these (perhaps) rational responses could not account for more than 5 to 10 percent of total-factor productivity differentials that range from 30 to 200 percent.

Thus even if some of the measured low RTFP overstates the difference between developing country and best-practice plants, there is still a considerable amount to explain. Moreover, the preceding discussion has given the benefit of the doubt to the strict neoclassical view by allowing, for argument's sake, that some of the observed deficiencies are attributable to cost-minimizing responses rather than to the absence of knowledge or of interest in economizing. Many of the observed practices are relatively unambiguous, however: most of the observed performance gaps that account for poor productivity, particularly in the Philippines, do not appear to be responses to economic incentives (or therefore movements along the production function). Rather they represent a downward shift in the production function, and rectifying them would considerably reduce unit costs, even at current input prices. Without still more detailed engineering and economic information for each firm, this assertion is difficult to validate directly by the use of a multifactor production function. Indirect confirmation is possible, however, and several types of evidence can be adduced to support the hypothesis that most of the firm-specific sources of low productivity represent examples of x-inefficiency. Three instances of deficient practice that confirm this view are discussed below: the small number of fiber bales used at the beginning of the spinning process, the type of fiber purchased, and the inventory of spare parts that firms maintain.

Of the three illustrations, only that of the insufficient stocking of spare parts can be related directly to one of the generally important productivity depressants measured in chapters 4 and 5, namely low loom efficiency in Philippine weaving sheds. Many similar instances could be adduced from the evidence collected, however (for example, the failure to employ simple and well-known methods to correct for excess humidity). The major point of these examples is that, given the ease and low cost with which the deficiencies could be corrected, it is particularly tempting to conclude that their continuation reflects a lack of maximizing behavior, bounded rationality, or both, rather than a negative decision based on a careful calculation of benefits and costs (see Leibenstein 1976, 1978, and Nelson and Winter 1982). The main reason for caution before we accept this plausible alternative to the conventional view of economists is that the benefit-cost calculations presented in the next few pages include only immediate or narrowly defined direct costs of altering the existing situation. They do not include implicit and explicit overhead, such as the cost of revamping the organizational structure so that performance gaps are in fact perceived as a problem and addressed. In some of the specific cases considered, these indirect costs may be substantial. A more inclusive benefit-cost ratio, including some allowance for these organizational expenses, will be carried out in chapter 8.

Blending Routines

Consider the marginal costs and benefits that would accrue from the use of, say, forty rather than three bales of raw fiber to supply the opening machines. Although the benefits are difficult to quantify (Lord 1981; Subramanian and Garde 1974), it is known that improved blending raises productivity at all stages of spinning. A rough indicator of potential benefits is the increase in revenue that could be obtained from improved speed in Philippine plants. From table 5-6, it can be seen that perhaps a 5 percent increase in total output could be realized in two vintage groups, 1960–70 and 1970–77.

What marginal costs, apart from a minor rise in power use as speed increases, are associated with obtaining these benefits? The two major costs of enlarging the number of bales from which the openers are fed are expansion of the factory floor area devoted to opening and the interest cost of the growth in the steady-state inventory. The data on utilization of space show that plants that use a small number of bales typically have much greater than average square footage per unit of equipment. Moreover, this excessive footage characterizes all stages of spinning, not just opening. Thus rather than engaging in a tradeoff between space and yarn quality that would support the economizing hypothesis, the firms in question are technically inefficient in the use of space throughout the plants. Indeed, in all cases the current size of the opening room would permit a large expansion in the number of bales from which the opening line is fed.

With respect to the potentially greater interest cost associated with higher inventory levels, the firms' balance sheets and income statements show no systematic interfirm differences in inventory-sales ratios—if anything, the firms with worse blending behavior have slightly larger overall inventory-sales ratios. Interfirm differentials in borrowing costs might warrant varying ratios, but most firms report very similar short-run borrowing costs. The qualitative picture is thus fairly clear: firms with poorer blending forgo the potential benefits of a different routine, but the departure from the best-practice procedures does not reflect an effort to economize on either inventory costs or space. It is a purely x-inefficient practice rather than a cost-minimizing response to substitution opportunities.

Fiber Quality

A similar conclusion results from examination of another source of poor performance, the purchase of fiber that is not consistent with the design of existing equipment. Although the specific instance cited here was noted in UNIDO (1972b), my interviews and other recent studies of the Philippine textile industry suggest that similar problems remain (see Philippines, Board of Investment 1979; Philippines Interagency Technical Subcommittee 1978a, 1978b). A firm encountering considerable difficulty in spinning requested help from the Philippine Textile Research Institute, a joint government-industry venture whose purpose is to improve productivity. It was found that the chief financial officer, who handled fiber purchases, often chose the cheapest fiber available without consulting the technical staff in his spinning department. The fiber being purchased, however, was too short a staple to be spun by the plant's existing equipment. Because the degree of substitutability between fiber of different qualities (below some threshold) and the equipment currently in place was nil, no economically efficient substitution was possible. This again was a case of x-inefficiency rather than one of optimization along a more disaggregated isoquant.

Spare Parts Inventory

A third, more detailed example may consolidate the point being made. As noted in chapter 5, lack of spare parts is a major source of poor relative total-factor productivity in the Philippines, particularly in weaving. The average rate of loom efficiency for all firms is 63 percent, whereas the attainable rate at current loom-labor ratios and end breakage rates is about 91 percent. Assume that improved maintenance by itself could raise the current average efficiency rate to 70 percent. Then the loss in efficiency and hence in output per loom largely attributable to inadequate supplies of spare parts is equal to roughly 30 percent of current output. Denote by v the ratio of variable cost (materials, electricity, and so forth) to the price of this additional output. No more labor is required to produce the expanded output, as potential efficiency has been calculated for the existing labor-loom and breakage rates. More spare parts would, in fact, reduce labor requirements per machine, as looms could be operated without the current level of attention to warp breaks and pirn depletion. Let i equal the current cost of short-term borrowing, β the inventory-sales ratio, α the ratio of spare parts to all inventories, and R total sales. The marginal net revenues from storing enough spares to realize potential efficiency is

$$(6\text{-}1) \qquad \Delta R = R \left(\frac{\Delta e}{e} \right)(1 - v)$$

where $\Delta e/e$ is the achievable percentage change in the utilization rate.

The marginal cost of holding additional inventories of spare parts is

$$(6\text{-}2) \qquad \Delta C = i\beta \, \alpha \left(\frac{\Delta \alpha}{\alpha} \right).$$

Information from the seven Philippine firms for which detailed income and balance sheet data are available yields the following average values for the relevant variables: $i = 0.15$, $\beta = 0.54$, $\Delta e/e = 0.30$, and $1 - v = 0.38$. Values of spare parts inventories, α, are not reported by any firm. Assume a very high value, such as 0.20. Then, given the value of the other variables in equation 6-2, a doubling of spare parts inventories would result in additional annual costs equal to 1.6 percent of current sales, whereas equation 6-1 suggests that the increase in efficiency of 30 percent permitted by greater availability of spares would result in an increase in net revenues of 11.4 percent of current sales. The annual benefit is thus 7.1 times the annual cost. The sectorwide average, as indicated by evidence from individual firms, suggests that inadequate stocks of spares are more likely to represent the absence of a marginal benefit-cost calculus than a cost-minimizing effort.

If sectorwide values for the variables are replaced by the firm-specific values for the variables, the marginal benefit-cost ratios for the seven mills are 5.6, 24.6, 18.6, 5.0, 7.0, 19.6, and 11.0. Thus even the firm that exhibits the lowest ratio, 5.0, is currently forgoing a one-year rate of return of 400 percent (if it is assumed that all of the increase in stock occurs at the beginning of the year and the additional output is forthcoming at the end of the year). These figures are offered only to suggest orders of magnitude; they are probably conservative, however, as the assumed ratio of spare parts to total inventory is probably overstated severalfold. Firm inventories consist of fiber, finished goods, and work in process. Given the magnitude of fiber requirements, it seems unlikely that spare parts would account for even 5 percent of total inventories.

The Persistence of Poor Performance

Why have defective practices not been corrected? One important strain in the international trade literature attributes such laxity to a degree of protection from competitive forces that allows manager and owners, if not workers, to obtain part of their enhanced real income in the form of low work effort. In this view, the necessary conditions for raising productivity are liberalization of trade restrictions and intensification of competitive pressures. As Corden (1974) has noted, however, it is not analytically necessary that a monopolistic position leads to managerial failure to cut costs—as in other behavioral relationships there are income and substitution effects. Very specific assumptions about managerial utility functions are required to obtain a result showing that the entire blame rests on the absence of competition. Although most economists believe strongly in the role of competition in stimulating higher productivity, there have been no empirical studies of changes in sectoral factor productivity in the wake of trade liberalization.[15]

The detailed examples given above suggest that even relatively simple procedures could substantially reduce firms' costs. Not only are such actions feasible in principle, but they have been brought to the attention of plant managers in the Philippines and the expertise to correct the existing flaws was offered at zero cost.[16] Nevertheless there has been no progress in this or other directions in a decade. It is possible to argue, though implausible in the specific cases noted, that the organizational cost of considering, adopting, and implementing the required changes is significant and the decision is consistent with global cost minimization. I think it is necessary to seek other explanations, however. Nelson and Winter place a related issue within a context of bounded rationality:

> There is similarly a fundamental difference between a situation in which a decision maker is uncertain about the state of X and a situation in which the decision maker has not given any thought to whether X matters or not, between a situation in which a prethought event judged of low probability occurs and a situation in which something occurs that never has been thought about, between judging an action unlikely to succeed and never thinking about an action. The latter situations in each pair are not adequately modeled in terms of low probabilities. Rather, they are not in the decision makers' considerations at all. To treat them calls for a theory of attention, not a theory that assumes that everything always is attended to but that some things are given little weight (for objective reasons). (Nelson and Winter 1982, p. 67.)

The observations from the Philippines suggest that precisely such a theory of attention is needed. The entire burden of explanation could be placed on the protective trade regime and firms behaving as satisficers, but as noted above, there are income and substitution effects, and it is not obvious that the failure to engage in such simple activities returns much in the way of an easier life.

More generally, it is evident that many firms simply do not understand the fine points of the production function with which best-practice firms operate. The firms' own technologists, particularly in the Philippines, are insufficiently trained in a formal sense, do not adequately appreciate the relevance of readily available information for their own plants, and do not bring knowledge about international best-practice production engineering to their work. To the extent that firms learn by doing, there is little diffusion of this knowledge within the textile industry itself (again in the Philippines), partly because there is little interfirm mobility of technicians (a reflection of the firms' origin in local family businesses) and partly because secretiveness is engendered by the perception that the market is an oligopolistic one in which any competitor's improvement may come at one's own expense. In short, the Philippine firms are not on the international technical frontier but do not know this or are unable to move there. Furthermore, they do not augment their technical and organizational abilities to enable them to move toward the technical frontier despite the almost certain improvement in profits obtainable from such a move.

A critical issue from a policy perspective is whether these firms would try to learn about the practices necessary to attain this frontier if they were subjected to competition. It seems to me that the only sensible view on the probable outcome is skepticism, pending a study of the results of liberalization in some areas that are currently inefficient and protectionist. The success of textile industries in Hong Kong, the Republic of Korea, and Taiwan does not, I believe, demonstrate that liberalization would guarantee a move to sufficiently high levels of productivity to permit world competitiveness. In particular, entrepreneurs and technical managers in these countries have had quite long experience with textile production, in contrast to their counterparts in both Kenya and the Philippines (see Chin 1965; Koh 1966; Stifel 1963; and United Nations 1953). Indeed, in Kenya there was little in the way of traditional hand spinning and weaving before the advent of large mills. Productivity improvement may require specific technological intervention as well as a more competitive trade regime, an issue discussed at length in chapter 8.

Costs and Profitability

One other interpretation of performance gaps that must be directly addressed is the possibility that high production costs are consistent with global profit maximization. Given the constraints on total organizational resources, firms may be spending their scarce managerial abilities on activities, such as marketing or manipulating the trade regime, that yield a greater increase in profitability than would further efforts to raise allocative and technical efficiency. Thus plants might show similar profitability despite variations in production costs. Do firms neglect to remedy production deficiencies because other pursuits are more profitable?

Firms were, not surprisingly, unwilling to divulge any information on profitability other than statements submitted to various government agencies. Most of the data throughout this study have a large number of built-in technical consistency checks and could also be partially verified with observations on the plant floor; this is not the case with income statements and is reason to have less confidence in them. Even if firms made a goodwill effort to depict their global profitability accurately, problems would arise from the fact that many textile manufacturers are part of vertically integrated firms. Depending on specific tax provisions and the effective tax rate in each sector in which they operate, transfer prices might be altered to show greatest profits in the low tax sectors.

There is thus no reliable evidence against which to test the hypothesis that rates of return are similar across firms. Available income statements show low profits on sales; rate of return on equity defined by profits relative to any of several measures of capital is not meaningful given the absence of efforts to revalue historical data for inflation. The recorded profits-sales ratios are not systematically related to the cost and productivity measures shown in chapter 5, but given the limitations of the income statements, the absence of such a relation is not particularly significant.

It is also possible to try to infer something about profitability from the pattern of firm expansion and contraction. (Local Philippine lore suggests that any relationship between the two would be considerably attenuated by the propensity of high-profitability firms to reinvest in the financial sector.) Most of the growth in physical capacity occurred during the 1950s and 1960s (Philippines, Interagency Technical Subcommittee 1978a, 1978b). Since then only a small amount of additional spinning and weaving capacity has been installed, mostly in newly established mills. This fact, along with only slight growth in physical output during the period, implies that most existing plants expanded production by little during the past fifteen years. And there is no evidence that any firms went bankrupt during the same period. Although detailed historical data on the output of each mill are not available, the aggregates suggest that large changes probably did not occur in market shares in response to rates of return. Rather each firm's total output was probably relatively constant regardless of profitability, because tariffs precluded the existence of a selection environment in which profitability determined growth patterns. Hence, it is all the more impossible to determine whether growth patterns and low unit production costs are related. If rates of return do in fact vary with unit cost, some firms are obtaining very high rents. Conversely, the existence of high costs does not imply that, despite them, firms are somehow obtaining normal profits and the failure to reduce costs is part of some global maximization strategy. Although there is a puzzle about why plants with presumably low returns remain in the sector, such behavior is hardly unusual among firms in the textile and other sectors in the OECD countries.

Spare Parts

There is an extensive literature on the difficulty of obtaining spare parts for older equipment and the implications of this problem for the choice of appropriate technology. The view that this literature embodies is too simple, and the question that it poses about choice of technology must be rephrased to focus on the benefit-cost ratio of establishing spare parts capacity. In both Kenya and the Philippines, but most prominently in the latter, the availability of spare parts is a critical determinant of total-factor productivity. Indeed, it may accurately be claimed that the ability of firms to obtain an adequate supply of spare parts is a good predictor of their total-factor productivity.

The best firms in the Philippines have helped several medium-size machine shops (with about one hundred employees) to begin manufacturing needed parts. This aid has included the provision of drawings and close interaction to assure correct dimensions. Other mills with relatively good productivity have been creative in establishing relations with producers of spare parts in India and Taiwan. In contrast, the least efficient firms bemoan the absence of any local supplies and typically do not carry inventories of parts from the original manufacturers. When questioned about the possibilities of establishing a local machine shop as a supplier, they adduce many ad hoc reasons why such a step would be impossible. It is not surprising, then, that the weaker plants are those most anxious to modernize; modernization is an admission of their shortcomings rather than a cure for it.

Notes

1. Many of the most interesting descriptions and insights are, unfortunately, available only in unpublished documents. See, for example, Byrd and Tidrick (1984).

2. Tensile and tear strength, elasticity, durability, wrinkle resistance, color, luster, softness, and so on. Much of this discussion is based on Fiori (1965) and Enrick (1980).

3. Automatic bale pluckers are available, but these make little economic sense at Kenyan and Philippine relative factor prices if we assume that supervisors can be trained.

4. It will be recalled that drafting involves the use of a series of rollers moving at successively higher speeds, so that the sliver is elongated.

5. A World Bank study in 1975 provided an independent and similar confirmation of the state of Indian plants.

6. Standard checklists for loom settings exist; see, for example, Enrick (1980), chap. 21. Incorrect settings largely affect product quality, although some may decrease productivity as well.

7. For accounts of quality-control possibilities, see Enrick (1980), Lord (1981), pt. 6, and Ormerod (1979), chap. 3. There are instruments for checking weight gain from humidity, for automatically weighing samples of laps, for calculating the coefficient of variation of the sliver's count (the Uster percentage), and so on. Also, some types of processing equipment introduce control features as an integral part of the production process. Thus the autoleveler has been developed for use in drawing. It measures the count of the sliver produced in the first stage of drafting, "compares it to a standard and sends out an error signal which is proportional to the difference. The error signal causes the draft ratio to be altered to correct the error" (Lord 1981, p. 59). Nevertheless, the autoleveler cannot completely correct for all deficient practices

at earlier stages, as it can redress errors only within a limited range that is likely to be exceeded when earlier procedures are very defective.

8. Nelson and Winter (1982) label the information conveyed "tacit knowledge."

9. For the Philippines, a firm-by-firm documentation of the incidence in 1972 of some of these deficient practices is contained in UNIDO (1972b). Many problems had not yet been corrected by 1980, according to the textile engineer R. Grills of the Shirley Institute, who accompanied me on the visits to the plants.

10. The 1972 UNIDO study notes that 7–20 percent of laps are rejected, but only when supervisors are present.

11. For a detailed discussion of the nature of the required settings and the consequences of ignoring them, see Marks and Robinson (1976).

12. On the importance of firmwide atmosphere, see the summary by Nelson (1981). One effort to measure firm efforts in these more subjective dimensions is that of Marsh and Mannari (1976).

13. In many cases the assessments reflect those of R. Grills.

14. This firm and the few others that had obtained or established a good local spare parts supplier were more reluctant to divulge the latter's name than any other single piece of information—hardly a surprising reaction, in view of the competitive advantage conferred by these supplies.

15. There has been little direct effort, and even less success, in demonstrating a link between trade regime and factor productivity within sectors. A recent exception is Nishimizu and Robinson (1984). A survey of the issues is provided by Pack (forthcoming). Most attention has been given to intersectoral allocation effects. Most analyses of potential sources of x-inefficiency, such as those stemming from excess inventory holdings or low-capacity utilization, have considered aggregate effects rather than those manifest in individual sectors. For a summary of one major set of studies, see Bhagwati (1978), chap. 5.

16. UNIDO (1972b) describes many technical problems that were identified in each mill and discussions with senior management and technicians. Offers to help rectify deficient practices were almost never considered by the firms.

CHAPTER SEVEN

Comparative Analysis

THIS CHAPTER considers the findings of chapters 4-6 in a broader framework and relates them to the existing theory of production and firm-level behavior. Many of the phenomena presented in the earlier chapters are not easily explained within the neoclassical model usually employed in firm-level analysis. Because this format provides the standard analytical framework and vocabulary for discussing productivity, I will first present a stylized version of an augmented neoclassical production model. This will be used to help explain intracountry and intercountry differences in productivity that are often ignored in conventional analyses. I will then provide data on the extent of such variations in productivity within and between countries, concluding with observations on the role of proprietary information in the achievement of high productivity.

The Availability and Cost of Technology

Neoclassical production theory attempts to explain both the growth of an economy over time and differences in observed productivity at a given point in time. Most analyses of the sources of growth over time focus on aggregates: they implicitly assume that a changing technology is adopted by a set of identical firms, so that observed variations in aggregate growth rates for an industry or the entire economy stem solely from differential growth of natural (or augmented) factors, economies of scale (often not mentioned in theoretical analyses but noted in empirical analyses such as Denison 1972), and other factors, broadly categorized as technology, that affect all firms in an identical manner. In effect, the economy or the industry consists of the Marshallian representative firm writ large; variations between constituent firms have generated limited interest. Studies of international productivity differences have been carried out in the same spirit, typically utilizing sectorwide data and analyzing the individual industry as if it were a large firm.[1] Studies of this latter type have often neglected intraindustry dispersion because the only available source of data was sectorwide, but the root of the omission in some cases goes beyond data scarcity and reflects an implicit theoretical model.

If technology is costlessly available and assimilable, any intraindustry variation in total-factor productivity that is not attributable to national and industry sources is presumably small. Because such variation is hypothesized to be largely due to differences in equipment vintage and incomplete adjustment to changed technology, it is a not very interesting phenomenon.[2] Differential abilities of firms and the costs they face in learning about various technologies are omitted. Although the suppression of these relatively complex aspects has facilitated the development of a powerful set of theoretical insights in growth theory and major breakthroughs in empirical measurement, excluded factors that may be of limited importance in the analysis of the growth of advanced countries become very important when poorer countries are being analyzed. Intraindustry differences in unit costs of 77 percent in spinning and 142 percent in weaving, for example, are observed in the Philippines. They cannot be explained by the different vintages of equipment used by the firms concerned.

The data presented in chapters 4 and 5 permit an exploration of the usefulness of the fiction of the representative firm and an examination of the extent and nature of intraindustry variations in productivity. Moreover, because very detailed data characterizing the machinery in use were collected, it is possible to go beyond the date of manufacture in order to explain the impact of specific equipment on observed productivity. Thus the present study has greater explanatory power than some of the previous research on productivity, which assumed that diversity in vintage was the major explanation of measured differences among firms.

The three preceding chapters demonstrate that firms using essentially identical equipment achieve widely varying levels of both single factor and, more important, total-factor productivity. The decomposition procedure identified and measured the proximate sources of productivity differences relative to best practice. If technology were costlessly available and assimilable, and if firms acted to minimize their costs, the relatively large interfirm variation in productivity-reducing factors (other than specialization) should not be observed. One objective of this chapter is to compare the level and variation of these factors for Kenya and the Philippines and to infer, if possible, the most likely underlying sources of differential firm-level performance.

The preceding chapters have compared the productivity of Kenyan and Philippine producers to a conveniently available set of detailed U.K. best-practice standards. It is also useful to provide an additional perspective by comparing these sets of productivity measures with those achieved in other countries. A plausible conjecture based on the assumption of a costlessly available international technology is that the better firms in each country, say, those in the highest quartile, should exhibit similar productivity (apart from differential specialization), particularly in a technologically mature sector such as cotton textiles.[3] Even if disembodied technology is not "in the air" or in journals, individuals who understand the relevant technical or organizational skills are internationally mobile and hence allow equalization of total-factor productivities. Single-factor productivities would, however, still reflect differences in relative factor prices that themselves stem from different relative factor endowments.

International equality of total-factor productivity among the better firms may coexist with substantial international variation in average sectorwide productivity if there is nonsymmetric intracountry variation. Moreover, international dispersion may also be reflected in intracountry dispersion. One has only to consider the possibility that each domestic firm learns (through licensing agreements, technical advice from purchasers of its products, and so on) from a representative sample of foreign companies. If each of the purveyors of technology is itself a best-practice firm within its own country, then any intercountry variations in productivity that exist among best-practice plants may be replicated in, say, the Philippines. Such replication would result if the technical mastery of each domestic developing country firm is more closely related to these external sources than to the knowledge (costlessly available) within its borders.[4] Evidence of either substantial variations in firm-specific productivity of the kind found in Kenya and the Philippines, or of significant variations between the better firms in different countries, undermines the plausibility of the usual, very convenient assumption of an identical, freely available international production function along which all firms are able to move.

An important question, separate from intracountry variations, is the level of peformance of Kenyan and Philippine firms relative to each other. Although the large-scale textile sector in both countries arose after World War II, the Philippine firms are generally older than those in Kenya and might be expected to have achieved higher productivity levels if infant industry arguments are correct.[5] Thus bilateral comparisons are of interest for the light they throw on this question as well as on the efficacy of alternative modes of international technology transfer.

An Augmented Neoclassical Model

The foregoing discussion of the sources of variation in international and intraindustry productivity can be represented in a number of ways. A simple augmented neoclassical model can capture the essence of the argument. Assume that the production function is

(7-1) $$Q = Q(K, L, T, O)$$

where Q is net output, K is plant and equipment, L the number of production workers, and T and O two types of knowledge, which we will call technical and organizational. Technology as employed here consists of such information as the optimal number of bales to be used in opening, desirable humidity levels, standard preventive maintenance routines, and so on. It can be learned from books and periodicals or obtained by hiring individuals in command of such knowledge. Organizational knowledge includes the ability to motivate, coordinate, and implement—activities that determine the intensity of various productive efforts within the firm and link them. There is no simple way to separate the two sets of skills. Whatever the form in which technical knowledge is obtained, someone will have to incorporate it into the routines of the firm; this may be the individual embodying the knowledge or someone else. The main reason for noting them separately is that, in principle, technical knowledge can be obtained from many sources, whereas organizational competence will always be embodied in people. Inevitably there are gray areas, for example, some types of coordination such as production scheduling routines can be obtained in written form; nevertheless, improvements in this dimension depend on ensuring that various departments adhere to the schedule, an organizational problem requiring individual supervision.

Technology is a factor of production that partly determines the productivity of capital and labor; such knowledge can be purchased externally (as journals, consultants, computer programs, or new personnel possessing the relevant skills) or can be obtained through expenditure of internal resources (study of journals) or as a combination of the two (sending present staff members to study in other plants or in training institutes). Whatever the combination of implicit and explicit costs, technology is costly to obtain. In contrast, the standard model assumes that knowledge is costlessly available to shift the production function or to augment the productivity of one or another primary factor.

The first-order condition for maximizing output for a given cost is

(7-2) $$\frac{F_K}{h_K} = \frac{F_L}{h_L} = \frac{F_T}{h_T} = \frac{F_O}{h_O}$$

where F_i denotes the partial derivative of Q with respect to each factor and h_i the marginal cost to the firm of employing each factor. Both F_i and h_i are affected by the firm's initial endowments and a succession of decisions that alter these over time. The marginal productivity of new technical information will be greater in those firms that have implemented organizational changes that allow effective use of new knowledge. New quality-control procedures, for example, will have greater marginal productivity if a firm's organizational structure permits senior management as well as technical supervisors to be informed about important operating problems. In noncompetitive markets, h_T will be affected by the firm's knowledge of suppliers of alternative technology as well as by its bargaining skills.

Organizational abilities and technical knowledge can be accumulated only as a result of explicit firm decisions. Interfirm variations in this area may be attributable to differences in time preference, initial managerial ability that determines the values of F_i early in the firm's life history, credit rationing that results in different interest rates for each firm, and so on. The main point is that these considerations would not be relevant if the conventional production function, defined in terms of capital and labor only, were everywhere the same and the cost of knowledge were zero.

If firms are currently maximizing output for a given cost, increased total-factor productivity, defined in terms of L and K alone, can be obtained in the short run only by an increase in costs associated with obtaining additional "nonstandard" inputs. Given the conventional result that each element in equation 7-2 equals the inverse of short-run marginal costs, MC, the use of more T or O increases MC because of falling marginal productivity or rising marginal factor cost.[6]

If $h_T = h_O = 0$, the output obtainable from capital and labor will be the same in every plant or country (if we assume cost-minimizing behavior), because all firms can costlessly achieve best-practice standards in the use of equipment and labor by employing sufficient quantities of T and O—in this case the standard neoclassical shift version is a useful fiction.[7] If knowledge is not costlessly available, then differing quantities of T and O will be utilized, depending on their marginal cost in various countries and firms and differences in F_T and F_O. The cost of T and O to a firm will, at a minimum, reflect the opportunity cost to sellers—that is, their marginal cost of transmitting knowledge (for example, the cost of time spent conferring with buyers). The cost may also include an economic rent whose size will depend on the extent of competition in the specific market for knowledge and the relative bargaining skills of buyers and sellers. Firms whose managers are unfamiliar with the technical and organizational requirements of production or with the technology market (including the bargaining process) thus suffer from two disadvantages: they perceive a price that considerably exceeds the seller's reservation price, and they probably underestimate the productivity of additional units of T and O. The net effect is likely to be that they employ less of these factors[8] and obtain correspondingly lower productivity of equipment and workers.

The resulting variation in the intensity of use of T and O may be as pronounced among firms within a country as it is between firms in different countries. Because the quantities of T and O used by companies cannot be measured directly, such differences can only be inferred from observed interfirm variations in specific aspects of production that are more likely to be related to one or the other factor.

The model just outlined provides one simplified view of some sources of interfirm productivity differences. It differs from the standard neoclassical model by implying that firms in the same and different countries may not operate with the same productivity defined solely in terms of K and L and by attributing this phenomenon to variations in the amounts of T and O employed. The height of the production function in terms of primary inputs is here viewed as a function of other inputs, rather than as being the same in all countries or a function of an exogenous variable, "the state of knowledge." Even with a suitably expanded list of inputs, including technology and organizational abilities, the same production function may not hold in different countries if F_T and F_O differ as a result of previous decisions of the firm that affect them.[9]

The preceding discussion has been based on the cost minimization represented by equation 7-2 and is not consistent with some of the observations of inefficiency and calculations of the profitability of redressing specific shortcomings noted in chapter 6. The examples presented there suggest that, in some dimensions, firms are not paying attention to fairly egregious deficiencies and that a theory is needed to explain how specific shortcomings enter into the purview of management. In contrast, the formulation of this section implies that the defects cited in chapter 6 and the entire set of firm-specific productivity depressants may reflect the failure of firms to invest enough in organizational and technical abilities. It might be argued, however, that even if such acquisition had been attempted, a combination of bounded rationality and satisficing could limit the relevance of the cost-minimizing formulation.

It is difficult to discriminate empirically between these alternative formulations of firm behavior. A weak test is suggested in the next chapter, in which each company's benefit-cost ratio from investments in improving its production engineering capabilities is calculated, but the results are inconclusive. Although the potential importance of behavioral propensities is not captured in the cost-minimizing approach, this approach nonetheless permits some clear-cut and plausible inferences about the source of interfirm differences in the components of production engineering competence. A still better understanding could be obtained by using the bounded rationality–satisficing paradigm to extract systematic insights from the same set of data. Unfortunately, the empirical implementation of this approach still lies beyond the capacity of economists.[10]

Intracountry-Intraindustry Variations in Productivity

If technical and organizational skills were costlessly available, measures of their impact would be the same for all firms; that is, firm-specific and task-level productivity-depressing (or residual-depressing) factors presented in the earlier chapters should vary relatively slightly between plants using roughly the same equipment. If firms differ in either their marginal acquisition cost of these factors or their ability to absorb available knowledge (F_T and F_O), however, then interfirm productivity at a disaggregated level should also differ. Some of the data presented earlier permit these questions to be addressed. In the Philippines there are eight observations of plants using spinning equipment of a similar vintage (1960–70) and nine observations of weaving sheds employing looms that use essentially the same method for injecting the weft. In Kenya, four weaving sheds use similar looms; however, only two plants use each of two vintages of ring frames, so that it is difficult to employ these observations in the general discussion.

Spinning

Tables 7-1 and 7-2 present the relevant data for spinning and weaving, respectively. First consider Philippine spinning plants using 1960–70 equipment. These plants differ considerably in their labor and spindle requirements per unit of output as well as in their spindle-labor ratios (see the coefficient of variation).[11] These differences arise primarily not from movement along an identical isoquant in response to variation in relative factor prices but from interfirm differences in total-factor productivity, as can be inferred from the relatively large coefficient of variation of total-factor productivity for the 1960s mills. Examination of the variance in productivity-reducing factors gives some insight into the nature of the differences between plants.

Specialization, twist multiple, and machine efficiency have relatively low coefficients of variation, whereas speed and task-level productivity vary considerably. Given that improvements in all productivity depressants have the same payoff in additional output and therefore in marginal revenue, the lower variation in the twist multiple and spindle efficiency implies either that interfirm variation in the cost of mastering them is less or that there is less diversity in the firms' marginal productivities, F_T and

Table 7-1. *Characteristics of Selected Spinning Firms in Kenya and the Philippines Relative to Best Practice*

Country	Input			Relative total-factor productivity ($\sigma = 0.5$)	Specialization	Productivity-reducing factor			Task-level productivity ($\sigma = 0.5$)
	Labor	Spindles	Spindles per labor hour			Speed	Twist multiple	Machine efficiency	
Kenya									
1950s	2.63	1.09	0.43	0.74	0.94	1.17	0.81	0.97	0.77
1970s	4.51	1.07	0.24	0.65	0.75	1.01	0.97	0.95	0.96
Philippines									
Pre-1950	1.87	1.28	0.71	0.66	0.81	1.23	0.98	0.85	0.86
1960s	1.99	1.33	0.69	0.69	0.77	0.94	1.00	0.89	1.09
Coefficient of variation	0.22	0.25	0.28	0.19	0.06	0.22	0.01	0.11	0.23
1970s	2.73	1.30	0.47	0.57	0.84	0.95	1.00	0.99	0.82

Note: The coefficient of variation has been provided only for the group containing more than three observations.

133

Table 7-2. *Characteristics of Selected Weaving Firms in Kenya and the Philippines Relative to Best Practice*

| Country | Input | | | Relative total-factor productivity ($\sigma = 0.5$) | Specialization | Productivity-reducing factor | | Task-level productivity ($\sigma = 0.5$) |
	Labor	Spindles	Capital-labor ratio			Yarn quality	Loom efficiency	
Kenya								
Conventional automatic looms	4.62	1.05	0.24	0.68	0.63	1.00	0.98	1.11
Coefficient of variation	0.30	0.17	0.19	0.19	—a	0	0.08	0.14
Philippines								
Conventional automatic looms	4.53	1.51	0.40	0.52	0.70	0.95	0.75	1.02
Coefficient of variation	0.48	0.19	0.47	0.21	—a	0.05	0.09	0.13

a. All firms are assumed to exhibit the same level of specialization.

F_O. Variation in spindle efficiency (as discussed in chapter 2) largely reflects differences in planned maintenance and "housekeeping" activities such as dust removal. Although the coefficient of variation (0.11) indicates that all firms do not command identical abilities, its relatively low value suggests that the largely technical skills required to achieve a given level of efficiency are more evenly diffused than the technical and organizational skills necessary to achieve best-practice speed and task-level productivity, the coefficient of variation of these being 0.22 and 0.23.[12] The former requires competence in quality control early in the spinning process. Where quality control is poor, higher speeds, which even under the best conditions produce greater breakage rates, will have an even greater impact. Significant levels of both technical and organizational abilities (such as ensuring that quality-control results are actually used) are needed.

It will be recalled from chapters 2 and 6 that defective skills in the early stages of spinning (opening, carding, and drawing) can be partly rectified in spinning proper by imparting a higher twist to strengthen the yarn and by running spindles at a lower speed in order to reduce the stress placed upon the roving. The twist multiple and speed must be considered jointly. Although there is very little diversity in the twist multiple about its high average level, there are considerable differences in speed relative to best practice. The lack of mastery over early operations in spinning manifests itself in some firms in reduced speed and the effort to limit breakage rates, although other factors such as poor maintenance also contribute to this outcome.

Because firm-level deficiencies in opening, carding, drawing, and roving are proximately technical and much of the requisite knowledge is well understood and standardized,[13] interfirm variance in marginal factor cost is unlikely to explain the significant observed speed differentials. Indeed, records of earlier technical aid missions to the Philippines (UNIDO 1972b) document in detail the free information readily available to firms and their unwillingness or inability to use it despite ready access to it. Although it is easy to ascribe this failure to the absence of incentives because of the high levels of protection for the sector, the variance in speed relative to best practice indicates that some firms did in fact use such knowledge. Moreover, even with protection, the marginal firms had low rates of return and would have benefited from improved productivity unless the managers had strong preferences for an "easy life." A more plausible explanation is that the firms had done little to accumulate the necessary organizational capacity to apply the readily available information in their plants; that is, F_T was relatively low because of the low level of O, the complementary factor.

The above suggests that without a mechanism to ensure proper organizational responsibility for the necessary technical activities, knowledge will not be adopted or will be little utilized, even when it is available at low cost. It may, for example, make a critical difference whether a firm's technical department perceives management as taking a serious and sustained interest in quality control and responding to any sustained deficiencies. Seemingly mundane details, such as whether the laboratory reports to upper management or to the spinning and weaving director, may significantly affect plantwide attitudes toward obtaining high productivity as well as the approach of key subsections such as spinning and weaving. In sum, a technical production characteristic such as speed relative to best practice may vary considerably and can depend critically on the capacity of the organization to absorb and act on relevant technical knowledge, even when the know-how necessary to attain best-practice performance is available at low and uniform cost.

There is considerable interfirm variation in task-level productivity (assuming some systematic component within this residual) relative to best practice, and the activities needed to strengthen this productivity are likely to have a largely organizational basis. Recruiting, training, modes of supervision, and the establishment of productivity norms and connection of them to wage incentive systems all depend on high-quality organizational abilities and interpersonal interactions (see chapter 6).

Weaving

Relevant data on weaving are available for ten Philippine weaving sheds and four Kenyan ones, all of which use quite similar looms. In the Philippines (table 7-2), interfirm variation in loom efficiency is low, as is its level relative to best practice. The low variation is not surprising; information on how to obtain greater loom efficiency is readily available in the literature of equipment manufacturers, trade journals, and special publications of textile research institutes. It is one of the easier skills mastered by all textile engineers. Differences in the marginal cost of this information cannot be large. Most firms are able to master such simple organizational skills as ensuring that machines are cleaned, lubricated, and tuned well enough for looms to function without an unusual number of stoppages.[14] Most firms thus cluster around a low average level, the major exceptions being the few firms that successfully maintain an adequate supply of spare parts.

In contrast, high average task-level productivity is accompanied by substantial interfirm variance—some firms devoted considerable resources to accumulating skills in recruiting, screening, and training, whereas others have not. These differences are presumably reflected in the current organizational capacities of the firms. Although the details of particular deficiencies and their variation are interesting (see chapter 6), the most striking feature of the Philippine weaving data is the large interfirm variance in task-level productivity. The major variation among firms in the Kenyan weaving sector (table 7-2) is also task-level productivity.

Comparisons of Kenya and the Philippines

The relevant data for spinning firms in each country using similar vintages of equipment are shown in table 7-1. As noted in chapter 5, Philippine firms are more productive relative to best practice when they employ older (pre-1950 and 1960s) equipment. The same pattern emerges in Kenya, but for different reasons. In the Philippines, the 1970s plants have lower RTFP than do those of older vintage because of their lower than best-practice speeds or their lower task-level productivity. The lower productivity of the newer Kenyan plants arises primarily from their inability to realize long production runs rather than from any technical or organizational deficiency. The older Kenyan spinning plants suffer less from specialization losses, probably because of their better ties to wholesalers and retailers. Moreover, the older plants benefited historically from speeds exceeding best practice, which suggests a good mastery of the earlier stages of spinning. The failure of the newer plants to realize speeds above best practice lies in their very closeness to the frontier and the fact that greater speeds are not easily (physically) achievable.

Thus the poorer performance in both countries of newer spinning equipment is not related to characteristics of technology embodied in machines. In the Philippines, the potential gains from newer vintages are reduced by the firms' limited capacity for quality control in the early stages of production (rather than difficulty in operating new spindles) and by organizational deficiencies that make it hard to get high labor performance. In Kenya, the pattern results mainly from shorter production runs as newer firms attempt to enter the market.

Consider now the relative performance of weaving sheds in the two countries (table 7-2). In Kenya, weaving sheds using automatic looms operate, on the average, at close to best-practice standards in all dimensions except specialization, whereas the Philippine sheds exhibit poor loom efficiency as well as low specialization. At the plausible value for the elasticity of substitution, 0.5, Kenyan plants exhibit considerably greater RTFP despite their more recent origins, largely because of the difference in loom efficiency.

The fact that Kenyan firms using the same spinning or weaving equipment as those in the Philippines display higher total-factor productivity in both spinning and weaving provides some clues about the nature of technology transfer and the requisites for successful industrialization. Because the Kenyan firms are newer, they might have been predicted to exhibit lower productivity, given conventional arguments about learning by doing, although in neither country have there been competitive pressures to improve productivity. The surprising success in Kenya is almost certainly due to the presence of international managers of high quality who have been able to implant the procedures followed by some of the better firms of India, Japan, and Western Europe. These abilities, embodied in five to twenty expatriates per firm, have been critical to Kenyan success, as manifested in the high level and limited variation in most determinants of total-factor productivity. In effect, for most of the Kenyan firms the marginal cost of acquiring additional technical or organizational skills was close to zero once these expatriates were present, and the marginal productivity of such knowledge was high. Where the staff did not possess technical information it knew where to identify relevant sources quickly and cheaply and how to incorporate such information productively within the plant—hence the closeness to best practice and limited interplant variation in most dimensions.

In contrast, the textile sector in the Philippines has not benefited from a similar infusion of international expertise. Although a few firms have employed two or three expatriate managers (on fixed-term contracts) from other countries on an ad hoc basis, most plants have relied on domestic managers whose training has rarely included sustained exposure to international best practice. Should an unusual production problem arise, it is more easily rectified internally by the Kenyan firms. Where external help is required, the search process is almost certainly quicker and less expensive than in Philippine firms.[15] Whether the issue involves unusual spare parts or evaluation of the utility of a new process, the Kenyan firms also have a better idea of the appropriate price, whereas the Philippine firms may be discouraged by an initially high quotation that is merely a bargaining price.

Although the sustainability of industrialization based on foreign technical expertise may be questioned, the Kenyan experience provides a basis for optimism for countries desiring rapid industrialization; the road to internationally competitive productivity levels is not necessarily slow.[16] As indicated in chapter 4, the evidence suggests that a change of international trade policies could well make the Kenyan industry capable of sustained exporting. The same is true of many individual Philippine firms: the industry has existed for a much longer period in that country, and if learning by doing is a plausible model, Philippine textile firms should exhibit considerably greater total-factor productivity than technically comparable Kenyan firms.

International Comparisons

Spinning

For a reliable indication of the productivity of the Kenyan and Philippine textile plants relative to those in other countries, it is necessary to obtain data similar to those used in the preceding comparisons. The data on individual plants' operating characteristics must show sufficient engineering detail to instill some confidence that comparisons are not being made between mills with very disparate equipment. Although sectorwide aggregates are often used in international comparisons, the necessary assumptions about the deflation of capital stock and value added and about the translation of local currencies into a common one entail uncertainty about the robustness and interpretation of such results (Kravis 1976). Fortunately, data with the requisite technical information were collected for a number of countries in the late 1960s. They are presented in the U.K. study (Textile Council 1969) that I have used in previous chapters to obtain estimates of best-practice coefficients and thus implicitly allow the comparison of Kenyan and Philippine productivity in 1980 with that achieved elsewhere during the late 1960s. It is likely that the best-practice plants have achieved still higher productivity levels since the 1960s, in part because of improved technology embodied in new equipment (see chapter 3) and in part because of disembodied technical progress. Thus, although the results are helpful for analyzing the evolution of productivity, they cannot be used to infer current comparative advantage.[17]

Table 7-3 presents indexes of unit labor and capital requirements for upper-quartile firms[18] in each country and an index of total-factor productivity; a Cobb-Douglas function with the same output elasticities used in chapters 4 and 5 is assumed, and a CES function with $\sigma = 0.5$. For reasons given earlier, I believe that the latter value is a more realistic reflection of the possibilities of substitution after a basically similar technology has been installed in each of the firms represented in the sample. The capital-output ratios shown reveal a relatively small variation around the mean of 0.94, the coefficient of variation being 0.15; they do not increase with a rise in the capital-labor ratio. Simultaneously, there is a high positive correlation, 0.91, between total-factor productivity and the

Table 7-3. *International Productivity Comparisons: Spinning*

Country	Unit input requirement		Capital-Labor ratio	Total-factor productivity	
	Capital	Labor		$\sigma = 0.5$	Cobb-Douglas
United Kingdom	1.00	1.00	1.00	1.00	1.00
United States	0.93	0.31	3.01	1.94	2.02
Austria	0.87	0.91	0.96	1.13	1.12
France	0.91	0.74	1.23	1.20	1.24
Holland	0.91	0.71	1.28	1.22	1.27
Portugal	0.98	2.26	0.43	0.79	0.64
Germany, Fed. Rep.	0.83	0.71	1.17	1.29	1.32
Hong Kong	0.80	1.22	0.66	1.08	0.98
India	1.19	2.69	0.44	0.65	0.53
Japan	0.74	0.93	0.80	1.24	1.19
Pakistan	1.16	2.33	0.50	0.60	0.58
Mean	0.94	1.25	1.04	1.10	1.08
Coefficient of variation	0.15	0.63	0.70	0.33	0.39
Kenya	1.05	4.51	0.24	0.66	0.42
Philippines	1.30	1.74	0.75	0.68	0.65

Note: All data were collected in 1967, except those for Kenya and the Philippines, which were collected in 1980. Also see note 18 in chapter 7.

Source: Textile Council (1969), vol. 2.

capital-labor ratio; the variation in the latter arises mainly from variation in the labor-output ratio.

These relationships can be placed within a simple production function framework in which, for simplicity, a Cobb-Douglas function is assumed. The capital-output ratio can be written as $Q/K = P(K/L)^{\alpha - 1}$, where P is the total-factor productivity index. A rise in the capital-labor ratio that would, other things being equal, reduce Q/K is offset by a simultaneous increase in P. Countries with greater capital endowments relative to labor do not experience a decrease in average (or marginal) capital productivity, a result that parallels the intertemporal results for aggregate production functions in advanced economies (Solow 1957). This interpretation of the results assumes cost-minimizing behavior. An alternative view is that firms apply the amount of labor necessary to realize the standard engineering norms, kilograms per spindle hour in spinning and meters per loom hour in weaving.

If an engineering rule of thumb is indeed generating the observed limited variation (which also holds in weaving) in the capital-output ratio, firms are incurring costs that are greater than necessary. In figure 7-1, for example, the developing country plant operates with lower TFP along $a'a'$

Figure 7-1. *The Effect of Rules of Thumb on Firm Costs*

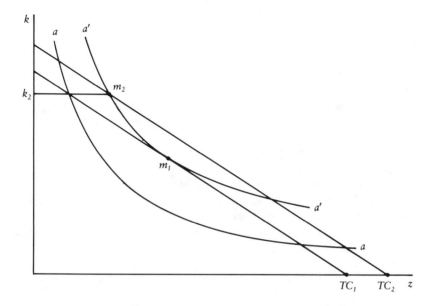

than its developed country counterpart. Nevertheless, it aims for the same capital-output ratio, k_2, and produces at m_2 rather than minimizing costs at m_1. The excess cost of applying the rule of thumb is $TC_2 - TC_1$.

Clearly, there is no simple way to discriminate between the two interpretations of the extremely low variation across countries in the capital-output ratio.

Intercountry differences in productivity manifest themselves mainly in unit labor input and in total-factor productivity, their coefficients of variation being 0.63 and 0.33 (when $\sigma = 0.5$ is used). Not surprisingly, the correlation between unit labor input and total-factor productivity is 0.90. If the same relationships prevail in other industries that have similar production characteristics,[19] labor productivity may not provide a bad approximation for total-factor productivity, and many existing sectorwide studies of the former would acquire new interest.

Little of the observed variation in total-factor productivity can be ascribed to dissimilarities in the type of machinery employed. Indicators of the vintage and probable productivity of equipment include such machine-embodied properties as the size and width of the spinning rings and potential speed. Although these characteristics can vary somewhat (between the Western European countries and the United States, on the one hand, and the Asian countries plus Portugal, on the other), the differences are surprisingly small and could not account for even 10 percent of measured differences in total-factor productivity. The homogeneity of equipment is rather surprising, given that the data were collected from firms facing widely differing relative factor prices that militate in favor of the purchase of disparate machinery. The international diffusion of engineering knowledge seems to engender uniformity in behavior among the better (upper-quartile) firms, which is manifested not only in the type of equipment purchased but also in the remarkably small variation in their capital-output ratios.

The dominance of engineering over economic desiderata is not complete, however. Firms in different countries do use different quantities of labor with the same equipment, as is shown by the substantial variation in capital-labor ratios (presumably in response to differences in relative factor prices). A cross-country regression of the logarithm of the capital-labor ratio on the logarithm of the wage-rental ratio yields a regression coefficient of 0.42, not significantly different from the value of 0.5 for the short-run elasticity of substitution suggested by engineering considerations (chapter 3 appendix). The regression coefficient is significantly different from zero at the 1 percent level.

Table 7-4 shows three characteristics of the spinning mills: the speed at which the spindles are operated, R; twists per inch, T; and spindle efficiency, e. It will be recalled from chapter 2 that the expression $(R/T)e$ is equal to the output per spindle and that each component of this expression reflects an endogenous decision of the firm. One way of raising output per spindle is to increase speed and simultaneously raise the labor-spindle ratio in order to forestall a decline in the efficiency rate; this practice is most likely to make sense where a low wage rate prevails. To what extent have the developing countries included in table 7-4 taken this step and moved along an efficient, high-productivity isoquant?

The last column of the table presents the value of $(R/T)e$ indexed on the value for the United Kingdom. It can be seen that firms in Hong Kong and Japan operate their spindles at very high speeds that are not offset by a high T or a low e; they employ large amounts of labor per spindle to maintain spindle efficiency.[20] The ability to substitute labor for capital in response to lower wages and to maintain high TFP distinguishes these two countries from other low-wage producers (India, Kenya, Pakistan, the Philippines, and Portugal) in which a lower capital-labor ratio is accompanied by low total-factor productivity (table 7-3). The inability of the second group of countries to move along an efficient isoquant reflects the effect of the factors considered in the decomposition of total productiv-

Table 7-4. *Selected Characteristics of Technical Operation*
of Upper-Quartile Spinning Firms across Countries

Country	Speed (1)	Twists per inch (2)	Spindle efficiency (3)	Index of $\frac{(1)}{(2)} \times (3)$ (4)
United Kingdom	1.00	1.00	1.00	1.00
United States	1.17	1.12	0.99	1.11
Austria	0.97	0.98	0.94	1.00
France	0.92	0.98	0.96	0.98
Holland	1.02	0.98	0.96	1.07
Portugal	1.07	1.02	0.98	1.11
Germany, Fed. Rep.	1.07	0.95	0.96	1.17
Hong Kong	1.19	0.90	1.01	1.44
India	0.97	1.14	0.98	0.90
Japan	1.34	0.98	0.98	1.45
Pakistan	0.97	1.02	0.90	0.92
Kenya	1.00	1.03	1.05	1.05
Philippines	1.00	1.00	0.93	0.89

Note: All data were collected in 1967, except those for Kenya and the Philippines, which were collected in 1980. Also see note 18 in chapter 7.
Source: Textile Council (1969), vol. 2.

ity differentials in preceding chapters. In spinning, the major source of deviation from best practice in Kenya was seen to be the lack of specialization, whereas both this variable and firm-specific technical inefficiencies were substantial in the Philippines. Without similarly detailed data for other poor countries, it is impossible to determine the sources of their low total-factor productivity. Given the nominal indexes of productive potential such as ring size and rated speed, inferior equipment is certainly not to blame.

The performance of the better Kenyan and Philippine firms can now be assessed, not only relative to the best-practice standard used in earlier chapters but also within a broad international context that includes observations from other developing countries. The newest of the developing-country producers, Kenya, comes closest to achieving international norms while exhibiting roughly the same level of RTFP (assuming that $\sigma = 0.5$). This result probably reflects the fact that the Kenyan firms yielding the observation are subsidiaries of multinational corporations, whose managers are well aware of international norms and are quite capable of achieving high levels of firm-specific technical performance. Thus, despite the relatively recent establishment of the textile sector in Kenya and its workers' lack of previous experience in either home or small-scale factory production, its better spinning firms have equaled the productivity of those in India and Pakistan—countries with considerably longer histories of factory textile production and general industrial experience.[21] This result will be seen below to hold for weaving as well; it is probably attributable not only to the fact of multinational corporation management noted earlier but also to the nature of textile manufacturing, which makes it unusually suitable for a successful transplant of technology. In particular, textile production requires relatively little interaction (compared with other sectors) with other domestic industrial suppliers.[22] Although spare parts are necessary—as witness the difficulties in some Philippine firms—they can be obtained abroad, and even when large inventories are held, they do not constitute a major cost.

Weaving

Table 7-5 shows the relevant data for weaving. Both labor and loom coefficients per unit of output have been adjusted for differences in loom speed, the major machine-embodied characteristic that varies among looms.[23] Because all the looms used by the upper-quartile firms are conventional automatic ones, and if it is assumed that upper-quartile firms maintain their equipment adequately and stock sufficient inventories of spare parts, most of the remaining variation in productivity is attributable to disembodied productivity-reducing factors. Again, the very small variance in loom-output ratios, k, is striking, the coefficient of variation being 0.03 around the mean of 1.05. In contrast, the mean unit labor requirement (z) in the sample equals 2.10, and its coefficient of variation is 0.58. The range of RTFP is thus strongly affected by that of z, and its coefficient of variation is 0.29. The correlation coefficient between z and RTFP is .91, which confirms the conclusion reached in the case of spinning that the use of labor coefficients may be a cheap and accurate substitute for more elaborate calculations of total-factor productivity.

The figures for total-factor productivity in Kenya and the Philippines in 1980 put both countries close to or above the position of Hong Kong in 1968. Although the latter has undoubtedly improved in the succeeding period, the fact that its earlier level of productivity has been matched is of considerable interest. Given the rapid progress of Hong Kong's production and exports from its 1967 base, it can be inferred that Kenya and the Philippines have at least moved toward the starting position for the international race. Their task is to transform this potential into current international competitiveness through increased technological and organizational competence and changes in the economic policy environ-

Table 7-5. *International Productivity Comparisons: Weaving*

Country	Unit input requirements		Capital-labor ratio	Total-factor productivity	
	Capital	Labor		$\sigma = 0.5$	$\sigma = 1.0$
United Kingdom	1.00	1.00	1.00	1.00	1.00
United States	1.06	0.59	1.80	1.34	1.32
Austria	1.02	1.45	0.70	0.83	0.80
France	1.04	1.56	0.67	0.79	0.76
Holland	1.02	1.30	0.78	0.87	0.85
Portugal	1.12	3.07	0.36	0.59	0.50
Germany, Fed. Rep.	1.03	1.23	0.84	0.89	0.88
Hong Kong	1.05	2.88	0.36	0.63	0.54
India	1.09	3.92	0.28	0.57	0.44
Japan	1.04	1.91	0.54	0.73	0.68
Pakistan	1.08	4.19	0.26	0.56	0.43
Mean	1.05	2.10	0.69	0.80	0.75
Coefficient of variation	0.03	0.58	0.64	0.29	0.36
Kenya	0.92	3.47	0.26	0.78	0.52
Philippines	0.95	3.27	0.29	0.76	0.52

Note: All data were collected in 1967, except those for Kenya and the Philippines, which were collected in 1980. All looms are conventional automatic. Also see note 18 in chapter 7.
Source: Textile Council (1969), vol. 2.

ment. Indeed, it seems likely that the better firms in Kenya and the Philippines would be able to compete successfully in international trade at current productivity if their countries' trade regimes were reformed (see the closing section in chapter 4).

The result for Kenya also suggests that it would be interesting to examine the past performance of the sector to determine whether the high level of productivity around 1980 reflected its rapid growth from a low base or whether firms had begun at high levels, with limited learning in the ensuing years. The fact that the only significant productivity-reducing factor among the better firms was their inability to achieve specialization bodes well for the establishment of exports if these mills were faced with a neutral policy regime.

The quite respectable performance of the upper-quartile Philippine firms (if we assume that $\sigma = 0.5$), the high variation in the sector as a whole (table 7-2), and the allocative inefficiency cited in chapter 5 all emphasize the need for greater diffusion within the Philippines of knowledge already available in better firms. It could hardly be an objective of policy to force these firms to share the capabilities derived from their prior investments, however, and indeed learning so imparted might not be absorbed. Specific policies designed to increase absorptive capacity are needed, along with incentive structures to generate a business environment in which firms ignore such know-how at their peril.

The Importance of Proprietary Information

There is currently much concern about the allegedly excessive cost to developing countries of acquiring proprietary technical information. (For discussion of the issues and an extensive bibliography, see Cortes and Bocock 1984.) Such costs, it is claimed, retard the industrial development process in developing countries. In textiles, however, almost all the information relevant for achieving high productivity is not proprietary. Most operational deficiencies that can be remedied by acquiring technical information fall under the rubric of production engineering. For a relatively low fee, a large number of individuals, consulting firms, experts employed by international agencies, and other purveyors of information are readily obtainable. Nevertheless, developing country firms at the upper quartile typically exhibit lower total-factor productivity than do firms from developed countries; it is not known how much this feature reflects firm-specific factors affected by technology as opposed to factors beyond the control of firms.

Another result suggesting the limited importance of proprietary technical knowledge is the fact that RTFP varies more widely within the Philippines than it does among the upper-quartile firms of the developed countries (tables 7-3 and 7-5). Given the low intra-Philippine variance in firm-specific technical abilities and the large variation in organization-related productivity, still greater access to production engineering knowledge is of less importance than an augmentation of the organizational abilities of weaker firms. Considerable gains in productivity could be obtained in the Philippines by successful transmission to weaker firms of the organizational competence of stronger firms now operating in the country. Transfers of this kind are far from easy, however, and cannot be realized by the provision of organization charts and manuals. Indeed, the whole issue of the mechanisms and requirements for diffusing organizational skills is not understood with any certainty.

Summary

- In a mature industrial activity in which most technical advances result from incremental improvements in a basically unchanged technology (this restriction limits the discussion to ring spinning and conventional weaving), and in which most production engineering knowledge is widely available at very low marginal cost, substantial shortfalls from developed country total-factor productivity may still be experienced by developing country firms. Analysis of the sources of this deficiency indicates that both the economic environment within which firms operate (specialization effects) and a lack of organizational skills (for example, the ability to ensure adequate inventories of spare parts) are important phenomena.

• Organizational ability is not only lower in developing countries but also unevenly diffused. Even in those activities in which average performance is good (for example, task-level productivity in both spinning and weaving in the Philippines), substantial interfirm differentials are revealed by the high coefficient of variation in these activities.

• The identification of organization as the critical element is supported by the high average levels of Kenyan firms in most of the disaggregated measures of productivity and their relatively small variance despite the recent establishment and growth of the sector. Except for the effect of specialization, which largely reflects national economic policy, international management teams have been successful in achieving high levels of relative total-factor productivity.

• The preceding observations imply that neither increased diffusion of new equipment nor lower charges for narrowly defined technology transfer are likely to be sufficient for successful industrialization, even in an industry in which most technological problems have a traditional and fairly simple mechanical and chemical basis. And in newer manufacturing sectors based on electronics and more advanced chemical and biological knowledge, the problem is compounded. Inadequate command over technology that is not embodied in machines does not bode well for the establishment of plants in these newer industries, because the technical problems inherent in nontraditional and rapidly changing know-how are added to organizational deficiencies.

Much of the preceding is consistent with a large body of work, recently summarized by Nelson (1981), that emphasizes the critical role of organizational behavior in the determination of productivity. As Nelson notes, within the broad framework of organizational analyses there are two views, classical and "new." The former, Taylorism (Taylor 1911), emphasizes the scientific management of physical production activity and the correct structuring of particular functions (centralized versus decentralized maintenance) as the major activities of management. In this view firms can identify the specific technical operations that need to be improved and can choose from well-defined alternatives for achieving higher productivity. In contrast, more recently developed management theory suggests that a firm is best viewed as a social system in which many critical dimensions of performance, such as worker effort, are not easily controlled by management. Rather, the firm's social system—a complex set of interactions among individuals, departments, and divisions—sets work norms, enforces them, and may resist management pressures to change.

Both of these perceptions contribute to an understanding of the preceding chapters. The relatively good performance documented earlier in firm-specific technical characteristics indicates that the easier management tasks, those identified under the older view, are often successfully implemented in many developing country firms; their low coefficient of variation indicates that most firms possess these abilities. But functions requiring substantial organizational ability are less uniformly present. Firms differ considerably in their ability to institute quality-control procedures and employ them fruitfully, to establish external suppliers of spare parts, and to ensure that adequate inventories from foreign suppliers are maintained. Unlike the management tasks that Taylor emphasized, these activities are intrinsically difficult to implement and are not likely to be evenly diffused unless firms have made conscious efforts to accumulate the relevant abilities.

Notes

1. Some studies, for example, Pratten (1976), present comparisons between single firms in different countries. Kravis (1976) offers a thorough survey of international comparisons of labor productivity through the mid-1970s.

2. Productivity differentials from this source would disappear if correct equipment prices were utilized.

3. As shown in chapter 3, the prevailing conception of textiles as a technologically stagnant and labor-intensive industry is not apt.

4. There is little personal contact among the employees of manufacturers in developing countries, in contrast with the considerable interaction in developed countries. Thus one of the potential benefits of industrialization programs, the reaping of Marshallian external economies, is largely absent. Such interaction is undoubtedly of great importance in transmitting knowledge (Arrow 1969); its absence is partly due to the typically small number and low regional density of firms in developing countries. With few manufacturers in a limited domestic market, firms view the market as having an oligopolistic rather than a competitive or monopolistically competitive structure. Under such conditions, to divulge any technical "secrets" may have more serious consequences than in a more competitive structure. The oligopolistic structure may also imply that firms cannot expect, in any statistical sense, to learn as much as they reveal. Similar arguments have long been used to explain the reluctance to train workers who may be lost to competitors. Leff (1978) has noted the pervasive importance of family-owned businesses in which key positions are held by family members. It is easy to spin out plausible scenarios about why such structures may generate less interchange of information than a more impersonal structure.

5. See Stifel (1963) for an analysis of the development of the Philippine textile sector through the early 1960s.

6. Leibenstein (1976, 1978) noting interfirm differences in (labor) productivity, postulates that x-inefficiency (a deviation from best practice) is attributable to deficient motivation or supervision, difficulty in contract enforcement, and so on. Stigler (1976), criticizing the concept of x-inefficiency, argues that firms are currently minimizing costs, having equated marginal revenue and marginal cost in each activity, although such minimization may yield low observed productivity in conventionally measured factors. In the terms used here, he is arguing that equation 7-2 is currently satisfied and that any improvement in current total-factor productivity would entail increased unit costs.

7. As noted earlier, Saxonhouse (1976) has documented the information-diffusion mechanism of the early Japanese cotton-spinning industry. The industry's monthly publication included detailed cost data for each plant, which, surprisingly, was identified. More thorough evaluations and criticisms were occasionally published. In addition, one major British spindle manufacturer accounted for a very high percentage of installed spindles, and its local representatives acted as important disseminators of technical knowledge. It is also shown that Japanese industrialists had considerable information about foreign practices from representatives of Japanese trading companies, overseas missions, and consular staffs. One consequence is that econometric testing (Saxonhouse 1974) cannot reject the hypothesis that all firms operated on the same production function, although it is not known whether this differed from international best practice. Saxonhouse's work thus supports the hypothesis that information acquisition costs may be an important determinant of the diffusion of the knowledge of best practice.

8. Unless F_T and F_O are greater where h_T and h_O are higher. Such a positive correlation seems unlikely. Firms lacking managers with the relevant skills should find it profitable to hire better ones, whereas managers should in turn be able to obtain higher wages in less well-endowed firms. These considerations partly explain the willingness of some developed country managers to locate in Kenya as well as some recent contracts signed by Philippine firms with nationals of developing countries that are currently more advanced in textile production methods. If factor markets were perfect, competition for able managers should yield rents to them and should equalize average cost across firms. The fact that such equalization does not occur suggests considerable imperfection in the market for such skills.

9. Thus if the underlying production function were of a Cobb-Douglas kind, the exponents of T and O would differ among firms at a given point and reflect prior efforts. In this case the marginal productivities of K and L would be affected.

10. Simulation with synthetic data does, however, offer insights about competitive processes. See Nelson and Winter (1982).

11. Although some slight differences in interest rates are reported by the firms, the resulting variation in the user cost of capital and in the wage-rental ratio could not generate the range of differences observed in capital-labor ratios.

12. "Abilities" is used to denote the skills determining the values of F_T, h_T, F_O, and h_O.

13. Technical details are widely available in engineering texts, in trade publications, and from consulting firms.

14. The underlying calculation for actual loom efficiency relative to best-practice loom efficiency has already adjusted for deficient yarn quality, a largely organizational phenomenon.

15. This statement is not inconsistent with the point made earlier about the low and uniform price of technical information as the result of various aid missions to the Philippines. There the reference is largely to routine quality-control problems that repeatedly manifest themselves, whereas the search costs referred to here are incurred to deal with extraordinary occurrences.

16. This discussion does not address a number of questions, in particular the net social benefit to the Kenyan economy of this form of industrialization. In the short term, the ex post benefits and costs of an industrial plant's operation can be evaluated by the criterion of the domestic resource cost, suitably expanded to reflect the foreign exchange cost of expatriate managers and repatriated profits. In the longer run, an important issue in many countries is the rate of transfer of the relevant technological skills from expatriate to domestic managers. The value attached to such diffusion reflects nonquantifiable objectives that may nevertheless be of considerable importance to policymakers. It is still too early to evaluate this dimension of Kenya's industrial experience.

17. Inferences about comparative advantage in chapter 4 employed recent best-practice production coefficients as the norm against which current Kenyan plants were compared.

18. Given the absence of a large sample or a census, I have used an average of the two best firms in Kenya instead of the upper quartile. In the Philippines, where the sample is larger, the coefficients in the upper-quartile firm have been employed. Thus in neither case are the figure contained in tables 7-3 and 7-4 to be found in the tables in chapters 4 and 5.

19. These would comprise machine-paced industries but not continuous-process ones such as chemicals. Examples of such processes can be found in many subbranches of food processing, printing, and shoe production.

20. Such behavior is rational only if hourly wage costs are relatively low. When the data were collected, the wage costs per hour indexed on the U.K. wage were United Kingdom, 100; Japan, 44; United States, 249; and Hong Kong, 33. Ranis (1973) documents the important role of the high speeds achieved in the Japanese development experience.

21. For careful studies of the development of other developing country textile industries, see Chin (1965) and Koh (1966).

22. In his well-known article on the product cycle, Vernon (1966) suggested that textiles would be a primary candidate for production in developing countries precisely for such reasons.

23. Loom speed is rarely altered from manufacturers' recommended levels, a feature that differentiates weaving from spinning.

CHAPTER EIGHT

Project Design

As INDICATED in the introduction, analyses of individual plants' productivity and the sources of their deficiencies can be used to formulate
and evaluate proposed industrial projects. In particular, low productivity
suggests the possibility of a type of industrial project that has not usually
been considered: one solely to improve the performance of existing plants
rather than to add to physical productive capacity.[1] This chapter describes
the type of project design and evaluation that becomes feasible if careful
attention is given to the collection and analysis of data from operating
factories. Such information provides the basis for a comprehensive
fomulation of industrial project analysis in which the social benefit-cost
ratio of a project to expand physical capacity is compared with that of
one for raising the productivity of existing facilities.

The technical characteristics of plants already operating in a country
also provide a benchmark for the plausibility of the technical input-
output coefficients contained in feasibility studies of proposed new plants
in the same nation. Coefficients considerably better than those currently
achieved in similar plants should initially be viewed with skepticism and
require explanation in terms of such variables as better management, new
quality-control procedures, or new or improved training programs.
Equipment containing new features is not among the more persuasive
justifications. Otherwise, a not overly conservative working hypothesis is
that of a regression to the mean, which assumes that the most probable
operating parameters of a new plant will be those currently manifested in
local firms employing roughly similar technology.

Formulation of Alternative Industrial Projects

Two of many possible examples of project analysis will be given in this
chapter. One is based on an actual case study of the desirability of build-
ing a completely new textile factory in Tanzania as compared with improving the effectiveness of existing plants. The second considers the

potential benefit-cost ratios to be obtained by improving the productivity of Philippine textile mills and uses some of the results of chapter 5. The Tanzanian project is typical of many industrial projects proposed in developing countries: adding a substantial new factory to a sector in which considerable production capacity already exists, albeit inefficiently deployed. The rich set of analyses of the sector that are available allows some confidence in the results obtained. In contrast, the issue in the Philippines is to assess the benefits to be derived from improving the productivity of existing plants in a large sector that is generally considered to operate inefficiently. Both types of analysis can be extended further, but the presentation here is mainly intended to indicate a way of evaluating industrial projects from a new perspective and to suggest that a broadened view of industrial project design should be an intrinsic part of every proposal to augment physical capacity.

There is only limited evidence of the success of attempts to improve productivity in existing firms. Early efforts by the ILO (Kilby 1962) resulted in substantial growth in labor productivity, apparently with no increase in equipment per worker. The permanence of the achievement was not investigated. A carefully described experiment in Indian weaving plants (Rice 1958) notes short-run increases in output of 19 percent and 100 percent in automatic and semiautomatic loom sheds solely as a result of rearranging equipment and work assignments. Again, the duration of this improvement is not known. Recent World Bank efforts along similar lines, often combined with loans to rehabilitate equipment, have yet to be systematically evaluated (de Vries and Brakel 1983).

Both the ILO and Indian improvements in productivity were obtained with a much less systematic program than that envisioned here at the firm level, and with no attempts to reorganize the industry or alter the economywide incentive structure. The initial success in these cases, despite their limited scope, provides an empirical basis for optimism about the potential benefits of a comprehensive program to increase productivity.

The Role of Individuals in Technology Diffusion

Individuals perform a critical role in the successful transfer of technology, and especially in the specific form envisioned in this chapter: a group of individuals hired by textile mills with low productivity to provide technical and organizational help for a number of years. Because other ways of raising production engineering skills exist, there is justification for a short discussion of why this method is likely to be superior to alternative ones such as centralized aid provided by a consulting group.

A considerable literature, based largely on historical evidence, suggests that the diffusion of technology—both new processes and new products—results mainly from the movements of individuals from firm to firm and from country to country.[2] The precise behavioral reason for the importance of person-to-person contact is rarely articulated (but see Arrow 1969): possible interpretations include the role of tacit or uncodified knowledge (Nelson and Winter 1982); the importance of an advocate of a particular change in breaking down an organizational equilibrium that favors the status quo (Pack and Pack 1977); and the reduction in uncertainty and in the cost of information acquisition when a person with production experience is on hand—as opposed to the abstract and untested technical possibilities available from other sources. Whatever ultimate combination of reasons accounts for the decisive role of individuals in the transmission of operational command over new processes and products, there is no evidence that the diffusion of best-practice routines can be effectively achieved by other modes. Information recently collected in the Republic of Korea confirms the role in knowledge diffusion of informal personal contacts, although other more formal modes, such as advice from purchasers of exports and knowledge obtained from recently returned Koreans with U.S. work experience, are also important (Westphal, Kim, and Dahlman 1984; Westphal, Pursell, and Rhee 1981).

There appears to be little interfirm mobility in middle and upper management in the Philippines, partly because of the family basis of many firms (see chapter 7, note 4). It can plausibly be argued that successful industrialization is characterized by a fairly uniform diffusion of best practice and is thus impeded by the absence of job switching among firms.[3] In addition to the absence of actual interfirm transfers embodied in individuals, there is also a loss of the kind of informal exchange of information that occurs as technicians suggest to each other that they might confer substantial benefits on another firm if they were to be hired. Anecdotal evidence suggests that such information exchange is important in some sectors of U.S. industry.

Given the absence of interfirm mobility, limited informal contact, and no transmission of foreign methods by returning nationals or purchasers of exports, some mechanism to substitute for such processes is desirable. Licenses, technical aid from foreign manufacturers, and a central consulting group composed of domestic technicians constitute alternatives to the long-term hiring of individuals by firms proposed in this chapter. Although a similar benefit-cost analysis could be carried out for any of these alternatives, this chapter reflects the view that any method that does not rely on individual contact on a sustained basis is unlikely to be effective. The nature of the problems discussed in chapter 6 suggests that changes in production engineering are not likely to be implemented on a one-shot or short-term basis; problems arising from the variation in products or the processing environment occur frequently. Changes in the nature of raw materials, new product designs, and new developments in production engineering will pose unanticipated problems whose solutions will differ from those obtained with earlier practices. Successful absorption of improved production engineering practices requires not only initial learning but also an ability to modify practices as circumstances change. Given the current levels of skill, it is improbable that a centralized pool of consultants or a foreign license accompanied by some initial personal help can instill the requisite adaptive ability. With skills initially higher, one-time infusions of this type from licensers or purchasers of a firm's exports may be adequate, but even in the case of Korea, individual mobility and employment in the firm seem to have been an important way of obtaining mastery in production engineering.

The Role of Competition in Obtaining Greater Productivity

A textbook view of industry dynamics might suggest that explicit policy efforts to spread knowledge are redundant. Faced with sufficient competitive pressure, firms will be compelled to devote greater effort to the search for the technical knowledge that will allow them to maintain profit rates equal to those in other endeavors. This position has much force and partly explains why any policy effort to promote the diffusion of information should be embedded within a wider framework (set forth in chapter 9) to increase competition; nevertheless, the view that competition is all that is required is too facile. Attribution of the success of the superexporters of East Asia solely to their reliance on market forces, for example, does not accord with the facts.[4] In these countries, competitive forces have been allowed full sway only after substantial technical learning has taken place. A liberalized economic milieu and a policy to increase technical competence are the two blades of the scissors, to use the Marshallian image, necessary to achieve decreased cost. Either is likely to be considerably less effective without the other.

In the present context, the most relevant argument for an explicit technology policy is the relatively low level of technical skills in Tanzania and, to a smaller degree, in the Philippines. Williams (1975) has documented the poor technical performance of the Tanzanian textile sector during the 1970s. Mlawa (1983) has presented detailed evidence of the poor preparation of technicians and the small number of individuals with relevant training. If the sector were exposed to competition without an attempt to improve its performance, most plants would probably go out of business. The fact that this is likely to be true of almost all industrial sectors—the Tanzanian example being just one instance of premature import-substituting industrialization—means that the following discussion of the benefit-cost ratio of improving existing technical competence in one sector has broad general significance.

Despite the noncompetitive nature of existing textile plants, still other additions to capacity are being considered. Below I consider the economic desirability of one very large project relative to a program designed to improve the performance of existing firms. I then address the issues more generally, using the results from chapter 5 on the Philippines and relating the question to more traditional infant industry arguments.

Cost-Effectiveness of Two Alternative Projects

The first case to be discussed is that of a proposed investment in a new US$100 million integrated textile mill in Tanzania in the late 1970s. The availability of detailed information on the specific project, together with a considerable amount of background data on the textile sector (Mlawa 1983; Williams 1975), permits an analysis of the cost-effectiveness of two alternative proposals: a new textile plant designed to increase annual output by 19 million linear meters and a project designed to raise the productivity of existing plants within the context of a general effort to improve industrial performance via internal and external liberalization. Rather than using benefit-cost ratios, the analysis compares the cost of obtaining the same target increase in output by each of the two methods. The cost-effectivness approach precludes the need to analyze the value of the increase in output, which is the same in both cases.[5]

In the case of the improvement project, five major textile plants existed at the time of the planned expansion in capacity. During the preceding five years, average labor productivity for these plants had declined by 28 percent, but the size of the capital stock remained roughly constant during this period in all plants.[6] For the two largest mills, accounting for two-thirds of total output, it is possible to calculate factor inputs relative to best practice as well as relative total-factor productivity calculated in the same way as the figures for Kenya and the Philippines. The relevant data are shown in table 8-1.

The capital-labor ratio in both spinning plants is higher than best practice, an anomalous result, given the country's low wage-rental ratio. Relative capital inputs are very high in both spinning and weaving (compare tables 7-3 and 7-5). At best, RTFP for both segments of textile production

Table 8-1. *Performance in Two Plants in the Textile Sector*

Performance relative to best practice	Weaving		Spinning	
	Firm A	Firm B	Firm A	Firm B
Unit labor input	3.54	6.08	2.06	2.18
Unit capital input	1.40	1.43	3.03	2.27
Capital-labor ratio	0.40	0.24	1.47	1.04
Relative total-factor productivity ($\sigma = 0.5$)	0.54	0.49	0.42	0.45

Source: Williams (1975), World Bank data..

in both plants is about 50 percent; these percentages probably exceed those of other mills, as firms A and B have experienced smaller declines in labor productivity than have other factories. In 1976, total output in the textile sector was 73 million linear meters. If all plants could be brought up to RTFP of 85 percent from an assumed optimistic average level of 50 percent, total additional output of 51 million meters could be obtained as compared with additional capacity of 19 million meters provided by the new mill. In deciding which route to pursue to obtain additional output, we must also estimate the investment in each case.

Given the argument voiced above, I assume that the main component of a productivity improvement effort is the introduction of a group of high-quality technicians into each of the five large mills currently constituting the sector.[7] Additional efforts that might be appropriate include domestic training institutes for operatives, foreign training for middle management, and the establishment of a central group of technicians capable of dealing with unusual production engineering problems. Although these activities are probably necessary in the long run, discussions of the problems of individual firms (Mlawa 1983) suggest that the main impediment to higher firm-level productivity is the limited production engineering ability of middle-level technicians. Although the following discussion and the ensu-ing benefit-cost ratios could be broadened to include some of the ele-ments of a more general program, the limited venture suggested here is more relevant in this particular context.

Assume that ten persons are employed in each firm for three years to improve operating methods, to implement organizational changes, and to train a group of successors. Moreover, assume that five of these experts are retained for an additional seven years, so that the total number of man-years involved is sixty-five. If the cost of each man-year is initially US$50,000 and increases 5 percent yearly, the present discounted cost per plant of the technical-help package, at a 10 percent real rate of interest, is

US$2.5 million. This figure will be used in calculations throughout this chapter, including those involving the Philippines. Although small cost increases might be incurred if the remedies for some inefficient practices—for example low current inventories of spare parts—require additional investment, my calculations suggest that these increases are minor. Thus the investment necessary to obtain 51 million meters of additional cloth per year from the five existing plants is equivalent to an investment of US$12.5 million; this figure contrasts with US$100 million estimate in the feasibility study that proposed producing 19 million meters of cloth in a new plant. Even if other institutional mechanisms, such as training institutes for operatives, were provided to improve productivity, they would probably not greatly narrow the gap between the costs of the two projects.

If the productivity improvement effort were limited to the two larger existing plants, the potential increase in output would be considerably larger than that anticipated from the new mill and would cost only US$5 million. Moreover, the projected output for the new plant is almost certainly too high, as the feasibility study is predicated on higher productivity than that currently realized in similar Tanzanian mills.

One possible justification for the new mill is the benefit conferred by the domestic output of a new product, polyester-cotton blends. Proponents of this argument would have to show, however, that the difference in consumer surplus between the two types of products would have a present discounted value of more than US$95 million, the difference in investment in the two projects, and that this increase in consumer surplus is most efficiently obtained by domestic production rather than by imports. Both assumptions are implausible.

Benefit-Cost Analysis of Productivity-Enhancing Projects

The above discussion has taken a cost-effectiveness approach where a productivity improvement project constitutes an alternative to a new factory. In many cases, however, the relevant question is likely to be the benefit-cost ratio of a productivity improvement project that is part of a larger program to improve the functioning of a particular sector. Other elements of the program should include liberalization of the trade regime (to provide a more competitive environment that encourages firms to make productive use of additional technical capacity) and explicit efforts to encourage greater product specialization. The relations between the elements of a productivity-enhancing program are considered in the next chapter. In the following section I discuss the relevant measure of benefits and other questions that arise in assessing the merit of such programs.

The Analytic Framework

Assume that the sector is initially in the equilibrium shown in figure 8-1. Imports of competing products are excluded by a made-to-measure tariff that is set so that the least efficient firm can survive and the more efficient ones collect rents.[8] Output is initially Q_1, domestic price P_1, world price $P_2 = P_W$, and the made-to-measure tariff P_1P_2. The productivity-enhancing project results in a downward shift in the supply curve to S_2, and tariffs are simultaneously eliminated, the project being embedded within a

Figure 8-1. *Benefits and Costs of Productivity Improvements*

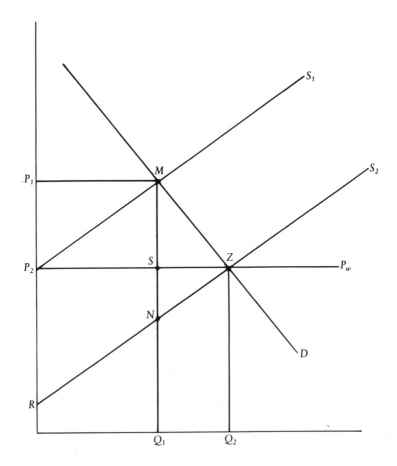

more general structural adjustment program. There are two effects of the liberalization-cum-learning effort: (1) an increase in consumer surplus of P_1P_2ZM and (2) a change in producer surplus of $P_2ZR - P_1P_2M$. The net gain is thus P_2MZR, which can be decomposed into two areas, P_2MNR and MNZ. A downward shift in the industry's supply curve reflects the shift in the marginal cost curves of the component firms. Thus P_2MNR represents the fall in the (private) marginal cost of producing initial output Q_1 and can be approximated by the decrease in the sum of the marginal costs of the firms constituting the sector. MNZ is the social gain from the expansion of output from Q_1 to Q_2 and consists of the additional producer surplus, SZN, and consumer surplus, MSZ.

Given that area P_2MZ[9] could, in principle, be obtained simply by the elimination of protection without a concomitant learning program,[10] should the entire gain, P_2MZR, be attributed to the productivity-enhancing project and its impact on the supply curve? The answer depends on an assessment of the probability of liberalization: if it is thought likely to occur without a productivity-enhancing program, P_2MZR overstates the social benefit from an investment in learning. The constellation of political forces, however, may preclude a reduction in tariffs without a simultaneous productivity-enhancing project, given the possible bankruptcy of influential but inefficient firms.[11] In this case, the total gains will be achievable only when a learning project is attached to the liberalization program. Because of the possibility that a number of workers and plant owners would be significant losers and therefore hostile to a pure liberalization effort, however, such policy changes are rare. The more inclusive measure of benefits is thus a defensible view of the gains stemming directly from the productivity-enhancing component. Nevertheless, the "pure" effect of the intensified learning effort should exclude P_2MZ, and only the remainder RP_2Z should be counted as a true benefit.

Some might argue that even the smaller measure represents an overstatement insofar as liberalization, even if not supplemented by explicit measures to encourage productivity, would cause a downward shift in the industry supply curve as individual firms facing more intense competition would seek to reduce costs on their own. Managements, for example, would try to improve their production engineering abilities, and greater competition would produce a more rational pattern of product specialization or, at the least, production for inventory and the cost reductions associated with larger lot sizes.

These outcomes are theoretically possible. Skepticism about their inevitability may be warranted, however, as such opportunities for profit already exist (see chapter 6) and have not been exploited. Moreover, the more competitive pricing induced by liberalization does not guarantee greater product specialization. Very little is understood about the dynamics of product specialization, the conditions under which it emerges, and the stability of any structure that is achieved.[12] It requires a fundamentalist's faith in the strength of the invisible hand to believe that the requisite specialization will develop, without guidance, simply from liberalization. Even the European Common Market countries, with considerably larger domestic markets than most developing countries, substantial exports, and much lower levels of effective protection, have recently resorted to explicit, legally sanctioned, cartel-like arrangements to encourage greater specialization in the textile sector.[13]

The implication is that the time required for adjustment of the supply curve is likely to be longer, and the ultimate height of the supply curve greater, if firms are left to their own devices than if a program focusing directly on productivity issues is implemented. If these views are correct, ignoring the potential shift in the supply curve that might result solely from liberalization is not likely to exaggerate benefits by much.

Given the preceding arguments, two measures of the gain from a learning program are calculated, RP_2MN and $\frac{1}{2}RP_2MN$. Use of $\frac{1}{2}RP_2MN$ is computationally convenient and provides a fair approximation of the actual value of RP_2SN as calculated from individual plant data. The larger of the two values would be correct if it were true that no liberalization would occur without a learning program. The smaller estimate, however, does not take into account the possibility that learning may occur in a free trade regime. Both measures omit MZN, all of which should be added to RP_2MN under the more comprehensive measure, whereas only part, SZN, should be added to $\frac{1}{2}RP_2MN$ under the more restricted view. Estimation of these areas requires supply and demand elasticities in the relevant range, both of which are unavailable. Calculations with plausible values of these parameters suggest that the omission decreases calculated benefits by a maximum of 15 percent and introduces a downward bias of this magnitude into the benefit-cost ratios.

It is of use to relate this discussion to the traditional infant industry case. The conventional argument is that initial social costs, P_2MZ, are incurred during a learning period, whereas benefits RP_2Z accrue later as learning shifts the supply curve from S_1 to S_2. To meet the Mill-Bastable criterion, the present discounted value of the benefits over some suitable period must exceed the present discounted value of the social costs. Similarly, the benefit from a productivity improvement program is the present discounted value of RP_2Z (calculated here as $\frac{1}{2}RP_2MN$), and the cost of obtaining this is the investment in the project rather than the present discounted value of P_2MZ. The supply curve shifts not as a result of passive but inevitable learning by doing over time, as in the infant industry argument, but in response to investment explicitly designed to shift it quickly. In the conventional view, the producer surplus RP_2Z, which constitutes the potential benefit, accrues over time even if nothing is done to force the pace of learning. If this were the likely evolution over time (for an evaluation of the realism of this view see Bell, Ross-Larson, and Westphal 1984), the benefit from the productivity-augmenting effort as measured here would be overstated, and the true benefit would consist of the discounted differences in producer surplus given by the two time paths of shifting supply curves.

Introduction of a New Product

The analytic framework just established allows a more precise analysis of the potential benefits and costs of local production of goods that must currently be imported. One of the alleged benefits of the new mill in Tanzania is its ability to produce blended yarns and fabrics, in this case polyester-cotton. Assuming for the sake of argument that it is difficult and therefore very costly to convert existing equipment to such production, how does the analysis of the preceding section change? The assertion that blended products are more desirable than pure cotton, perhaps because of their increased durability and easy care, implies that the demand curve for the good lies above that shown for pure cotton products in figure 8-1.[14] If the firm established to satisfy cotton-polyester demands were as inefficient as those producing pure cotton products, the forgone consumer surplus and excess production cost would thus be a loss still greater than that shown in figure 8-1. If consumers perceive the newly produced good to be superior, as is claimed, the potential economic loss from inefficient domestic production is particularly great. Rather than constituting an argument for initiating production, a higher demand curve suggests the need for an even more careful appraisal of the proposed plant.

An Application to the Philippine Textile Sector

The cost-benefit framework described above has been implemented using the data obtained from individual Philippine firms. The numerical estimates of benefits are derived by computing the reduction in current cost that would be obtained, with the prevailing output, if each firm could increase its relative total-factor productivity to 85 percent of best practice in both spinning and weaving. In addition, a quantitatively important benefit in weaving is the cost reduction obtained by moving from the current capital-labor ratio to the cost-minimizing one.

Benefits from Industry- and Firm-Level Improvements

It was noted in chapter 5 that the average reduction from improved allocational performance was 26 percent of current total weaving costs.[15] One of the tasks of technical personnel would be to capture these benefits in addition to those derived from the realization of higher total-factor productivity. Although not directly attributable to improved technical capability, the measured benefits include those obtained from greater specialization, because the productivity improvement program is assumed to be embedded in a general effort to rationalize the industry. Some of the implications of the inability to realize gains from specialization are presented in the next section.

Benefits are calculated as the present discounted value of the total reduction in cost over ten years, and a 10 percent discount rate is assumed. The cost of the program is based on the assumption (used earlier in regard to Tanzanian productivity improvement) that expatriate staff would be hired for several years. It is assumed that they are equally divided between the spinning and weaving sections, and the cost is allocated on this basis to each process.

In principle, the desired transfer of technological capabilities could be handled in other ways—for example, by acquiring foreign licenses for specific process technologies, by organizing a central pool of technicians, by establishing a worker training institute, and by hiring short-term consultants. Many of these approaches have already been tried without success in the Philippines, however (see chapters 6 and 7). It can plausibly be argued that their failure was attributable to the lack of any prior effort by the firms to improve their own ability to assimilate technology and that placing expatriate technicians at the firm level would be the best way of quickly expanding the stock of human capital to obtain greater absorptive capacity. Moreover, given the nature of the accumulated deficiencies, the expatriates must be present for a lengthy period—because their job is to provide a stock of skills that is otherwise nonexistent rather than to improve slightly the quality of an existing stock. Within the context of greater rationalization of the product structure and a more competitive environment (see chapter 9), this strategy seems the most promising source of greater firm-level productivity. Certainly the quite good comparative performance of the Kenyan firms seems to be based on the presence of such a group of technicians in each firm (see chapters 4 and 7).

The emphasis in this example on improved production engineering stems from the results of the decomposition of the sources of low productivity in the Philippines. As tables 5-6 and 5-8 show, firm-specific technical deficiencies are a major source of the deviation from best practice in both spinning and weaving. In contrast, task-level productivity is, on the average, about at best-practice levels. Nevertheless, as some of the examples in chapter 6 indicate, improved labor practices might help increase productivity in some firms. Rectification of deficiencies in this area requires skills different from those involved in production engineering; given the specificity of national attitudes and cultural patterns, these skills are not easily implanted from abroad. Internal diffusion of better labor practices is probably the way to raise performance in this dimension.

The results, for both the full benefits and half of this value, are presented in table 8-2, the logic of each having been discussed in the preceding section. The benefits and costs for each firm have been included in the sectorwide totals only for the activity (spinning or weaving), in which the benefit-cost ratio for each definition of benefit is greater than one. The last row indicates the percentage of firms exhibiting benefit-cost ratios greater than unity for both processes.

The narrower calculation (columns 3 and 4), comparing half of the benefits and all of the costs, yields a sectorwide benefit-cost ratio of 1.71 when benefits from an improvement in RTFP alone are included and 2.30 when allocative gains from improved choice of technique are included as well, the cost being the same. The range of individual benefit-cost ratios is quite large, the coefficients of variation being 38 and 26 percent, respectively. The benefit-cost ratios are quite high when compared with those projected in most industrial plan documents; they also have a fairly high probability of realization, because the activities envisaged (largely involving production engineering) are much narrower in scope than those required in establishing an entirely new plant.

Nevertheless, in light of the documented poor performance of the Philippine textile sector, some may view the benefit-cost ratios as low,

Table 8-2. *Potential Benefit-Cost Ratios Stemming from Productivity Improvement and Correct Choice of Factor Proportions*

| | 100 percent of benefits | | 50 percent of benefits | |
| | Move to RTFP OF 85 percent | (1) + move to correct capital-labor ratio | Move to RTFP of 85 percent | (3) + move to correct capital-labor ratio |
Item	(1)	(2)	(3)	(4)
Sectorwide benefit-cost ratio (B/C)	3.2	4.3	1.7	2.3
Coefficient of variation of individual firm values	0.48	0.36	0.38	0.26
B − C (millions of U.S. dollars)	48.7	71.1	14.3	26.1
Percentage of firms for which B/C > 1	83	92	75	83

although they are substantially greater than unity. As the first two columns in table 8-2 show, this is attributable to the conservative nature of the preceding social benefit-cost calculation insofar as the part of the gains that might be obtained simply from liberalization has been excluded in the last two columns. Including these gains as part of the benefit (columns 1 and 2) yields sectorwide benefit-cost ratios of 3.16 and 4.33 and absolute net benefits of US$49 million or US$71 million as compared with US$14 million and US$26 million when half of total benefits are included.[16]

Benefits Restricted to the Firm Level

Of the calculations that have been done, those with the more inclusive definition of benefits, full rather than half, correspond to what an individual firm would gain from an investment in technical and organizational upgrading.[17] If the potential benefit-cost ratios are so favorable (and on the assumption that financing is not a problem), why do firms not undertake productivity improvements on their own? Are they failing to minimize costs or to make rational investment calculations, or are they engaging in one form or another of nonmaximizing behavior?

One obvious possibility is that companies in the existing environment could not look forward to obtaining benefits accruing from greater specialization, because product specialization depends on explicit coordination among all firms. Without such industrywide changes, which have a public goods character and well-known attendant problems (Olson 1965), companies calculating the potential benefits from improving their own technical competence as well as their task-level productivity would anticipate an upper limit in their performance of perhaps 90 percent of best-practice total-factor productivity. If the absence of greater specialization in Philippine weaving is a given, for example, that sets a limit to RTFP of 70 percent, the best that individual plants might expect to attain is RTFP of $0.90 (0.70) = 0.63$. The private benefit-cost calculus can then be recalculated on the assumption that firms are successful in achieving this level.

To return to the question of the economic rationality of firms, an outcome consistent with cost minimization requires that individual plants exhibit a prospective benefit-cost ratio of less than one from undertaking their own improvement efforts. This criterion is weak, as it rests on the assumption that the posited minimum-cost level (based on the calculation that is given above) of the technical aid program is indivisible; companies with potential benefits below this fixed cost would not purchase such aid. In contrast, if technical aid could be bought in continuously variable amounts, each firm capable of obtaining any positive marginal benefits would engage in such purchases until the marginal benefit-cost ratio became unity. Firms for which a prospective benefit-cost ratio of less than one is calculated, and whose failure to invest in self-improvement appears "rational," might exhibit a benefit-cost ratio greater than unity if technical inputs, as they perceive them, are in fact available in smaller packages. Thus any inferences from the benefit-cost ratios about the extent to which companies engage in optimizing behavior are necessarily tentative.

Table 8-3 presents the benefit-cost ratios obtained when the gains from greater specialization are not included. The second column shows the sectorwide benefits and costs when it is assumed that individual firms proceed with their own productivity augmentation effort in either spinning or weaving if the private benefit-cost ratio (with a ten-year horizon and a real interest rate of 10 percent) is greater than unity—with benefits defined to include the reduction in costs attributable to improved capital-labor ratios. In this case the numerator consists of all benefits, because it is of no concern to each company that some of these gains would accrue in any event if liberalization were to occur (the reason used earlier to exclude half of the benefits). In tables 8-2 and 8-3, the impact of product specialization can be seen in the absolute difference in benefits minus costs, $71 million versus $37 million.[18] With respect to evaluating the economic rationality of firms, even without the prospective cost reductions stemming from greater specialization, two-thirds of all firms have a prospective benefit-cost ratio above unity (table 8-3, column 2) as com-

Table 8-3. *Potential Benefit-Cost Ratios Stemming Solely from Firm-Level Productivity Improvements and Correct Choice of Factor Proportions, without Gains from Greater Specialization*

| | 100 percent of benefits | |
| | Move to maximum RTFP[a] | (1) + move to correct capital-labor ratio |
Item	(1)	(2)
Sectorwide benefit-cost ratio (B/C)	2.6	4.0
$B - C$ (millions of U.S. dollars)	11.7	37.4
Percentage of firms for which $B/C > 1$	33	67

a. Maximum RTFP equals 90 percent of total-factor productivity of best-practice plants, except for the productivity-reducing effect of inadequate specialization, which is assumed to continue at its current level.

pared with 92 percent of firms when such gains are included in potential benefits. Not surprisingly, without the lure of gains from specialization and with the assumption of a minimum size for the technical effort required, a smaller fraction of firms will find it in their interest to undertake a productivity enhancement program of their own.

The fact that two-thirds of plants should currently find it worthwhile (column 2, row 3), given the assumptions made, to invest in their own improvement program, whereas only one-third are in least-cost equilibrium in the sense indicated earlier, might be viewed as a refutation of the neoclassical view underlying equation 7-2 and more generally as a rebuttal of the view that neoclassical theory, suitably extended, is an adequate model for the behavior of firms. I do not think that such strong conclusions can be drawn. Although firms may believe that outside help could improve their technical efficiency, for example, they may be doubtful about the possibility of altering existing machine assignments per worker; hence gains in allocative efficiency could appear less certain and might not be included in the calculus of prospective benefits. If this were the case, then only one-third of firms (table 8-3, column 1) would currently have anticipated benefit-cost ratios greater than unity.[19] The prospective benefit-cost ratios and the percentage of firms with ratios above unity vary with the assumption made. Although they are useful for delineating the range of issues involved in undertaking improvement programs, the data cannot be invoked to strengthen the claims of either those who view cost minimization as the only view of firm behavior or those who believe that a bounded rationality-satisficing model is superior. As in most serious issues, the result retains some ambiguity—except to those who hold strong prior views to which empirical information contributes only a small amount of additional insight.

The preceding calculations demonstrate the potential benefits of eliminating two common features of the developing country industrial landscape: firm-specific inefficient practices and efficiency losses that require the reorganization of the industry. The approach taken here implies that neither source of inefficiency can be eliminated without a conscious effort, whether it involves the introduction of technicians into individual firms to redress inefficient practices or a purposeful, industry-wide program to rationalize the division of products among firms. The opening of the sector to competitive forces is a necessary adjunct to these activities, but it is unlikely to be sufficient to guarantee the desired outcome. The size of the prospective gain from sectorwide reorganization is particularly important if the productivity improvement programs can be carried out only on a minimum scale. In this case, the prospective benefits of product specialization provide the necessary bonus that makes it economic for many firms to incur the cost of eliminating purely internal inefficiencies.

The method of achieving adequate product specialization is of particular importance.[20] In principle, adequate price competition stimulated by the entry of foreign products should encourage and enforce optimal specialization. When each firm produces a wide range of products, opening the economy to price competition should lead to a new situation in which each plant makes only a few products and obtains the advantage of long production runs. Although the comparative static equilibria are clear, the dynamics of moving from the initial situation to the final one are difficult to envision, and there is certainly no guidance from the literature on the likely adjustment process. Indeed, it is easy to imagine scenarios in which the path to the desirable equilibrium will be diverted time and again, so that its eventual achievement is thwarted.

A relatively direct approach could be a two-part policy of assigning products to plants and lowering tariffs to prevent monopolistic exploitation of each plant's position. The precise legal structure for assigning products cannot be given in detail here, but some issues can be foreseen and some precedents can be examined.[21] Questions clearly arise about the dynamic stability of such an arrangement: for example, in the face of declining international or domestic demand, forces similar to those that have led to the current fragmented state of production may reassert themselves. Such difficulties, and their likely costs, must be weighed against the gains from greater specialization (compare tables 8-2 and 8-3). The administrative costs associated with reorganization must also be considered. Nevertheless, to do nothing purposeful to foster the requisite specialization is to grant the possibility that quite substantial gains in real income will be forgone. As noted earlier, neither the size of an economy nor the competitive forces at work appear to have guaranteed the realization of gains from product specialization in other countries. Although the potential problems of administrative interference in the market must be examined carefully, the gains are sufficiently large to warrant careful examination of the approach outlined here.

Notes

1. For a recent survey of a number of World Bank efforts along these lines in the textile sector, see de Vries and Brakel (1983).

2. See Landes (1969) and Rosenberg (1976). Jeremy (1981) provides detail on the diffusion of textile technology in the nineteenth century. Also see Saxonhouse (1974, 1976, 1978).

3. An apparently contradictory argument often made in support of infant industry protection is that turnover is harmful because it reduces the incentive for firms to provide training to workers unless the cost is borne by trainees. Two issues associated with mobility are its impact on the level of privately financed training provided by the sector and its social benefit from the diffusion of knowledge. Whether high mobility reduces the incentive of firms to provide training depends on the incidence of training costs. In the case of technicians with considerable formal education, it is unlikely that firms bear much of the training cost, and mobility should have net beneficial effects on industrywide performance.

4. For documentation in the case of Korea and an analysis of the nature of the policies actually followed, see Pack and Westphal (1986).

5. In fact, as will be seen, the potential increase in output from improving the productivity of existing plants exceeds that obtainable from the proposed new plant. Proponents of the new investment would, however, argue that manufacture of a different product, polyester-cotton blends, confers a benefit that must also be included when evaluating the project. This issue is addressed below.

6. This figure for the decline is based on meters of cloth produced, divided by total plant employment. It is thus assumed that the plants were roughly balanced so that each was fairly self-sufficient in producing yarn for its own weaving needs. In this case, production of cloth provides a good approximation of total mill output.

7. It is not possible to learn from existing studies how much of the low current productivity is attributable to insufficient product specialization. If excess product diversity is one source of low productivity, it is relatively easy to effect a solution in Tanzania, where most textile plants are owned by the government. The role of greater specialization is explicitly discussed below.

8. The discussion would be similar within the more conventional geometric framework that depicts imports and domestic production occurring simultaneously, with the tariff set to yield a domestic price below the supply-demand intersection. The made-to-measure tariff is used because it portrays more accurately the current situation in the Philippines, the country for which the empirical analysis is carried out.

9. P_2MZ equals the net cost imposed by the initial protective regime, namely, excess production cost plus the loss in consumer surplus minus the increase in producer surplus.

10. Although, as depicted, domestic production would fall to zero, this result reflects an effort to keep the geometry simple. Under present conditions some firms would survive the exposure to international competition.

11. A good example of the fears of weaker firms thwarting the introduction of liberalization is provided by a recent account of Mexican efforts in this direction. See the *Wall Street Journal* (1985).

12. See Scherer (1980), pp. 133–38, and Scherer and others (1975). Some of the literature on intraindustry specialization sheds some light on general questions but fails to address the specific issues of interest in this study. See, for example, Grubel and Lloyd (1975).

13. *New York Times*, February 16, 1980, "U.S. Pricing Roils Europe Textile Makers." Examples of rationalization cartels are given by Scherer and others (1975), pp. 313–15. For a discussion of European efforts at industrial rationalization in the nineteenth century, see *Encyclopedia of the Social Sciences* (1934), s.v. "rationalization," and Landes (1969). For a recent study and many relevant citations, see Muller and Owen (1983).

14. Ad hoc arguments can be adduced on either side of the issue, and an empirical resolution requires the estimation of hedonic demand functions that include specific characterisics, such as durability, ease of care, and comfort of various fabrics. As far as I know, no such studies have been carried out.

15. In spinning, the potential gains from improved choice of technique are minor.

16. The benefit-cost ratio does not double when 100 percent rather than 50 percent of benefits are included, because in a few firms the increase in benefits still does not yield a benefit-cost ratio greater than unity; hence the benefits to these firms are not included in the sectorwide totals.

17. This statement assumes no loss to other firms of staff members trained in the program.

18. The large decrease in $B - C$ is not reflected in a commensurate decline in the benefit-cost ratio, because the number of firms for which the prospective benefits outweighs costs declines, and it is assumed that the costs of augmenting productivity are not incurred by those whose prospective benefit-cost ratio is less than unity.

19. One of the firms whose prospective benefit-cost ratio is greater than unity has, on its own initiative, already begun such a program, with initially impressive results.

20. This topic is also discussed in the following chapter.

21. See, for example, OECD (1982) and other annual reviews as well. For a brief survey of the magnitude of potential gains that may be realized in mergers, see Scherer (1980), pp. 33–38.

CHAPTER NINE

Conclusions

THIS BOOK set out to investigate two related issues, the appropriate choice of technology and the productivity with which specific technologies are employed within developing countries. Before discussing policy guidelines and the relevance of the evidence to broader issues of technology transfer, I present the main conclusions to be drawn from the detailed empirical analysis.

The Choice of Technology

The determination of the appropriate capital-labor ratio for manufacturing a given product has several components: the choice of machinery from the range of models that are currently manufactured, the choice between new and used machinery of the relevant type, and the choice of the amount of labor to be used with whatever machinery is finally decided upon. The empirical results confirm that none of these questions can be resolved simply by using the input coefficients supplied by machinery producers or those for best-practice firms in developed countries. Neither can one rely on input coefficients observed in operating developing country plants, because these may obscure some cost-minimizing choices that would be relevant if greater productivity could be achieved in individual plants. Thus two alternative calculations are appropriate: the economically efficient technology if current developing country productivity is maintained and the efficient alternative if it were possible to obtain productivity that approaches best practice.

Three broad conclusions emerge from this book.

• At both current and high productivity, new conventional equipment offers a cost advantage over new machinery from either the highest or the lowest end of the capital-intensity spectrum; thus in weaving, both water jet looms in the Philippines and semiautomatic looms in Kenya are inferior to conventional automatic looms. Radically new or very old designs are not competitive within the economic environments studied, although in other countries, for example Korea, new semiautomatic looms have been shown to be cost efficient (Rhee and Westphal 1977).

• Comparisons between new and used conventional equipment demonstrate that the latter exhibits some cost advantage at current productivity levels; the advantage stems from its lower price and the greater productivity, relative to its potential, achieved with it. At uniform high productivity relative to best practice, the advantage may lie with new or used machinery; in both countries, the margin of difference in either case is quite small. Obtaining a good price on used equipment is more important than any inherent differences in operating characteristics if high productivity can be realized. Firm-specific management skills are important in obtaining the cost advantages that exist, and the Kenyan multinationals achieve better results in production engineering than locally owned Philippine mills.

• Once a specific set of machines has been chosen, the correct choice of the amount of labor employed with them may result in a large cost saving, as in Philippine weaving.

Productivity

In spinning, both Kenyan and Philippine plants achieve roughly 70 percent of the total-factor productivity obtained from similar equipment in best-practice plants in the United Kingdom (table 9-1). In weaving, relative total-factor productivity is lower, at 55 percent (the Philippines) and 68 percent (Kenya), and a considerable part of the shortfall is attributable to

Table 9-1. *Productivity Summary for Kenya and Philippine Textile Mills Relative to Best Practice*

	Spinning		Weaving	
Item	*Kenya*	*Philippines*	*Kenya*	*Philippines*
Relative total-factor productivity	0.70	0.73	0.68	0.55
Sources of deviation from best practice[a]				
Specialization	0.85	0.79	0.63	0.70
Firm-level technical mastery	0.93	0.91	0.99	0.75
Task-level productivity	0.85	1.03	1.11	1.03

a. The higher the value, the closer the developing country plant to best practice.

inadequate product specialization. Firm-specific sources of low productivity are more significant in weaving than in spinning, particularly in the Philippines.

The empirical findings on productivity confirm results on productivity differences that have usually been established at more aggregate levels employing sectorwide averages rather than firm-level observations.[1] The productivity gap is attributable partly to intercountry differences in the extent of product specialization and partly to the absence of technological mastery in a number of aspects of production engineering (table 9-1). The failure of plants in the Philippines to achieve greater specialization, despite the large number of textile firms and the low concentration ratio within the country, is consistent with difficulties experienced in other countries, including developed ones. International experience suggests that a liberal trade regime is a necessary but not sufficient condition for realizing the economies of product specialization.

Detailed analysis in chapter 7 of the variation in intercountry technical performance suggests a reason for the deviation between developed and developing countries in a technically mature sector in which proprietary information is relatively unimportant. The variation reflects the failure of the developing country firms to invest in the accumulation of sufficient technical and organizational skills to absorb fruitfully a considerable amount of freely available knowledge. Technological mastery is the outcome of purposeful efforts and expenditures and does not appear to accrue costlessly simply as a result of accumulated past experience.

Guidelines for Policy

Chapter 8 presented benefit-cost ratios obtainable from productivity-enhancing projects. These projects must be part of a more general liberalization effort that increases competitive pressures upon all firms in an industry and perhaps on the industry relative to all other industries. It is envisioned that tariffs on both the inputs and the products of the sector would be lowered, with the goal of reducing the effective rate of protection to the same rate that applies to other sectors, a commonly accepted uniform level being 20 percent. The entire policy package should comprise four elements: (1) an imminent change in tariff rates and other forms of protection on both inputs and outputs would be announced; (2) the availability of collateral-backed loans for improving production engineering would simultaneously be announced; (3) the only condition for loan eligibility would be a firm's agreement to engage in product specialization;

(4) loans for new equipment or rehabilitation of older equipment would become available at the end of a prespecified period.

The analysis presented in earlier chapters of the sources of low productivity provides the basis for a specific set of recommendations about the sequence of liberalization measures. Before we embark upon a detailed discussion, it is worth asking whether productivity enhancement is necessary—why not simply liberalize and allow a competitive environment to eliminate inefficient firms from the industry? This may seem a particularly attractive option, given the great quantitive importance of product diversity in increasing production costs in the textile sector. One of the more probable results of liberalization, it might be argued, is the natural realization of the benefits of greater specialization as firms strive to remain competitive.

Evidence demonstrating the desirability of a productivity-enhancing program in addition to liberalization was provided in table 8-2, where it was shown that, when greater specialization is realized, the benefit-cost ratios from efforts to improve firm-level capabilities are, depending on the assumptions, 4.3 and 2.3. Few industrial loans to expand capacity offer the high rates of return implied by these ratios.

A more complex reason for pursuing productivity improvement involves the politics of liberalization. As noted in chapter 8, there will inevitably be a number of losers from any liberalization effort. The possibility of obtaining loans to improve firm-specific performance will give all firms a chance to survive in a more competitive atmosphere and is likely to mute opposition to the reform. This feature is particularly important, given the well-known difficulty of mobilizing the diffused potential beneficiaries of liberalization to support the program. The argument is not solely political, however. Public provision of information on how to improve performance and the reduction of firm-level costs of acquiring information are socially desirable on the assumption that economies of scale exist in the acquisition and dissemination of information.[2]

The program of liberalization and productivity enhancement envisioned here offers firms the opportunity to borrow from an industrial development bank to finance their efforts to augment productivity. It is likely that not all firms would take advantage of this offer. If collateral requirements are imposed, only companies with some reasonable prospect of postliberalization competiveness would enter the program. While the productivity-enhancing effort is being pursued, tariffs (or quantitative restrictions) should be reduced, first on inputs, then on the final product. Typical components of earlier rehabilitation efforts—the financing of spare parts and new equipment to break bottlenecks and of new machinery to augment capacity—should be delayed until the very end of the effort rather than being allowed to proceed concomitantly.

The first (temporally) component of a rehabilitation program should be to improve production engineering and task-level productivity by assigning individuals to a firm for sustained periods, as suggested in chapter 8. This process is likely to have its greatest impact if the addition of technical personnel is not accompanied by a parallel attempt to rehabilitate the existing equipment. Although such improvements may be necessary at some point, the management of the firm is unlikely to be able to absorb simultaneously the results of both nonembodied technology transfer and physical rehabilitation; their independent effects may be confounded by the potential beneficiaries. In particular, the introduction of new equipment to alleviate bottlenecks or the rehabilitation of older equipment may be mistakenly viewed as the sole source of improved productivity. This could encourage firms to believe (as many currently do) in the decisive role of reequipment. The perception of the contribution of production engineering and greater product specialization might therefore be lost, with a consequent diminution in future attention to both. Reequipment is appropriate only after the marginal gains from improving productivity without additional equipment is estimated to equal the marginal costs of further such changes; moreoever, the necessary funds should be obtained from conventional nonconcessionary financial markets rather than from a newly formed component of an aid program.

Before any new machinery is introduced, other macroscopic policies should be in operation to liberalize the trade regime and to organize the structure of production. The liberalization effort should be designed to reinforce the learning program by enabling firms to obtain inputs at world prices. Firms would thus learn the extent to which they could become competitive by moving toward best-practice productivity. Their improved competitiveness should reinforce their desire to absorb the ongoing technology transfer and should increase their confidence in their ability to withstand the gradual lowering of protection on their own output. To the extent that their existing equipment cannot make them competitive, even at high productivity levels and even with inputs purchased at lower international prices, some firms may face unpromising prospects. Recognition of this threat will force them, early in the program, to reassess their prospects of profitability in the period before loans for reequipment become available. A fairly long transition period before these loans become available will encourage the scrapping of truly dated equipment. In contrast, if reequipment begins after a short period, firms with either obsolete equipment (unit costs above world price even at best-practice productivity) or poor management may be willing to sustain short-term losses in the expectation that the promised machinery will soon save them.

Policies to increase product specialization are particularly difficult to formulate. It is possible to do nothing explicit and to assume that liberalization in both output and input markets, combined with improved technical abilities of firms, will inevitably result in an appropriate degree of interfirm product specialization. Unfortunately, as indicated earlier, there is little evidence on which to base such an optimistic prognosis either in developed or developing country experience.[3] Recently, the countries of the European Economic Community engaged in cartelization of their textile industries specifically to obtain greater specialization.

If there is to be an explicit concern with the range of products, there are two policy options: (1) a large country such as the Philippines might manufacture the entire range of products, but each firm would produce a very small subset of yarns and fabrics; or (2) the entire industry might specialize and all firms would produce a similar, small range of products; the industry would thus be compelled to export and products not manufactured locally would have to be imported. The relative merits of each outcome will not be set forth here. The important issue is the strategy for realizing a desirable industrial structure and the complementarity of this strategy with other policies.

The case in which each firm produces a different set of products is the more complex, the difficulty being how product allocation is to be decided. In principle, the firms can decide among themselves, basing their decisions on a presumptively superior knowledge of their own comparative advantage across products. But firms that are currently operating well below best practice may not be able to predict correctly their ultimate relative costs for different products; better forecasts may not be available until they are fairly far along their learning curves. Because part of the advantage among products should reflect differences in equipment-embodied specifications, however, there is some basis for attempting to determine relative costs early in the program. In any case, agreement on a narrowing of product range should be a prerequisite for a firm's participation in any restructuring program. It also should occur at the beginning of the program, because a considerable part of the learning process could profitably concentrate on a small range of products.

The lower costs arising from increasing specialization should reinforce the confidence that stems from improving firm-level productivity and lowering input prices toward world levels. The inevitable lowering of protection on firms' own output will be seen as less of a threat—but it should be emphasized that it will be implemented to prevent monopolistic rents from being earned in the domestic market because of a limited number of suppliers of any given product.

The need to encourage product specialization also militates against the early provision of additional equipment or rehabilitation of the existing stock. The opportunities afforded by the product specificity of new equipment may deflect attention from raising productivity and toward obtaining machines that might allow rents to be earned in a particular market segment. Although the eventual reduction of tariffs on all products should serve to deter firms from such behavior, past experience of failed liberalization efforts may make such a strategy particularly attractive and may subvert the productivity improvement program.

More generally, although the precise details of any industry restructuring will depend on country-specific circumstances, including current macroeconomic performance, the provision of new machinery should be low on the agenda of planned industrial policies. One of the most important lessons of the past two decades of development history and analysis is the relatively minor role of simple physical capital accumulation. The evidence and analysis presented here and much current research confirms this conclusion.

Some Issues in the Transfer of Technology

Many of the empirical results described in this book are relevant in analyzing the international transfer of technology (Mansfield and others 1982; Rosenberg 1976, 1982). In particular, they are helpful for assessing the cost of alternative modes of transfer (direct foreign investment, licensing, joint ventures, and turnkey plants) and the extent to which skills are transmitted to local managers and workers.

Modes of Technology Transfer

One striking conclusion to be drawn from the data is the ability of multinational management teams to bring Kenyan firms relatively close to international best practice in production engineering and task-level productivity within a relatively short time. Nevertheless, to demonstrate the social profitability of direct foreign investment as a mode of technology transfer, we must know something about its cost. It is at least theoretically possible that payments for foreign knowledge and management skills are sufficiently large to offset the relatively low production costs that they make possible. Some social profitability criterion such as domestic resource cost (DRC), corrected for factors beyond the firm's control (such as product diversification), would have to be calculated for each firm to establish the economic optimality of direct foreign investment.[4] DRCs have not been estimated in this book because the focus is on the determinants of private behavior, given existing price structures. Even if standard DRC calculations had been done, however, modifying them to incorporate the costs of technology transfers would require a major independent study. It is necessary to determine not only the nominal explicit costs (fixed fees and percentage of sales) but also the opportunity costs of restrictions such as the prohibition on exports to third markets.[5]

Although this study does not address these broader questions of evaluating alternative modes of technology transfer, one important cautionary lesson emerges: it is not sufficient to examine only the firms' realized cost, productivity, or expanded DRCs where they are available. Because the performance of companies will be affected by national and industry factors that are beyond their control, a meaningful evaluation of past successes of technology transfer requires some form of disaggregation of the elements affecting productivity to permit a detailed analysis of those that are truly controlled by the firm. Otherwise, a study might conclude that licensing or turnkey plants were inefficient and that an expensive local technology effort was warranted, when in fact the transfer was leading to high firm-specific and task-level productivity. Development of indigenous capability might still be warranted, but it should be encouraged only after consideration of more finely honed measures of the success of alternative methods of technological development. These considerations also apply to efforts to assess the validity of infant industry arguments. Firms that start from a position of firm-specific technical inferiority may close the gap between themselves and international best practice but may still be unable to compete in world markets because costs are raised by industry or national factors beyond their control. Analyses of the success of infant industries have often neglected this dimension of their evolution.

Transfer of Skills to the Domestic Labor Force

In Kenya it appears that nationals have not acquired critical production engineering skills, the capability to replicate existing plants, and the ability to modify products or processes.[6] Given Kenya's per capita income and the current degree of importance to its economy of the generation of additional modern sector employment, the transfer of such skills is not a matter of immediate urgency. If technology acquisition costs have not been excessive, the cost performance of multinational corporations may be all that is of interest. In countries with a larger stock of appropriately educated workers and a greater base of industrial skills, however, the transfer of additional technological capabilities will loom larger. Meanwhile, evidence from the Philippines suggests that there is no simple causal link between the nationality of ownership and the local absorption of skills. As seen in chapters 5–7, there has been little domestic acquisition of high-quality production engineering skills by locally owned firms in the Philippines, despite several attempts by international agencies to promote transfers of this kind. The failure of previous modes of technology transfer provides part of the basis for the precise form of the productivity-enhancing project suggested in chapter 8.

The observations in Kenya and the Philippines suggest that inquiries into the determinants of local accumulation of technological capability will have to go beyond simple dichotomies of ownership and toward more complex formulations. In particular, it will be necessary to specify the appropriate conditions for local absorption of technology and the methods for effecting its transfer; furthermore, the economic desirability of a technology transfer, compared with purely local efforts to accumulate such capabilities, must be carefully analyzed.

Notes

1. See, for example, the comparisons of the United States and the Philippines based on sectoral data from the national accounts in Pack (1984) and the references there to other studies of productivity. The differences in RTFP between the United States and the Philippines calculated from secondary data sources are greater than those implied in this book using the United Kingdom–Philippine comparisons in chapter 5 and the United Kingdom–United States comparison in chapter 7. Given the problems of collecting accurate sectoral data, converting exchange rates, and defining the sector, I have little doubt that the results reported in this study are the more accurate ones.

2. For a detailed discussion of this issue in the context of industrial development strategies, see Pack and Westphal (1986).

3. Some tentative evidence is beginning to accumulate in the study of recent efforts toward liberalization in the Southern Cone. See, for example, Corbo and de Melo (1983).

4. If a high DRC were the result of large payments for technology, the activity might become socially profitable if a lower set of technology charges could be obtained. Skilled bargaining rather than improved productivity as a source of lower DRCs suggests one drawback to using this criterion as a definitive standard in this context.

5. A full evaluation would also require measurement of improvements in productivity over time and detailed time series on performance characteristics used in this study. Use of time series requires an amplification of the DRC procedure. Research on intertemporal productivity changes at this level of detail has been undertaken by Katz and by others, but these interesting studies surveyed by Katz (1982) have been concerned largely with the domestic generation of technology rather than with the desirability of alternative mechanisms of technology transfer.

6. For a discussion of these issues, see Dahlman and Westphal (1981) and Katz (1982).

References

Acharya, S. N. 1974. *Fiscal/Financial Intervention, Factor Prices, and Factor Proportions: A Review of the Issues*. World Bank Staff Working Paper 183. Washington, D.C.

Aitken, J. B. 1964. *Automatic Weaving*. Manchester, Eng.: Columbine Press.

Alchian, A. 1959. "Costs and Outputs." In M. Abramovitz and others, eds., *The Allocation of Economic Resources*. Stanford, Calif.: Stanford University Press.

Amsalem, M. 1983. *Technology Choice in Developing Countries: The Textile and Pulp and Paper Industries*. Cambridge, Mass.: MIT Press.

Arrow, K. J. 1969. "Classificatory Notes on the Production and Transmission of Technological Knowledge." *American Economic Review*, vol. 59, no. 2 (May), pp. 29–35.

Arrow, K. J., H. B. Chenery, B. S. Minhas, and R. M. Solow. 1961. "Capital-Labor Substitution and Economic Efficiency." *Review of Economics and Statistics*, vol. 43 (August), pp. 225–50.

ATIRA (Ahmedabad Textile Industry's Research Association). 1977. *Modernization and Renovation in Textile Industry*. Ahmedabad.

Baer, Werner, and Michel Herve. 1966. "Employment and Industrialization in Developing Countries." *Quarterly Journal of Economics*, vol. 80, no. 1 (February), pp. 88–107.

Behrman, J. R. 1982. "Country and Sectoral Variations in Manufacturing Elasticities of Substitution between Capital and Labor." In A. O. Krueger, ed., *Trade and Employment in Developing Countries*. Chicago: University of Chicago Press.

Bell, M., B. Ross-Larson, and L. E. Westphal. 1984. "The Cost and Benefit of Infant Industries." *Journal of Development Economics*, vol. 16, no. 2 (October), pp. 101–28.

Bentancourt, Roger, and Christopher Clague. 1981. *Capacity Utilization: A Theoretical and Empirical Analysis*. Cambridge, Eng.: Cambridge University Press.

Bhagwati, J. 1978. *Foreign Trade Regimes and Economic Development: Anatomy and Consequences of Exchange Control Regimes*. Cambridge, Mass.: Ballinger.

Byrd, William, Gene Tidrick, and others. 1984. *Recent Chinese Economic Reform: Studies of Two Industrial Enterprises*. World Bank Staff Working Paper 652. Washington, D.C.

Caves, D. W., L. Christensen, and W. E. Diewert. 1982. "Multilateral Comparisons of Output, Input, and Productivity Using Superlative Index Numbers." *Economic Journal*, vol. 92, no. 365 (March), pp. 73–86.

Caves, Richard E. 1984. "Scale, Openness, and Productivity in Manufacturing Industries." In Richard E. Caves and Lawrence B. Krause, eds., *The Australian Economy: A View from the North*. Washington, D.C.: Brookings Institution.

Chenery, H. B. 1953. "Process and Production Functions from Engineering Data." In W. Leontief and others, *Studies in the Structure of the American Economy*. New York: Oxford University Press.

Chin, R. 1965. *Management, Industrialization, and Trade in Cotton Textiles*. New Haven, Conn.: College and Universities Press.

Christensen, L. R., D. Cummings, and D. W. Jorgenson. 1980. "Relative Productivity Levels, 1947–73: An International Comparison." In J. Kendrick and B. Vaccara, eds., *New Developments in Productivity Measurement and Analysis*. Chicago: University of Chicago Press.

Cooper, Charles, and Raphael Kaplinsky. 1975. "Second-hand Equipment in Developing Countries: Jute Processing Machinery in Kenya." In Ajit Bhalla, ed., *Technology and Employment in Industry*. Geneva: International Labour Office.

Corbo, V., and J. de Melo. 1983. "Measuring Technical Efficiency: A Comparison of Alternative Methodologies with Census Data." Washington, D.C.: World Bank, Development Research Department; processed.

Corden, W. M. 1974. *Trade Policy and Economic Welfare*. Oxford, Eng.: Oxford University Press.

Cortes, Mariluz, and Peter Bocock. 1984. *North-South Techhnology Transfer: A Case Study of Petrochemicals in Latin America*. Baltimore, Md.: Johns Hopkins University Press.

Dahlman, C. J., and L. E. Westphal. 1981. "The Meaning of Technological Mastery in Relation to Transfer of Technology." *Annals of the American Academy of Political and Social Science*, vol. 458 (November), pp. 12–26.

Daniels, Mark R. 1969. "Differences in Efficiency among Industries in Developing Countries." *American Economic Review*, vol. 49, no. 1 (March), pp. 159–71.

de Vries, Barend A., and Willem Brakel. 1983. *Restructuring of Manufacturing Industry: The Experience of the Textile Industry in Pakistan, Philippines, Portugal, and Turkey*. World Bank Staff Working Paper 558. Washington, D.C.

Duxbury, V., and G. R. Wray. 1962. *Modern Developments in Weaving Machinery*. Derbyshire, Eng.: Columbine Press.

ECLA (United Nations Economic Commission for Latin America). 1951. "Labour Productivity of the Cotton Textile Industry in Five Latin American Countries." New York: United Nations, Department of Economic Affairs.

———. 1965. *Economies of Scale in the Cotton Spinning and Weaving Industry*. New York: United Nations.

Enrick, Norbert L. 1978. *Industrial Engineering Manual for the Textile Industry*. 2d ed. Huntington, N.Y.: Krieger.

——— 1980. *Management Control Manual for the Textile Industry*. 2d ed. Huntington, N.Y.: Krieger.

Fiori, Louis A. 1966. "Blending." In D. S. Hamby, ed., *The American Cotton Handbook*, 3d ed. New York: Wiley.

Forsund, F. R., C. A. Knox-Lovell, and P. Schmidt. 1980. "A Survey of Frontier Production Functions and of Their Relationship to Efficiency Measurement." *Journal of Econometrics*, vol. 13, no. 1 (May), pp. 27–57.

Freeman, H. J., and J. V. Jucker. 1981. "Experimental Design for Comparing the Productivity of Traditional and Innovative Work Organization." In N. R. Adam and A. Dogramaci, eds., *Productivity Analysis at the Organizational Level*. Boston, Mass.: Martinus Nijhoff.

Gaude, J. 1975. "Capital-Labor Substitution Possibilities: A Review of Empirical Evidence: In Ajit Bhalla, ed., *Technology and Employment in Industry*. Geneva: International Labour Office.

Grills, R. 1978. "The Spinning Costs of Polyester-Cotton Yarns." *Shirley Institute Bulletin*, vol. 51, no. 4, pp. 81–84.

Grubel, H. G., and P. J. Lloyd. 1975. *Intra-Industry Trade*. New York: Wiley.

Hagen, E. E. 1975. *The Economics of Development*. Homewood, Ill.: Irwin.

Hamby, D. S., ed. 1966. *The American Cotton Handbook*. 2 vols. 3d ed. New York: Wiley.

Hillier, F. S., and G. J. Lieberman. 1967. *Introduction to Operations Research*. San Francisco, Calif.: Holden Day.

Hirschman, A. O. 1958. *The Strategy of Economic Development*. New Haven, Conn.: Yale University Press.

Hirshleifer, J. 1962. "The Firm's Cost Function: A Successful Reconstruction?" *Journal of Business*, vol. 35, no. 3 (July), pp. 235–55.

Horton, Susan, and Timothy King. 1981. *Labor Productivity: Un Tour d'Horizon*. World Bank Staff Working Paper 497. Washington, D.C.

ILO (International Labour Office). 1972. *Work Study in the Textile Industry*. Geneva.

Jeremy, D. J. 1981. *Transatlantic Industrial Revolution: The Diffusion of Textile Technologies between Britain and America, 1790–1830s*. Cambridge, Mass.: MIT Press.

Katz, Jorge. 1982. "Technology and Economic Development: An Overview of Research Findings." In M. Syrguin and S. Teitel, eds., *Trade, Stability, Technology, and Equity in Latin America*. New York: Academic Press.

Kilby, P. 1962. "Organization and Productivity in Backward Economies." *Quarterly Journal of Economics*, vol. 76, no. 305 (May), pp. 303–10.

Koh, S. J. 1966. *Stages of Industrial Development in Asia: A Comparative History of the Cotton Industry in Japan, India, China, and Korea*. Philadelphia: University of Pennsylvania Press.

Kravis, I. B. 1976. "A Survey of International Comparisons of Productivity." *Economic Journal*, vol. 86, no. 341 (March), pp. 1–44.

Krugman, P. 1981. "Intraindustry Specialization and the Gains from Trade." *Journal of Political Economy*, vol. 89, no. 5 (October), pp. 959–73.

Landes, David. 1969. *The Unbound Prometheus*. Cambridge, Eng.: Cambridge University Press.

Lazonick, W. 1981. "Factor Costs and the Diffusion of Ring Spinning in Britain Prior to World War I." *Quarterly Journal of Economics*, vol. 95, no. 1 (February), pp. 89-109.

Leff, N. H. 1978. "Industrial Organization and Entrepreneurship in Developing Countries: The Economic Groups." *Economic Development and Cultural Change*, vol. 28, no. 4 (July), pp. 661–76.

Leibenstein, H. 1976. *Beyond Economic Man*. Cambridge, Mass.: Harvard University Press.

————. 1978. *General X-Efficiency Theory and Economic Development*. New York: Oxford University Press.

Lord, Peter R. 1981. *Economics, Science, and Technology of Yarn Production*. Manchester, Eng.: Textile Institute.

Lord, Peter R., and M. H. Mohamed. 1976. *Weaving: Conversion of Yarn to Fabric*. Durham, Eng.: Merrow.

Lucas, Robert E. B. 1984. "On the Theory of DRC Criteria." *Journal of Development Economics*, vol. 14, no. 3 (April), pp. 407–18.

Mansfield, E., A. Romeo, M. Schwartz, D. Teece, S. Wagner, and P. Brach. 1982. *Technology Transfer, Productivity, and Economic Policy*. New York: Norton.

Marks, R., and A. T. C. Robinson. 1976. *Principles of Weaving*. Manchester, Eng.: Textile Institute.

Marsh, R. M., and H. Mannari. 1976. *Modernization and the Japanese Factory*. Princeton, N.J.: Princeton University Press.

Martin, J. P. 1978. "X-Inefficiency, Managerial Effort, and Protection." *Economica*, vol. 45, no. 179, pp. 273–86.

Mlawa, Hasa Mfaume. 1983. "The Acquisition of Technology, Technological Capability, and Technical Change: A Study of the Textile Industry in Tanzania." Ph.D. diss., University of Sussex.

Moore, W. E. 1951. *Industrialization and Labor*. Ithaca, N.Y.: Cornell University Press.

Morawetz, David. 1974. "Employment Implications of Industrialization in Developing Countries—A Survey." *Economic Journal*, vol. 84, no. 335 (September), pp. 491-542.

————. 1976a. "Elasticities of Substitution in Industry: What Do We Learn from Econometric Estimates?" *World Development*, vol. 4, no. 1 (January), pp. 11–15.

————. 1976b. "The Electricity Measure of Capital Utilization." *World Development*, vol. 4, no. 8 (August), pp. 643–53.

————. 1981. *Why the Emperor's New Clothes Are Not Made in Colombia: A Case Study in Latin American and East Asian Manufactured Exports*. New York: Oxford University Press.

Muller, J., and N. Owen. 1983. "Economic Effects of Free Trade in Manufactured Products with the EEC." Berlin: Deutsches Institut für Wirtschaftsforschung.

Nelson, R. R. 1981. "Research on Productivity Growth and Productivity Differences: Dead Ends and New Departures." *Journal of Economic Literature*, vol. 19, no. 3 (September), pp. 1029–64.

Nelson, R. R., and S. G. Winter. 1982. *An Evolution Theory of Economic Change*. Cambridge, Mass.: Harvard University Press.

Nerlove, M. 1967. "Recent Empirical Studies of the CES and Related Production Functions." In M. Brown, ed., *The Theory and Empirical Analysis of Production*. New York: Columbia University Press.

Nishimizu, M., and J. M. Page. 1982. "Total Factor Productivity Growth, Technological Progress, and Technical Efficiency Change: Dimensions of Productivity Change in Yugoslavia, 1965–78." *Economic Journal*, vol. 92, no. 367 (December), pp. 920–36.

Nishimizu, M., and S. Robinson. 1984. "Trade Policies and Productivity Change in Semi-Industrialized Countries." *Journal of Development Economics*, vol. 16, no. 1–2 (September–October), pp. 177–206.

OECD (Organisation for Economic Co-operation and Development). Various years. "Competition Policy." Paris.

Olson, Mancur. 1965. *The Logic of Collective Action*. Cambridge, Mass.: Harvard University Press.

Ormerod, A. 1979. *Management of Textile Production*. London: Butterworths.

Pack, H. 1975. "The Choice of Technique and Employment in the Textile Industry." In Ajit Bhalla, ed., *Technology and Employment in Industry*. Geneva: International Labour Office.

_____. 1981. "Fostering the Capital Goods Sector in LDCs." *World Development*, vol. 9, no. 3 (March), pp. 227–50.

_____. 1982a. "Aggregate Implications of Factor Substitution in Industrial Processes." *Journal of Development Economics*, vol. 11, no. 1 (August), pp. 1–38.

_____. 1982b. "Productivity during Industrialization: Some Latin American Evidence." In Frances Stewart and Jeffrey James, eds., *The Economics of New Technology in Developing Countries*. Boulder, Colo.: Westview.

_____. 1984. "Total Factor Productivity and Its Determinants: Some International Comparisons." In G. Ranis and R. West, eds., *Essays Presented to Lloyd Reynolds*. Boulder, Colo.: Westview.

_____. Forthcoming. "Industrialization and Trade." In Hollis B. Chenery and T. N. Srinivasan, eds., *Handbook of Development Economics*. Amsterdam: North-Holland Press.

Pack, H., and J. R. Pack. 1977. "Urban Land-Use Models: The Determinants of Adoption and Use." *Policy Sciences*, vol. 8, no. 1 (March), pp. 79–101.

Pack, H., and Larry E. Westphal. 1986. "Industrial Strategy and Technological Change: Theory versus Reality." *Journal of Development Economics* vol. 22, no. 1 (June), pp. 87–128.

Page, J. M. 1980. "Technical Efficiency and Economic Performance: Some Evidence from Ghana." *Oxford Economic Papers*, vol. 32, no. 2 (July), pp. 319–39.

Philippines, Interagency Technical Subcommittee. 1978a. "A Technical Survey of the Philippine Spinning Industry." Manila; processed.

_____. 1978b. "Textile Industry Status." Manila; processed.

Philippines, Board of Investments. 1979. "The Philippine Textile Industry." Manila; processed.

Pickett, J., and R. Robson. 1981. *The Choice of Technology in the Production of Cotton Cloth*. Edinburgh: Scottish Academic Press.

Pratten, C. F. 1976. *A Comparison of the Performance of Swedish and United Kingdom Companies*. Cambridge, Eng.: Cambridge University Press.

Ranis, G. 1973. "Industrial Sector Labor Absorption." *Economic Development and Cultural Change*, vol. 21, no. 3 (April), pp. 387–408.

Ranis, G., and Gary M. Saxonhouse. 1978. "Technology Choice, Adaptation, and the Quality Dimension in the Japanese Cotton Textile Industry." In *Japan's Historical Development Experience and the Contemporary Developing Countries: Issues for Comparative Analysis*. Tokyo: International Development Center of Japan.

Rhee, Y. W., and L. E. Westphal. 1977. "A Micro-econometric Investigation of Choice of Technique." *Journal of Development Economics*, vol. 4, no. 3 (September), pp. 205–38.

Rice, A. K. 1958. *Productivity and Social Organization: The Ahmedabad Experiment*. London: Tavistock.

Rosenberg, N. 1976. *Perspectives on Technology*. Cambridge, Eng.: Cambridge University Press.

———. 1982. *Inside the Black Box: Technology and Economics*. Cambridge, Eng.: Cambridge University Press.

Saxonhouse, Gary M. 1974. "A Tale of Japanese Technological Diffusion in the Meiji Period." *Journal of Economic History*, vol. 34, no. 1 (March), pp. 149–65.

———. 1976. "Country Girls and Communications among Competitors in the Japanese Cotton-Spinning Industry." In Hugh Patrick, ed., *Japanese Industrialization and Its Social Consequences*. Berkeley: University of California Press.

———. 1978. "The Supply of Quality Workers and the Demand for Quality in Jobs in Japan's Early Industrialization." *Explorations in Economic History*, vol. 15, no. 1 (January), pp. 40–68.

Saxonhouse, Gary, and Gavin Wright. 1983. "Two Forms of Cheap Labor in Textile History." In Gary Saxonhouse and Gavin Wright, *Research in Economic History*, Supplement 3: *Technique, Spirit, and Form in the Making of the Modern Economies: Essays in Honor of William N. Parker*. Greenwich, Conn.: Jai Press.

Scherer, F. M. 1980. *Industrial Market Structure and Economic Performance*. Chicago: Rand McNally.

Scherer, F. M., Alan Beckenstein, Erich Kaufer, and R. Dennis Murphy. 1975. *The Economics of Multi-Plant Operation*. Cambridge, Mass.: Harvard University Press.

Sen, A. K. 1968. *Choice of Techniques*. 3d ed. New York: Kelley.

Stewart, Frances. 1974. "Technology and Employment in LDCs." In E. Edwards, ed., *Employment in Developing Nations*. New York: Columbia University Press.

———. 1975. "Manufacture of Cement Blocks in Kenya." In Ajit Bhalla, ed., *Technology and Employment in Industry*. Geneva: International Labour Office.

———. 1977. *Technology and Underdevelopment*. Boulder, Colo.: Westview.

Stifel, L. D. 1963. "The Textile Industry: A Case Study of Industrial Development in the Philippines." Ithaca, N.Y.: Cornell University, Department of Asian Studies.

Stigler, George J. 1976. "The Xistence of X-Efficiency." *American Economic Review*, vol. 66, no. 1 (March), pp. 213-16.

Subramanian, T. A., and A. R. Garde. 1974. *End Breaks in Spinning*. Ahmedabad: Ahmedabad Textile Industry's Research Association (ATIRA).

Taylor, Frederick W. 1911. *The Principles of Scientific Management*. New York: Harper.

Teece, D. 1976. *The Multinational Corporation and the Resource Cost of International Technology Transfer*. Cambridge, Mass.: Ballinger.

Textile Council. 1969. *Cotton and Allied Textiles*. 2 vols. Manchester, Eng.

Timmer, C. Peter. 1971. "Using a Probabilistic Frontier Production Function to Measure Technical Efficiency." *Journal of Political Economy*, vol. 79, no. 4 (July–August), pp. 776-94.

UNIDO (United Nations Industrial Development Organization). 1967a. "Report of the Expert Group Meeting on the Selection of Textile Machinery." Vienna.

———. 1967b. "Technological and Economic Aspects of Establishing Textile Industries in Developing Countries." Vienna.

———. 1972a. "Quality Control in the Textile Industry." New York: United Nations.

———. 1972b. "Final Report to the Philippine Textile Research Institute." Manila: UNIDO; processed.

United Nations. 1953. *Handweaving in the Philippines*. New York: UN Technical Assistance Program.

Vernon, Raymond. 1966. "International Investment and International Trade in the Product Cycle." *Quarterly Journal of Economics*, vol. 80 (May), pp. 190–206.

Wall Street Journal. 1985. "Mexican Industry Is Opposing Plan That Would Open Mexico to Imports." April 9, p. 35.

Westphal, Larry E., Yung W. Rhee, and Garry Pursell. 1981. *Korean Industrial Competence: Where It Came From*. World Bank Staff Working Paper 469. Washington, D.C.

Westphal, L. E., L. Kim, and C. J. Dahlman. 1985. "Reflections on Korea's Acquisition of Technological Capability" In Nathan Rosenberg and Claudio Frischtak, eds., *International Technology Transfer*. New York: Praeger.

White, L. J. 1978. "The Evidence on Appropriate Factor Proportions for Manufacturing in Less Developed Countries: A Survey." *Economic Development and Cultural Change*, vol. 27, no. 1 (October), pp. 27–60.

Williams, David. 1975. "National Planning and the Choice of Technology: The Case of Textiles in Tanzania." Ph.D. diss., Harvard School of Business Administration.

Winston, Gordon C. 1973. "The Theory of Capacity Utilization and Idleness." *Journal of Economic Literature*, vol. 21, no. 4 (December), pp. 1301–20.

Index

Analytic model, 7–9; and best practice, 37–38, 39, 47–51, 63

Benefit-cost ratio, 131, 172, 173; defining benefits and, 164; Philippine analysis and, 152, 161–67; project design and, 157–61
Best practice: analytic model and, 7; capital and labor inputs and, 39, 40, 61–63; coefficients of, 37–38, 39, 47–51, 63; elasticity of substitution and, 50, 51–52, 63, 101; equipment and, 36–38, 39; firms and, 45–46, 48, 49, 177; industrialization and, 153; intracountry cost comparisons and, 53–55; Kenyan spinning and, 71–76; Kenyan weaving and, 76–80; looms and, 51, 59–60; national economy and, 42; Philippine spinning and, 87, 96–98; Philippine weaving and, 98–101; productivity-depressing factors and, 55–60; productivity in Kenya and Philippines and, 41–47, 50, 57, 60, 61–62, 63, 171; product specialization and, 43–45; relative total-factor productivity and, 48–49; returns to scale and, 52–53; shortfall relative to, 17; spinning and, 37, 39–40, 51, 56–59, 61–62; tariffs and quota barriers and, 3; task-level productivity and, 46–47; technology and, 36–38, 50, 176; weaving and, 40–41, 59–60, 62–63

Blending of fiber, 45, 104–5, 117–18

Capacity utilization, 42
Capital: best practice and, 61–63; in Kenya, 72, 75; excess, 47; finished fabrics and, 32; spinning and, 61–62; weaving and, 62–63
Capital-labor ratio, 1, 41; analytic model and, 8; best practice and, 61–63; international comparisons of, 139, 140–41; in Kenya, 72, 75; looms and, 25; project design and, 155; for spinning, 30, 140–41; for weaving, 31, 32; yarn quality and, 20–21
Chenery, H. B., 36
Cloth production. *See* Weaving
Cobb-Douglas production function, 35, 52, 63, 96, 99, 139, 140
Coefficients: for best-practice, 37–38, 39, 40, 49–51; for project design, 151, 163
Comparative analysis. *See* Firms; Productivity differentials; Spinning; Weaving
Competition, 3, 50, 166, 173; for Kenyan textile industry, 80–81; for Philippine textile industry, 101–2; productivity differentials and, 115; productivity and, 154–55, 157, 162. *See also* Trade
Constant elasticity of substitution (CES), 35, 52, 63, 101, 139
Consultants, 154
Corden, W. M., 120

The most recent World Bank publications are described in the catalog *New Publications,* which is issued in the spring and fall of each year. The complete backlist of publications is shown in the annual *Index of Publications,* which contains an alphabetical title list and indexes of subjects, authors, and countries and regions; it is of value principally to libraries and institutional purchasers. The continuing research program is described in *The World Bank Research Program: Abstracts of Current Studies,* which is issued annually. The latest edition of each is available from Publications Sales Unit, The World Bank, 1818 H Street, N.W., Washington, D.C. 20433, U.S.A., or from Publications, The World Bank, 66, avenue d'Iéna, 75116 Paris, France.